The ABCs of ERM

The ABCs of ERM

Demystifying Electronic Resource Management for Public and Academic Librarians

Jessica Zellers, Tina M. Adams, and Katherine Hill

LIBRARIES
UNLIMITED™

An Imprint of ABC-CLIO, LLC
Santa Barbara, California • Denver, Colorado

Copyright © 2018 by Jessica Zellers, Tina M. Adams, and Katherine Hill

Library of Congress Cataloging in Publication Control Number: 2017044500

ISBN: 978-1-4408-5580-1 (paperback)
       978-1-4408-5581-8 (ebook)

22 21 20 19 18   1 2 3 4 5

This book is also available as an eBook.

Libraries Unlimited
An Imprint of ABC-CLIO, LLC

ABC-CLIO, LLC
130 Cremona Drive, P.O. Box 1911
Santa Barbara, California 93116-1911
www.abc-clio.com

This book is printed on acid-free paper ∞

Manufactured in the United States of America

Contents

CHAPTER ONE

So What Are Electronic Resources Anyway?

It used to be so simple.

If you wanted to borrow a book, you went to the library. That was the point of libraries. They had books you could borrow for free. There were other things, too—newspapers, microfilm readers, collections of magazines packaged in unattractive cardboard covers—but for most people, libraries were all about the books.

Then the internet happened.

The impact of the digital revolution on library collections cannot be overstated. Card catalogs gave way to online catalogs, vastly improving the accessibility and searchability of libraries' holdings. Journals moved online and electronic databases sprang into existence, allowing ordinary people to become researchers without the need for librarian intervention. And when the online behemoth retailer Amazon released its first Kindle e-reader in 2007, electronic books went from irrelevancy to mainstream contenders, nearly overnight.

People still associate libraries with books. It doesn't matter how many instructional classes you offer, how many papier-mâché crafts projects you host, how many databases you subscribe to. When people think of libraries, they think of row after row of physical books. And they're not wrong, exactly; apart from a few places pushing the envelope with experimental collections, libraries do indeed offer shelves of books, neatly arranged and easily findable.

But the simple days of yesteryear are gone. Library patrons, regardless of their own technical expertise, need and want electronic resources. Not so long ago, most patrons met their informational and recreational needs with books (or, in academic libraries, with books and journals). The other formats were optional frills for the average person.

Electronic resources, in contrast, are essential for nearly everyone. Researchers depend on e-journals, e-books, databases, and general internet websites. People who use the library for pleasure reading can avoid e-books, but they cannot avoid the electronic catalog if they want a specific call number—not unless they ask for help.

And that is the other big piece of the puzzle. We who work in libraries ensure that patrons can access the resources they need and want. That's our job. It makes absolutely no difference whether those resources are physical or electronic.

Except, of course, it does.

Libraries were providing access to books back when they were written by hand and illustrated with charming gold inlays. We have long-established relationships with vendors and book jobbers and processes for acquisition, description, and classification that have worked reliably for decades on end. Some library employees learn about the system in library school, whereas others learn on the job; either way, much of the learning comes naturally. No one has to be taught what a book is.

Electronic resources have a much steeper learning curve. They're just as important as their physical analogs, but they don't have decades and centuries of tradition underpinning them. Everyone knows what a book is, but not everyone knows what a database is. Concepts surrounding electronic resources are addressed thoroughly in some library programs but not in others, and none of that matters anyway for people who do not have library degrees, or who earned their degrees when electronic resources were nascent.

This book was written to bring clarity to electronic resources and to help people navigate the steps of managing them. We'll start by looking at some definitions.

Definitions

The area of electronic resources is riddled with lingo, which can be disconcerting for new librarians. We've gathered some of the more common terms here:

Big Deals are bundled collections of e-journals, usually marketed to academic libraries. As with cable packages, some content will be more desirable than other content.

Databases are thematic collections of electronic resources. Some offer original content, such as Ancestry Plus, a genealogical database. Other databases are aggregators, which pull together many disparate resources into one searchable interface. These general aggregators are often the starting place for research questions. Examples include ProQuest Central and JSTOR.

Downloadable Audiobooks (also e-audiobooks) are digitized audiobooks that may be downloaded to a computer or handheld device.

DRM (Digital Rights Management) refers to copyright management for electronic resources. DRM is set by the publisher or distributor and can include restrictions on the number of users and the ability to save, print, and share.

E-books are digitized books that may be read on a computer or handheld device.

E-journals (also electronic journals) are digitized journals that may be read on a computer or handheld device. They include popular magazines as well as scholarly journals.

Electronic resources (also e-resources) are digitized versions of intellectual content, as compared to physical versions such as print, microfiche, and DVDs. Common examples are databases, e-books, e-journals, and downloadable audiobooks.

E-readers are handheld devices that can be used to read e-books and other digital media. Some devices, such as the Kindle and the NOOK, are dedicated e-readers whose primary or exclusive function is to serve as a platform for e-books and e-journals. Alternatively, multipurpose smartphones, tablets, laptops, and computers can be used as e-readers.

The internet often gets overlooked in discussions of electronic resources, even though internet access is one of the most valuable services that libraries provide. Whether patrons bring their own devices or use library equipment, they can use the library to access the vast world of electronic resources. This includes the e-journals, databases, and other electronic resources, selected by librarians, that are the subject of this book; personal computing applications like email and social media; and websites in general. Some of these freely available websites are as valuable to librarians as fee-based resources, and libraries will often draw attention to them by linking to them in LibGuides or catalog records.

Open Access (OA) refers to intellectual content that is freely available to end-users, often with few or no restrictions for its use.

Open Educational Resources (OER) are a subset of Open Access Resources used in the classroom and other academic settings. They are particularly popular in distance-learning classes.

Serials, in most contexts, is just another word for "journals." This term is a holdover from the time when all serials were journals and all journals were serials. The word can also refer to databases, however, because most databases have dynamic content and require an annual renewal fee. Thus a Serials Librarian likely deals with print journals, e-journals, and databases.

Streaming media refers to resources that are "streamed"—continuously delivered over a live connection—as opposed to resources that are first downloaded and then watched by viewers. Films and television are the most common types of streaming media in libraries.

Who's Who: The Major Players

When it comes to electronic resources, vendors and organizations abound. We've pulled together some of the biggest names here:

EBSCO: One of the three biggest database providers, along with Gale and ProQuest.

Gale: One of the three biggest database providers, along with EBSCO and ProQuest.

Hoopla Digital: A provider of streaming and downloadable movies, music, e-books, audiobooks, comics, and television shows.

Kanopy: A provider of streaming movies, mostly documentaries and classic films.

NASIG: North American Serials Interest Group. An organization that promotes the distribution, acquisition, and long-term accessibility of information resources.

NISO: The National Information Standards Organization develops, maintains, and publishes technical standards.

OCLC: A cooperative library that got its start in interlibrary loan (ILL). It remains best known for facilitating ILL, but it also provides many other services and products, including EZproxy.

OverDrive: A provider of downloadable e-books and audiobooks.

ProQuest: One of the three biggest database providers, along with EBSCO and Gale.

RBdigital: A provider of downloadable audiobooks and e-books from Recorded Books. Formerly One-Click Digital.

Swank: A provider of streaming movies, including feature films.

The Electronic Resources Life Cycle

In 2013, Jill Emery and Graham Stone wrote about six Techniques for Electronic Resource Management (TERMS), a project that had been brewing for several years. Developed in part by crowdsourcing ideas from the library community, the six TERMS describe the life cycle of electronic resources (Emery & Stone 2013, 8). We've listed those steps here, along with brief descriptions of what they mean:

- **Investigating New Content for Purchase/Addition:** Your first step includes comparing products and getting price quotes.
- **Acquiring New Content:** Once the decision to purchase has been made, you must negotiate terms and sign licenses.
- **Implementation:** This stage includes testing the bugs, setting up local and remote access, training staff and users, and marketing the electronic resource.
- **Ongoing Evaluation and Access:** This stage involves assessing electronic resources and ensuring their accessibility.
- **Annual Review:** For subscription resources, you will need to evaluate whether to keep or cancel subscriptions every year.
- **Cancellation and Replacement Review:** Finally, when you cancel subscriptions, you need to communicate with stakeholders and patrons.

As of 2017, the TERMS are undergoing revision. TERMS 2.0 will collapse the "Evaluation" and "Annual Review" stages into one and add a new stage, "Preservation" (Emery, Stone, & McCracken 2017). This book draws its inspiration from the first iteration, however: not only does the original life cycle remain a valuable framework, but the new emphasis on digital preservation currently has limited applicability to public libraries.

NASIG Core Competencies

There are many aspects of electronic resource management that can include everyone from a Systems Admin to the Head of Public Services, as can be seen in the earlier section. The contents of this book are based both on TERMS and on the NASIG core competencies for Electronic Resources Librarians. Realizing that this was a growing position with a lack of a strong job definition, NASIG put together a task force to examine job descriptions that included electronic resource management in their title or main duties. The task force identified trends across the requirements and duties and used these trends as a springboard to create a list of core competencies.

The full list of core competencies, available at the NASIG website, is extensive. You may be forgiven for wondering how one person is supposed to do it all. We have whittled down the list, collecting and summarizing the main issues that Electronic Resources Librarians should understand:

Life Cycle of Electronic Resources: The Electronic Resources Librarian should be very familiar with TERMS, as described earlier, and be able to act as the bridge between all the different moving parts and departments who might touch an electronic resource. They need to have a broad understanding of all the phases a resource goes through, from acquisition to preservation. This includes managing electronic resources budgets, licensing electronic resources, creating access points via the catalog and other methods to these resources, and developing systems for maintaining and tracking all of these parts.

Technology: Because electronic resources are online, Electronic Resources Librarians need to be able to use and manipulate the underlying hardware and software that supports access. This includes understanding networking technology; common standards and protocols such as OpenURL, Shibboleth, and IP; how to design a basic database; and how to use specific software such as link resolver software, discovery services, and Electronic Resource Management (ERM) systems.

Research and Assessment: The Electronic Resources Librarian needs to be able to analytically and thoroughly look at collection decisions, electronic resources problems, and other issues. This includes being able to gather information about potential purchases from patrons and fellow librarians, using usage statistics to make informed decisions on renewals and future avenues of collecting, and understanding how the numerous publisher and library systems talk to each other in order to pinpoint potential and current trouble spots for patrons.

Effective Communication: Electronic Resource Librarians need to be open in their communication. They need to be able to switch contexts easily from patron to vendor to librarian and provide translations for each of those groups. They also need to be able to communicate their research and evaluation in such a way as to be persuasive to stakeholders.

Supervising and Management: Even if Electronic Resources Librarians are not directly managing staff, they often are involved in project management and developing unit-wide procedures and workflows. As such, they need to have strong project management skills; be able to keep projects on time; and be able to analyze workflows and procedures and revise, repeal, or replace them as necessary. They also need to be able to communicate library policy concisely and clearly to patrons based on the situation at their library.

Trends and Professional Development: The world of the Electronic Resources Librarian is constantly in flux. Therefore they need to commit themselves to professional development, especially in areas like new standards (COUNTER and KBART, for example), changes and updates to copyright law, trends in scholarly communication, and new digital tools and initiatives that could be useful, like SUSHI and OpenURL.

If that sounds like a lot, that's because it *is* a lot. Just remember, you are taking the first awesome step by reading this book. We will make sure to help you along the way so you can eventually claim the title of NASIG-competent Electronic Resources Librarian!

Who Should Read This Book?

In news that should surprise no one who's ever been to library school, a study of the preparedness of entry-level Technical Services Librarians found a disconnect between what is being taught in library schools and what is needed in the workforce (Mueller, Thompson, & Valdes 2015). Library administrators found 0.9 percent of their new hires to be unqualified, 18.5 percent to be poorly qualified, and 35.2 percent to be adequately qualified, compared to 32.6 percent who were moderately qualified and 12.9 percent who were extremely qualified (Mueller et al. 2015, 13). Among the qualities and skills that library administrators desired, but did not always get, were familiarity with contract and license negotiations, awareness of current trends and options for electronic resources tracking and management, and experience with ILS software (Mueller et al. 2015, 11).

This book is for people with library degrees and without. It is a handbook for anyone who has ever felt bewildered by electronic resources, written especially for people working in public and academic libraries. The three authors of this book have each worked as Electronic Resources Librarians and wish this manual had existed when they were starting their jobs. Although the focus is on the behind-the-scenes, technical aspects of collection development, acquisitions, and management, it will prove useful to frontline staff, library administrators, and students in library school.

A note on language: We use the term "librarian" a lot because it's clunky to say "librarians, paraprofessionals, and support staff" each time we want to make a point. We know that the particulars of job titles and degrees aren't always important. In some libraries, volunteers answer reference questions and troubleshoot electronic resources. We use "librarian" to refer to anyone who currently works in a library or hopes to someday.

Our purpose is not to overwhelm you with in-depth details or high-concept philosophies, though we do provide suggestions for additional reading in each chapter, if you're a glutton for theory. Instead, we provide practical advice and just enough background information to get you up to speed.

Additional Readings

Hamlett, Alexandra. 2016. "Keeping Up with the Flow: Electronic Resource Work-flow and Analysis." *Serials Librarian* 70, no. 1–4: 168–174.

Imre, Andrea, Steve Oberg, Scott Vieira, and Lori Duggan. 2016. "The Future Is Flexible, Extensible, and Community-Based: Stories of Successful Electronic Resources Management." *Serials Librarian* 70, no. 1–4: 204–210.

Rinck, Elan May. 2017. "Coming to TERMS with Electronic Resource Management: An Interview with Jill Emery, Graham Stone, and Peter McCracken." *Serials Review* 43, no. 1: 51–54.

Ross, Sheri V. T., and Sarah W. Sutton. 2016. *Guide to Electronic Resource Management.* Santa Barbara, CA: Libraries Unlimited.

Sutton, Sarah W., and Paula Sullenger. 2017. "The Development and Use of the NASIG Core Competencies for Electronic Resources Librarians." *Serials Review* 43, no. 2: 147–152.

Weir, Ryan O., ed. 2012. *Managing Electronic Resources: A LITA Guide.* Chicago: ALA TechSource.

References

Emery, Jill, and Graham Stone. 2013. "Introduction and Literature Review." *Library Technology Reports* 49, no. 2: 5–9.

Emery, Jill, Graham Stone, and Peter McCracken. 2017. "Getting Back on TERMS (Version 2.0)." TERMS Techniques for Electronic Resource Management. https://library.hud.ac.uk/blogs/terms.

Mueller, Kat Landry, Molly Thompson, and Zach Valdes. 2015. "Ready, Set, Hire! Perceptions of New Technical Services Librarian Preparedness." *Library Leadership & Management* 29, no. 4: 1–33.

NASIG Executive Board. "Core Competencies for E-Resources Librarians." July 26, 2016. www.nasig.org/site_page.cfm?pk_association_webpage_menu=310 &pk_association_webpage=7802.

CHAPTER TWO

Vendors Are Your Friend

Vendors, which we define as all the entities from whom we purchase content and software, have always played an important role for libraries. Without them publishing and making creative expressions available, the library as we know it today would not exist. With the expansion to licensed (and not just owned) electronic content and the development of extensive integrated library systems (ILS), the librarian's relationship to vendors has increased in complexity and importance. Carlson (2006, 8), in his *Relationships Between Libraries and Vendors*, sums it up well: "the dependence of modern libraries on vendors is unprecedented."

The importance of good vendor relationships cannot be overstated. If you examine the life cycle of an electronic resource as laid out in the TERMS model (discussed in the introduction), you will see that interactions with vendors take place in every step. You talk to vendors, set up meetings with them, and visit them at conferences to investigate new content for purchase. You negotiate terms of use and price with vendors in order to acquire new material. You exchange information to technically implement resources correctly. You work closely with them as you try to troubleshoot access problems. And you discuss renewals and possible cancellations with them when it is time for evaluation. Strong communication and relationships with vendors are an essential part of being an effective Electronic Resources Librarian.

Vendor interactions are mentioned frequently throughout this book, as they are an integral part of day-to-day work, but this chapter focuses on a few fundamental aspects:

- **Types of Vendors:** A basic introduction to the different types of vendors and their role in the library.

- **The Ideal Vendor Relationship:** Methods of starting and maintaining good relationships.
- **Negotiating with Vendors:** Getting into the negotiation mind-set, theories of negotiation, and negotiating tips and techniques.

We're focusing on these specific topics due to their inclusion in NASIG's core competencies for Electronic Resources Librarians (Sutton et al. 2016). Because these core competencies were chosen based on how frequently these skills were mentioned in Electronic Resources Librarian job ads, their mention indicates how essential they are to the everyday work of electronic resources. They were also chosen because these topics and skills are relevant to all types of libraries, though the specifics might be different.

Types of Vendors

Before you jump into the world of meeting all the vendors as an Electronic Resources Librarian, it is helpful to know the different types of vendors with which you can and most likely will work. Understanding what type of vendor you are working with can help you determine how much leeway you have in negotiating costs and terms of use and can help you understand who to get in contact with if you are interested in specific types of products.

It's worth noting, however, that some vendors—especially the huge ones—serve numerous roles. For example, EBSCO and their various holdings can fill the role of the subscription agent, the aggregator, or the publisher, depending on the product. Before you begin interacting with a vendor, try to identify what role they are playing at that point in time.

Given the different types of vendors offering products, you frequently can get the same intellectual content from numerous different sources. Different sources have different advantages and disadvantages. For example, you might be able to get certain content more cheaply through an aggregator, but they might be missing the latest year of content. Before you decide to purchase content through one source, be sure to understand what that source means and what other options are available. We'll be talking about ways to research alternatives later in this chapter.

Publishers

These vendors directly publish the material that they are offering for sale electronically. They can be both nonprofit (most academic society presses and university presses fall in this category) or for-profit (as is the case with most of the popular press publishers). Either way, they work directly with copyright holders to publish material and then sell it to libraries, either on an individual title basis or, more commonly, in a large full-text package.

Because they often own the copyright to the materials they are selling, publishers can have greater flexibility when negotiating terms of use. They also have more control on what digital locks are put in place. This means that purchases from publishers will have more lenient terms (though not always, of course). The downside is that the materials you get from publishers only contain material they publish.

Aggregators

These are vendors who do not directly publish materials but instead license content from publishers. They have permission to use materials, but they do not own the copyright. Although aggregators do include content from big publishers, they often include a lot of content from small publishers who would otherwise not have the human resources or budget to reach a large audience. Aggregators therefore can offer a wide variety of content from many different publishers, all accessible using the same interface and terms of use.

But because aggregators do not own the copyright to their content, they have limited room to negotiate terms of use, because they need to please all the various publishers they work with. This means that often the strictest terms from represented publishers are the ones that are put in place for the entire product. Although negotiating terms of use can be challenging with this type of resource, price negotiation is absolutely something you should do. Finally, due to the lack of copyright, the other issue with these types of resources is that materials can be removed suddenly if the aggregator loses their license to the copyrighted material.

Subscription Agents (aka Book Jobbers)

These vendors act as intermediaries between publishers and libraries. They provide an interface for librarians to select journals or books they're interested in subscribing to, after which the subscription agent contacts the publisher to get price quotes and set up access. Sometimes general terms of use can be set up to cover everything subscribed to through the vendor, but in some cases, special agreements must be signed before you can request to purchase resources from the different publishers.

Subscription agents are great for managing many individual purchases, especially for a wide variety of small publishers. However, working through them does limit your ability to negotiate price and terms directly. Instead you negotiate through the agent and hope for the best. Most of these services also cost the library a fee.

Consortia and Buying Clubs

Incredibly important for most public libraries, these are generally nonprofit state- or library-run groups that work together to negotiate price and sometimes license terms for their members. The hope is that by pooling resources and gathering a lot of potential subscribers, vendors will be more likely to offer better prices to all members. Many states also have organizations that purchase and negotiate terms for a collection of resources. These subscriptions are paid for with state funds and then offered for free to public institutions, such as public libraries, community colleges, and public universities.

As an individual member of a consortium, you generally (though not always) pay a fee to belong, and you can often opt in and out of deals. Although you cannot negotiate price if you get something through a consortium, some consortia allow individual negotiation of terms of use. See also Chapter 12 for an in-depth discussion of consortia.

Platform Providers

Generally, you will not need to negotiate directly with these vendors, as they tend to work strictly on the publisher support side. However, it is useful to know how to contact the major ones that publishers use in case there are technical or administrative access issues. Platform providers create the back-end technology to support the hosting of publisher content. A good example of a platform provider is Atypon (www.atypon.com).

The Ideal Vendor Relationship

Within libraries, there are a lot of different opinions about what the correct attitude toward vendors should be. Vendors and libraries do have some different priorities; for example, vendors want to protect their product from copying or theft, because their control over the supply of these products is key to their existence. They also want to keep solvent, which requires selling their products at enough of a markup to make a profit.

Libraries focus on sharing information to their patrons. The broad sharing of ideas and information, as well as the right to privacy, is so essential to the library that it is encoded in ALA's Code of Ethics. Libraries also want to make as much quality information as possible available to patrons, though they are restricted in purchasing power by an often very limited budget. These opposing goals can cause tension and conflict between the sides.

Though the methods of operating might not always be similar on both sides, we do ourselves a disservice when we in libraries treat vendors as frenemies. Ideally, librarians and vendors constitute two sides of a mutually dependent, professional partnership. When viewed this way, librarians have actual leverage when negotiating and working with vendors. It is true that we need publishers, vendors, and aggregators in order to get important content for our patrons . . . but they also need us.

Libraries are currently the largest customer base for many publishers, especially those catering to academic markets. Vendors rely on libraries to acquire their content and make it available to the intended audience of readers. In the end, libraries and vendors both share the goal of making information accessible to those who need it. When you see vendors in this light, as a partner with whom you can disagree but with whom you share common goals, negotiation and working with publishers becomes far less scary.

Professionalism is essential in this endeavor. Although you can be social with vendors and even become friends with them (yes, it is true, this is possible!), keep in mind that making vendors your friend is not your ultimate goal. Realize that disagreements may happen and that these disagreements are about professional matters and are not an indictment of you as a person. Work against the tendency to become defensive and to take all negative feedback as personal. In most vendor discussions, it simply is their job to try to get as much money for their product and protect their product as much as they can.

Building Strong Working Relationships with Vendors

One of the first goals when you buy a new product or begin working at a new job is to identify your main contact. Most vendors assign a main point of contact for each library, a person who often is referred to as the library's sales representative or customer representative. Depending on the structure and size of the company, there can be one representative for an entire country or type of library, or you can have a representative who is responsible for libraries of a certain size in a certain geographic area. A rep might serve community colleges in three states, or all libraries in one state.

Large publishers can also have an additional representative called the account representative, who is also assigned to specific libraries. The sales representative is generally who you will contact for information about new products, licenses, and price negotiations, and the account representative is the person you will contact if you need an invoice or if you have any questions about access. Finally, there may be numerous sales representatives representing different products offered by a company; you might have one person who is your sales representative for databases, one who represents e-books, and one who represents e-journals.

If this seems confusing, that's because it is. The key to untangling these relationships and contacts is to home in on just one person at a company. Send them your questions, even if you are not sure they are the right person. Most will be glad to forward you on to someone who can help, thus letting you know who to contact next time.

If you unintentionally contact the wrong rep and they express frustration, ask for a different rep. This advice holds for any shoddy treatment. Part of the money you pay for electronic resources is for the satisfaction of a good customer experience.

Of course, this approach requires you to be able to find an initial contact in the company. There are few ways to go about this:

- Some libraries keep records of past vendor contacts. Ask your supervisor or someone else who has worked in a department for a long time if there is such a list and if you can access it. It's also possible the information is stored in your ILS or in your Electronic Resource Management tool, if you have one.

- If no list exists, find colleagues who have worked in collections management and acquisitions for at least a few years at your institution. Identify the major vendors you have products with, and ask them if they can find contact information for you. Often contact information will be tucked away in an email folder. Start with the top 10 to 20 vendors with which your library works. (Hint: The more money you spend with a vendor, the more important it is to have their contact information.) As new questions arise or new products become of interest, ask for new vendor contacts at the point of need.

- Contact librarians who deal with electronic resource management at libraries near you and of a similar type and size. Often these libraries will be assigned the same representatives and will be glad to share with you their list of names and emails.

- Though not advised for urgent questions, you can always gather missing contact information by approaching vendors at conferences, especially local conferences. Often the people at local conferences will be your representative. If they are not, you can still get the contact information of an actual person in a company and use that as a point of entry.

- If all else fails, look on the vendor's website. Specific personal contact information will normally not be provided, but even a general orders or sales email contact is better than nothing and will hopefully lead to a more direct contact in the future.

As a best practice, store contact information for vendors in a location that is sharable and editable by numerous people. If you have an Electronic Resource Management (ERM) system, there may be a section for storing vendor information. If you don't, a Google spreadsheet or even an Excel spreadsheet shared via a system like Dropbox can work well. Whatever system you choose, be sure to include the person's name, email, phone number, company, and position in the company. It's also valuable to record gender and preferred pronouns, even in cases where this information seems apparent.

Besides email and conferences, there are other ways to get in touch with vendors and even influence the directions of their products and business decisions. Vendors recognize that librarians are willing to provide critical feedback, have a direct conduit to patrons, and have a great deal of purchasing power. If a librarian receives poor service or an underdeveloped product, there are numerous listservs, conferences, and networks to which that librarian can air grievances and hurt a vendor's reputation. Because of this, vendors often seek ways to get feedback and interact more with librarians.

Oftentimes, vendors will seek beta testers when they are trialing new products. Volunteering to be a beta tester lets you make suggestions for the interface, get one-on-one help with trouble spots, and develop some good contacts in the technical side of the company. The best way to be invited to beta test is by reporting problems thoroughly and courteously when they arise and by asking questions of sales representatives that show you've researched the product they're selling beforehand. Of course, if representatives mention that they are creating a new product or platform, volunteering to help beta test is a good idea, too.

Vendors also hold open feedback sessions on products, often at larger conferences, but occasionally at consortia annual meetings or smaller, more specialized state meetings. Be on the lookout for feedback sessions hosted by those vendors whom your library works with regularly. They're often called "vendor sponsored sessions," and they provide a good way for you to start a relationship with a vendor.

If you are interested in talking to a specific vendor, invite them to your library to have a conversation. Vendors often tour around their states and will look to make appointments with your library. Depending on the structure of your library, you might be the main contact; alternatively, they might communicate to someone else, like your library director or head of collections. Be sure to talk to the librarians who hold these positions in your library and let them know you want to be invited to in-person meetings, conference calls, and webinars with vendors. And when you are invited, be sure to spend some time beforehand exploring the products and coming up with a few questions for the vendor.

Finally, one of the most in-depth and influential ways you can build relationships with vendors is by serving on an advisory board. Advisory boards are generally formal groups created by companies whose purposes range from advising on the general strategy of the company to focusing on specific products or platforms. Boards generally advise on product development and improvement, marketing research and strategy, and unmet needs of the community.

For librarians, serving on a board is a chance to give advice and suggestions directly to a company and to see new products before they hit the general market. The behind-the-scenes perspective gives board members a clearer understanding of current market trends and pressures that vendors might be facing.

It should be noted that usually you need to have a strong relationship with a vendor, cultivated through the other methods mentioned in this chapter, before you are asked to join an advisory board, because vendors tend to ask people they know well and whose opinions they feel are thoughtful and insightful. Don't despair if you are not asked to join an advisory board in your first few years. Building these kinds of relationships takes time.

Jumpstarting Relationships at a New Library

Beginning a new job or getting the new responsibility of managing electronic resources often leaves a librarian scrambling to dig up information known by previous staff. Finding out the names of your vendor contacts and reaching out to the ones your library considers important is a vital early step. How do you figure out which vendors are "important"? Brevig (2008, 22–32) suggests examining a vendor's complexity and criticalness. Complexity, she says, is how many individual relationships one must maintain with a vendor, the variety of products you subscribe to, and how fragmented the company is. Criticality is the negative impact on your library if you did not license a product from a vendor.

With these ideas in mind, start by going through a list of your electronic resources. You can find lists like this in a knowledge base, if your library has one; your database A–Z list; or a list of licenses that are currently active. As you go through, make note of which vendors supply the most content to your library. If you can, also determine with whom you spend the most money. Finally, think about any special populations or needs you are serving and identify the resources that specifically fill those needs. The vendors that come out on top in these questions are the ones you should focus on contacting within your first few months on the job.

When contacting those chosen vendors, the simplest way is to send an email that introduces who you are and explains what your role at the library is in terms of working with vendors. Ask if you could either meet at your library or at an upcoming conference. Most vendors will be delighted that you've proactively reached out, and this will begin your communication on a positive footing.

Negotiating with Vendors

Developing a strong relationship with vendors not only can help you influence products and fix problems more quickly, but it can also build a strong foundation for one of the more challenging parts of being a librarian involved in electronic resource management: negotiation. This is the process of mutual give and take in which two or more parties seek to find an outcome that is acceptable to all concerned. It does not mean a process in which everyone leaves happy, and it does not mean a process in which one side wins while the other loses.

This process of negotiation is often required for librarians, but is rarely taught in library school. As Ashmore, Grogg, and Weddle (2012, 22–25) point out, most librarians feel that negotiation is a scary, conflict-filled thing. This section will teach you some models and best practices that will help you face negotiation with more confidence.

Depending on your library, you might be called to negotiate with vendors directly; you might be part of a negotiation team; or negotiation might mostly take place at a higher level of the organization, or even offsite through a consortium. At some point in your career in this field, however, you will likely find yourself needing to negotiate something with a vendor. The negotiation of appropriate terms governing resource use, legal rights, and business terms, generally encapsulated in a document referred to as the license, is one of two main areas where Electronic Resources Librarians need to negotiate. The other main area is the price of a product. This negotiation more regularly happens at the library director or head of collections level, but the methods of negotiation work for both.

Note that this chapter deals with general advice on negotiating. See Chapter 3 for the gritty details of licenses.

Adopting the Negotiation Mind-Set

Negotiation does not have to be scary, but it takes practice. Though this section contains good advice that has helped many librarians who frequently engage in negotiation with vendors, there is no magic formula that will work every time. Therefore, look for chances to practice and observe negotiation.

If you have recently been tasked with negotiations as part of your job, or if you want to grow in confidence, ask to observe other negotiations that might take place in your library. These don't necessarily need to be negotiations for electronic resources; any price negotiation will do, perhaps for new furniture or spine labels. If you are the only negotiator in your library, try to find another librarian, perhaps one from a local library, who has done negotiation before, and ask if you can do mock negotiations with them for practice.

Practice and observation are important, but—according to the main writers about library negotiation (Ashmore et al. 2012; Dygert & Parang 2013)—the most important determiner of success is mind-set. When entering a negotiation, it is vital that you remember that the negotiation is about the deal in front of you. It is not, in any sense, personal. Though you can be confident, strong, or even forceful in your suggestions, you should never feel personally angry or hurt during a negotiation.

To help facilitate the right mind-set, start your own negotiation in a professional, confident, and friendly manner. Remember that you share with vendors the goal of making content accessible to patrons. Approaching a negotiation in a nonantagonistic, nonpersonal manner will help you keep your focus on the ultimate goal of the whole process: meeting your library's needs.

Of course, sometimes things can get heated, and taking criticism or perhaps antagonism from the other side is not easy. If you do start to take it personally, ask to step away from the negotiation for a time. This could be a matter of leaving the room for five minutes and getting a drink of water, or it could mean restarting the negotiation on a different day. If the situation does not get any better, and especially if you feel that the other parties are not acting in a professional manner, you are within your rights to report this to their management and request an alternative person. You can only bring the best mind-set you can.

Theories of Negotiation

Much of the theory shared in library negotiation guides, such as *Gateway to Good Negotiation: From Computer Mediated Communication to Playing Hardball* by Ashmore et al. (2012), *Honing Your Negotiation Skills* by Parang and Dygart (2013), and *Buying and Selling Information: A Guide for Information Professionals and Salespeople to Build Mutual Success* by Gruenberg (2014), comes from outside the library world, and the terminology may be unfamiliar to most librarians. These methods and theories can help you think about your negotiation in a more organized way and are mentioned repeatedly in other texts concerning negotiation. This section will introduce you to their basic principles.

Method One: Principled Negotiation

This method of negotiation comes out of the book *Getting to Yes: Negotiating Agreement without Giving In*, by Fischer, Ury, and Patton (1991). It has five main principles:

Separate the People from the Problem. This is another way of saying that negotiations are not personal. Both parties are trying to solve a problem, and personal feelings should be left out of the equation. Techniques to achieve this include trying to put yourself in the opposite party's position; acknowledging emotions when they arise and being willing to discuss them; and engaging in active listening, including paraphrasing others' statements to check for understanding.

Focus on Interests, Not Positions. This principle asks you to try to understand what core company interests lie behind a position. If a person states a position, ask "Why or why not?" Instead of challenging a position, state "yes and," followed by your own thoughts. See if you can get to their interests, and be willing to also openly discuss your own interests. Once interests are clear, discuss them, acknowledging the validity of both parties' interests.

Invent Options for Mutual Gain. Before you give up, invent a potential alternative solution that gets at their interests while protecting your own. Use phrases like "what if" to test out solutions. Be willing to try a lot of different solutions. Use a brainstorming process between parties as you try to develop solutions, and do not get fixated on a single answer. Once many solutions are proposed, look through the solutions together and agree on the most appropriate ones.

Insist on Using Objective Criteria. This principle means that you should develop some sort of standard or checklist of things that must be part of an agreement before entering negotiation. This will allow you to fall back on your document when you are trying to hold up your own position.

Know Your BATNA (Best Alternative to Negotiated Agreement). A BATNA is a term you will see thrown around a lot. It refers to your alternative solution, should you be unable to reach an agreement. One good way to think about it is to consider how you would meet a need if the product under negotiation were not available. Have a BANTA defined clearly before entering negotiation. This will allow you to recognize when the negotiated solution becomes worse (in terms of price, labor, conforming to your objective standards, or meeting needs of your patrons) than the BATNA. This is the point where you walk away from the negotiation. For example: You might be negotiating a package deal for a group of e-books. Your BATNA might be that you could go with an e-book aggregator for at least part of the content.

Method Two: The WHAT Method

This method of negotiation has four main principles:

W: What, What Else, Why, and What For? This is the step where you make sure you understand why the other party is invested in its position. This is also where you seek to clarify any parts of the agreement being negotiated that you do not understand. In short, your first step is to ask a lot of questions.

H: Hypothesize. This is the brainstorming phase, where you suggest possible solutions to help solve points of disagreement. You come up with a lot of ideas, but do not commit to any particular one.

A: Answers. This is the phase where you provide answers for the vendor in terms of your own interests and positions. Even though you are in the answer stage, don't be afraid to ask more questions; in fact, it is often best to follow up a question with another question. For example, if the vendor asks you what price is acceptable, ask the vendor what prices other peer institutions are receiving.

T: Tell Me More. When you answer their questions with more questions, or when you are initially asking questions, listen actively to their answers and prompt them to elaborate. Do not be afraid of silence, as pauses can lead to further revelations.

Tips and Techniques

Understanding the concepts of WHAT, principled negotiation, BATNA, and the power of mind-set are all powerful tools to bring to negotiation. Although your own style of negotiation will develop over time, the following techniques may be helpful. Many of them incorporate the theories discussed earlier. The techniques are presented here in a linear fashion, though it is important to note that negotiation is often a process in which steps get repeated or jumbled.

Also note that this is an ideal process. The truth is that sometimes you just do not have time to complete all these steps. Figure out which steps are essential to your feeling of comfort in the negotiation process and which steps you can sometimes skip.

Research the Company

You can better judge the company's interests, and negotiate with more empathy, when you do your research. It's worth your time to ask these questions:

- What is the company's current position in the market?
- What is the company's current profit margin?
- What deals have they offered to other similar libraries? (This could be tricky, but it is still worth asking around!)
- What are their recent acquisitions?

Answers to these questions can give you ammunition as you push for your own interests. You'll glean valuable information from company profiles, found in databases such as Hoovers, PrivCo, Mergent Online, and Morningstar. Don't be afraid to ask friendly business librarians how to use these products.

Develop a Checklist

Make a checklist of terms and price caps that must be in an agreement. This step ensures that you have objective guidelines to fall back on. Often these checklists are developed for all negotiations a library performs, though additional requirements can be added for certain situations.

In libraries, two main types of guidelines are generally used. The first consists of price caps. These set a limit on how much you're to pay for a product and how much of a price increase is acceptable from year to year for continuing resources. For example, you might have a written policy that you'll automatically consider cancelling any resource that has a price increase of more than 5 percent in a single year. The other guidelines tend to focus on terms and will be discussed in Chapter 3.

Research Your Alternatives

In order to create your BATNA, you need to know which alternatives exist. Look for reviews of other library products that might fill a similar need in places like *Library Journal* or *Choice*. Talk to other vendors who sell to a similar market and ask them questions about their competing products. Investigate how much using something like document delivery or interlibrary loan would cost compared to buying a product.

Strategize Beforehand

Create your main areas of negotiation before you enter a room or send an e-mail. Make more suggestions, not fewer, to give you room for compromise. Be thorough when reading through a contract or other deal you are negotiating, and write suggestions, alternative wordings, possible compromises, and questions on the document.

If you are unsure about what something means, be sure to highlight it and write down a question so you remember to ask. Don't be afraid to cover a document in comments and red ink. Making more suggestions will give you more room to negotiate, as you can compromise on some of the less important points in exchange for standing firm on the essentials.

Commit to a Communication Style

Recognize your weaknesses, and stick with a communication style that you feel strong in. Partner with those who can cover for you. Some people like to talk face to face, and some prefer email. Know the method of communication you prefer and default to that. If you suffer from phone anxiety and a vendor calls you, it's polite to speak to them, but it's perfectly acceptable to arrange a time to talk in person or to ask if you may email them a response later that day.

Go to the Source

Determine who among your vendor representatives has the decision-making power and attempt to negotiate with them directly, rather than with a surrogate. Often your contact will be the sales representative.

Having a good relationship with the sales rep can make them a major advocate for you and your needs, so use them!

However, sales reps often are not the ones who can make the final decisions on price and contract terms. Be sure that you eventually talk directly to the person (their boss or one of the company's lawyers) who can make these decisions. Try to email them or talk to them directly in order to decrease miscommunication and speed up the process.

Give and Take

Recognize your essentials (which should be documented on your checklist, described earlier). These are the terms you must have in order to agree to a deal. Be willing to compromise, but make sure that you are clear on what is necessary. For example, if you work at a state institution, you may be forbidden to sign any agreements that put you under another state or country's legal jurisdiction. You will be completely unable to budge on any agreement that calls for a different area of jurisdiction, but you might be able to compromise on a different aspect, such as interlibrary loan availability.

Get It in Writing

Get all agreements in writing. Having only said something and shaken hands does not make an agreement. With no documentation to prove that something was agreed to, the other side can easily insist that they did not agree to something or that they agreed to something slightly different. Even if you do not have a formal license or contract, if you agree to anything, such as price or even additional titles being added to a collection, make sure you have that written down from the vendor. Following an in-person or telephone discussion, it's a good idea to soon thereafter email the vendor with your understanding of the agreement, and to ask for a confirmation email in return.

Delay Tactics Are Totally Acceptable

If something gets difficult, be willing to delay. "I will have to ask my boss" is a good strategy. Sometimes you need to bring in a lawyer. If you feel pressured to do something you are unsure of, if the other negotiator is refusing to listen to your compromise or is acting in a rude or belligerent manner, or if they do not agree to enter into any kind of negotiation, realize that you can always delay and say you need to consult with others at your library. You may even need time to consult with the lawyer representing your institution (most colleges have a university attorney, and public libraries have the city or county infrastructure).

Be Prepared to Walk Away

Sometimes you can't come to an agreement. Sometimes you realize your BATNA is better. Sometimes one of your essentials will not be met. Sometimes your lawyer will say you can't agree to terms. You should be willing to walk away, and mean it. This can often get a vendor to reconsider the point of contention—and if not, because you have alternatives, you can still move forward with a new plan.

Conclusion

Developing and maintaining good relationships with library vendors is crucial. Sometimes the work is easy—chatting together about new products or grabbing a cup of coffee—and sometimes the work is intense. Learning about their companies and their products takes time, and negotiating with your sales reps can be an intimidating prospect. Use the advice in this chapter to give yourself a confidence boost for all of your interactions with vendors, from the conference hall to the negotiating table.

Additional Readings

Brooks, Sam. 2006. "Introduction: The Importance of Open Communication Between Libraries and Vendors." *Journal of Library Administration* 44, no. 3–4: 1–4.

Flowers, Janet L. 2004. "Specific Tips for Negotiations with Library Materials Vendors Depending upon Acquisitions Method." *Library Collections, Acquisitions, & Technical Services* 28, no. 4: 433–448.

Fries, James R., and John R. James. 2006. "Library Advisory Boards: A Survey of Current Practice Among Selected Publishers and Vendors." *Journal of Library Administration* 44, no. 3–4: 84–93.

Ginanni, Katy, et al. 2015. "Yer Doin' It Wrong: How NOT to Interact with Vendors, Publishers, or Librarians." *Serials Librarian* 68, no. 1–4: 255–261.

Johnson, Peggy. 2014. "Conducting Business with E-Content and Service Suppliers." In *Developing and Managing Electronic Collections: The Essentials.* Chicago: ALA Publications. 83–100.

Raley, Sarah, and Jean Smith. 2006. "Community College Library/Vendor Relations: You Can't Always Get What You Want . . . Or Can You?" *Journal of Library Administration* 44, no. 3–4: 187–202.

Stamison, Christine, Bob Persing, Chris Beckett, and Chris Brady. 2009. "What They Never Told You About Vendors in Library School." *Serials Librarian* 56, no. 1–4: 139–145.

References

Ashmore, Beth, Jill E. Grogg, and Jeff Weddle. 2012. *Librarian's Guide to Negotiation: Winning Strategies for the Digital Age.* Medford: Information Today, Inc.

Brevig, Armand. 2008. "Getting Value from Vendor Relationships." *Searcher* 16, no. 9: 28–34.

Carlson, David H. 2006. "Introduction: Forging Lasting Symbiotic Relationships Between Libraries and Vendors." *Journal of Library Administration* 44, no. 3–4: 5–10.

Dygert, Claire T., and Elizabeth Parang. 2013. "Honing Your Negotiation Skills." *Serials Librarian* 64, no. 1–4: 105–110.

Fischer, Roger, William L. Ury, and Bruce Patton. 1991. *Getting to Yes: Negotiating Agreement Without Giving In.* New York: Penguin Books.

Gruenberg, Michael L. 2014. *Buying and Selling Information: A Guide for Information Professionals and Salespeople to Build Mutual Success.* Medford: Information Today, Inc.

Sutton, Sarah, et al. 2016. "Core Competencies for Electronic Resources Librarians." NASIG. http://www.nasig.org/site_page.cfm?pk_association_web page_menu=310&pk_association_webpage=1225.

CHAPTER THREE

Licenses: The Fine Print

License negotiation is a common form of negotiation for Electronic Resources Librarians, especially those who work in academic libraries. Indeed, the core competencies for Electronic Resources Librarians published by NASIG list knowledge of electronic resource licensing and negotiation as one of the top 10 requirements for an Electronic Resources position. Yet as they point out, it is the requirement least likely to be taught in library schools.

Licenses can be defined as written contracts, agreed to by both parties, that outline the legal rights and restrictions of the use of content. They currently are the main governing law for electronic resources, due to the model of purchase for most electronic content. Because of the law of first sale, when a library purchases a physical item, full and perpetual ownership of that item is transferred to the library, with legal rights guided by the federal laws of copyright and fair use. Because most electronic resources are rarely or never locally hosted by the library, the library does not own these resources, but instead leases access to them through a vendor.

Because of this, the default law covering the use of electronic resources is contract law, in the form of licenses. There has been some resistance to this model by libraries, but at the moment, it is the most common way to get access to resources. Contract law trumps standing federal law. This means that what legal rights library users have can vary greatly by product and can be much more restrictive than standard copyright. This change in access makes the understanding of license terms essential for Electronic Resources Librarians.

Although this chapter cannot include everything there is to know about licenses, it hits the most important points:

- **A Note on Public Libraries:** Where license negotiation is comparatively easygoing
- **Preparing to Negotiate:** Doing your homework
- **Definitions and Examples:** The lingo of licenses
- **Authorized and Unauthorized Uses:** Interlibrary loan; scholarly sharing; printing, copying, and downloading; electronic reserves and course packs; fair use
- **Business Terms:** Routine business transactions that help the library's processes
- **E-book Licenses:** Special terms and issues
- **Streaming Media Licenses:** Special terms and issues
- **Current Trends in Licensing:** Shared Electronic Resource Understanding (SERU), ONIX-PL, and data and text mining
- **You Are Not Alone:** Additional resources
- **Housekeeping:** License management and preservation

The amount of negotiation you will need to do will vary by job. In many academic libraries, license negotiation is a given for librarians working with electronic resources. In public libraries, negotiation might be handled more by consortia or the state library system. But even if you don't actively engage in the negotiation of licenses, the ability to read licenses and understand what they mean for your users is vital. This chapter is worth a read, whether you currently negotiate licenses or not.

A Note on Public Libraries

Public libraries typically devote far less attention to licensing than do their academic counterparts. If you work in a public library, the level of detail in this chapter may seem like overkill, particularly for those public libraries that do not handle their own licenses. You do not need to be fluent in the intricacies of negotiation if all of your electronic resources are negotiated by a third party, such as a consortium or the state library.

But public libraries that handle some or all of their negotiations in house often have a, shall we say, *relaxed* attitude toward negotiating. An attorney will review the license to make sure there are no egregious legal problems, but librarians commonly suggest few or no changes, accepting the license precisely as the vendor presented it.

Public libraries that do not currently spend quality time reviewing and negotiating licenses should evaluate their approach. It could be that change is unnecessary, difficult, or undesirable, depending on the staffing and culture of any given library. But a change in process may well be worth the effort. The time and headache of negotiating can yield ample dividends in the form of cost savings and superior terms.

Preparing to Negotiate

Before you dive into license negotiation at an institution, there are a few things you need to find out:

- Discover who has signatory authority at your library. Usually this will be the library director or dean, the head of collections, or the lawyer or legal department. Whatever you negotiate will need to go through the signatory authority, so it's important to know who that is.
- Inquire about the current legal climate at your institution and what specific legal rules might be in place. Some libraries might have certain terms or phrases that they will always try to remove or add. These terms might come from the library director, the library board, or state law. Ask your library director and your institution's lawyers what terms must be included, what terms must be removed, and what terms are nice but not mandatory.
- Determine how to proceed should a vendor prove unwilling to agree to one of the required terms. Depending on your institution, you might need to directly involve lawyers, you might need to get permission from higher levels to make an exception to standard procedure, or you might have to give up on licensing the product.

Once you have gathered this information, you can create a document called a licensing checklist or licensing guide. It should include, at a minimum, four pieces of information:

- **Examples of licensing language that should be changed.** Your document should describe why this language should be changed and provide suggestions for possible modifications. Group these descriptions into three main categories: required license elements, language that is unacceptable, and license elements that are preferred but are not essential.
- **Business terms.** Include a list of business terms in a license that should be included for the library's own records. This includes information like price, renewal cycle, authorization method, title lists, late fees, ownership, access methods, and definitions of the licensee and licensor.
- **Special rules.** Identify special rules for specific types of licenses, like e-books, streaming media, or click-through licenses.
- **Special permissions.** Explain how to get special permission for unacceptable language or lack of required language, if such a process exists.

You can create a licensing checklist or guide from scratch, or you can also ask a library serving a similar population for their checklist, which you can then modify. This latter option will save you a lot of work, obviously; just be sure it includes the elements described earlier.

Definitions and Examples

Finding out about your institution's requirements and building off an existing license document are good ways to start. Sometimes, however, you may encounter license terms that are not yet accounted for in your institution's existing licenses guidelines. It's also possible that your institution simply doesn't have guidelines. And even if you're working with a good set of guidelines, the person who wrote them might have struggled to explain what different license terms mean.

To help, this section offers examples and definitions of license terms that are confusing or that frequently need a lot of negotiation. This is not an extensive list of every term that should be examined, as entire books have been written about this topic; see the end of this chapter for some additional readings. But it is a good starting point to help you better understand licenses and to assist with the creation of your own licensing guide.

Curing a Breach

A breach happens when either party violates the terms of the contract in some way. Curing a breach is the act of fixing that violation. It describes what either party will do to stop a breach from continuing and details any legal or fiscal compensation the breaching party must provide.

For example, a vendor noticed that someone at the University of North Carolina at Greensboro had downloaded over 200 resources within five minutes. The vendor threatened to permanently shut off access and void the contract. Fortunately, the university had successfully negotiated for a 30-day window for taking corrective actions and was able to resolve the problem to everyone's satisfaction within that time frame.

- Make sure that any breach language only refers to a material breach. A material breach is a violation that occurs when a party knowingly goes directly against a contract. The aggrieved party collects damages that result from that one mistake, nothing more.
- Be sure to not allow the licensor to collect direct damages.
- Add in language (if it does not exist already) that gives the library 30 days to remedy the breach themselves before any action against them is taken.

- If there is any mention of terms like "irreparable harm from a breach," attempt to remove this language. This language allows the vendor to ask for far more damages than the actual breach would justify.

Example of Language: "Either party may terminate this License by written notice with immediate effect if the other party materially breaches any of the terms and conditions of this License and/or the Copyright Policy and the License shall terminate forthwith where such breach cannot be rectified, or if it can be rectified, the License shall terminate where the party in breach fails to rectify such breach within sixty (60) days of receipt of the aforesaid notice stating the breach and the action required to rectify it."

Indemnification

"Indemnification" is legalese for "compensation." In an indemnification clause, one party agrees to hold the indemnified party harmless and will not require them to pay any fees in case of a breach or any other legal matter. If a library indemnifies a vendor, this means they relinquish the right to seek damages against that vendor.

- In general, it is best to completely remove any clauses that require the library to indemnify the vendor.
- If this is not possible, talk to your legal counsel about possible language referring to state laws that might overrule this and refer to them in the document. This works especially well if you are at a state or federal institution.
- If you cannot get rid of it, also try to write in a clause that says you cannot be held responsible for the actions of third-party users—that is to say, your patrons.

Example of Language: "The licensee shall indemnify the licensor against all claims, causes of action, losses, liabilities, and damages (including costs and expenses of legal representatives) incurred by defending a claim arising from: any unauthorized use or dissemination of the licensed materials by the licensee or any authorized users."

Warrantees

In library licenses, warranties are where the licensor guarantees that they have the permission of copyright holders to license the materials on offer.

- Problems can arise if the license does not list a warranty. You do not want to be held liable for the licensor forgetting to get the correct permissions.
- If the license does not list a warranty, be sure to insert language (like that provided in the following example) into the license.

Example of Language: "Licensor warrants to the Licensee that it is duly licensed to use, in accordance with the terms and conditions hereof, the Licensed Material and that the Licensed Material, if used as contemplated in this License, does not knowingly infringe any copyright or other proprietary or intellectual property rights of any natural or legal person."

Jurisdiction

The jurisdiction clause states which laws govern this license and under what court system any legal disputes will be settled.

- Be sure that the jurisdiction is listed as the state where your library is located or that the license is silent on jurisdiction. Especially if you are at a state-run institution, having the wrong jurisdiction will generally be a deal-breaker.
- This is an extremely common change that libraries have to make, because many licensors list their own location as the governing jurisdiction.

Example of Language: "This Agreement shall be governed by and construed in accordance with the laws of the State of [fill in your state here]."

Authorized Users

This language defines who has permission to use the resources you license.

- You want this to be as broad as possible.
- For academic licenses at public institutions, make sure you have the license include walk-in users, meaning nonaffiliated members who are physically at the library.
- For public libraries, make sure you define your users as anyone who has a library card, as well as anyone who walks into the library building, even if they don't have a card.

Be sure to have it include offsite users who would otherwise be authorized. In public libraries, this means library cardholders in good standing;

in academic libraries, this means current faculty, students, and staff, but usually not alumni or retirees.

Example of Language: "'Authorized Users' means faculty staff and students or users affiliated with the Licensee in some other capacity whereby they are permitted by the Licensee to access such services as are available to faculty, staff, students, and library patrons whether from a computer or terminal on the Licensee's secure network or offsite via a modem link to the Licensee's secure network, as well as users at terminals located in the library facilities of the Licensed Site."

Limitation of Liability

Limitation of liability governs what kind of damages and the amount to be paid to the licensee in a remedy for breach of the license. It is often used by vendors to make sure they are not responsible for as much as they might otherwise be in a court of law.

- If possible, remove any limitation of liability.
- If not possible, you want to make sure that the limitation of liability mentioned in the contract does not contradict state and federal laws that are put in place to govern contracts. In this case, add a phrase like "So far as permitted by the law of the State of X" before the clause.

Example of Language: "Where permitted to do so by law, the licensor limits its liability under this license to the value of the initial fee and/or any renewal fees paid to X during the previous twelve (12) months."

Primacy of the Signed License

The presence of this language indicates that what is in the signed license is the final say in all legal questions, no matter what any online terms of use or previous emails have stated. It allows the library to refer to the license if any legal disputes arise.

- The most common problem with this clause is its absence. If this language is not present, be sure to add it to your license.
- You might also see statements that say that the licensor can make changes to the terms at any time without notifying the licensee. Strike this language and replace it with language that says something similar to "all changes to this license must be submitted to the licensee and signed by both parties."

Example of Language: "The terms and conditions of this Agreement override all online click-through agreements, any click-wrap agreements, any automatic update agreements, and any other agreement, of whatever kind, whereby users of the Licensed Materials purport to enter into or accept contractual terms or conditions that are different from, or in addition to, this Agreement."

Policing Users

Language about policing users, especially in conjunction with the phrase "best effort," is often found in licenses, generally under the "Licensee Obligations" section. It attempts to hold the library responsible for all users and asks the library to police their behavior.

- Libraries should never hold themselves responsible for user actions and should never agree to police users, as this would be a huge burden on the library. If you see a clause like this, attempt to replace any instances of "best effort" or other definitive words like "shall" or "will" with the phrase "use reasonable effort."
- Include a statement saying that you cannot be held responsible for the actions of third-party users and that you cannot police their actions.

Example of Language: "Subscriber will restrict access to the Licensed Materials to Authorized Users. Subscriber will use their best effort to not permit anyone other than Authorized Users to use the Licensed Materials."

Authorized and Unauthorized Uses

The previous section addressed those parts of the license that are most likely to be confusing or in need of negotiation. The part of the license that lists authorized and unauthorized uses is less confusing and less contentious, but it nonetheless deserves close scrutiny, because it may be missing key user rights.

Interlibrary Loan (ILL)

Endeavor to make sure that ILL is permitted. If possible, also try to make sure that electronic resources can be transmitted electronically and do not need to be printed out and then rescanned. (Yes, this is very common.)

Example Language to Insert: "Licensee may fulfill requests from other libraries, a practice commonly called Interlibrary Loan. Licensee agrees to fulfill such requests in accordance with Sections 107 and 108 of the U.S. Copyright Act. Requests may be fulfilled using electronic, paper, or intermediated means."

Scholarly Sharing

It is important that authorized users be allowed to share resources with unauthorized users. In academic libraries, this might mean colleagues at other institutions; in public libraries, this might mean study partners who don't have library cards. Try to make sure that this type of use is allowed.

Example Language to Insert: "Authorized Users may transmit to a third-party colleague, in paper or electronically, reasonable amounts of the Licensed Materials for personal, scholarly, educational, scientific, or research uses."

Printing, Copying, and Downloading

If possible, make sure that users can fully print and download resources. This is especially important for e-books, because vendors and publishers often subject them to artificial limits.

Example Language to Insert: "Licensee and Authorized Users may electronically display, download, digitally copy, and print the Licensed Materials."

Electronic Reserves and Course Packs

For academic libraries, make sure that resources can be printed out for course packs and placed online in electronic reserve systems.

Example Language to Insert: "Licensee and Authorized Users may use the Licensed Resources for print and electronic reserve readings in connection with specific courses of instruction offered by Licensee."

Fair Use Clause

This usually is not included in licenses. Add it wherever possible.

Example Language: "Nothing in this license will override the principles of Fair Use as outlined in Section 107 and 108 of U.S. Copyright law."

Business Terms

This is arguably the driest section of the license, which is really saying something. "Business terms" is a blanket description for routine business transactions. Though vendors commonly omit some of these terms, they are essential for a library's smooth operations. Include as many of them as you can.

List of Items Covered by License

It is useful to know what you are getting, so make sure a list is attached to the license, if possible. This may not be practical with e-books, though, if you are buying everything a publisher releases annually; at the time of signing, they might not even know what they'll be publishing that year. In that case, have them write something like "all books published by X publisher in YEAR."

Aggregators also generally cannot give you a title list, as their lists tend to be in flux, but they should at least be able to provide a list of which databases and aggregated collections you are licensing.

Guarantee of Usage Statistics

It is best if the vendor writes down the type of usage statistics available to the library and how they will be made available. Ideally, vendors will provide COUNTER statistics (discussed in Chapter 8). If COUNTER is not explicitly mentioned, ask the vendors if they provide these statistics; if so, insert that into the license.

Guarantee of MARC Record Delivery

Especially for e-books, it is important for vendors to regularly give you updated MARC records for your catalog. The license should list how those will be delivered and the frequency of the delivery.

Renewal Terms

Make sure the license states when you will be notified of the new renewal price and how soon after a renewal notification the invoice will be due. When possible, remove any language about automatic renewals and replace it with notification of renewal either 30 or 60 days before the end of the subscription.

Authentication Methods

Check that the license states how offsite users will be authenticated. This is up to the library, though most institutions prefer IP authentication.

Inflation Cap

This is a statement that says a price can only increase by X amount per year over the life span of the contract. Unsurprisingly, this tends to not exist in most contracts unless you add it, and its irregularity will require a decent amount of negotiation on your part. Aim for locking in price increases of 5 percent or less. Be aware that this might not fall under license negotiation and may instead be handled during pre-negotiation.

Early Cancellation

This section lists the reasons either party might leave a contract early. It generally includes failure of either party to correct a breach or financial insolvency of either party. It is best if a warning in writing is delivered at least 30 days before early cancellation.

Perpetual Access

This section lists which content the licensee may continue to access if the contract is terminated and the mechanisms for granting that access. Not every license will include such information, but this is an extremely important component to try to include. You want to get as much access to the resource as possible, so shoot for complete access, either via a locally hosted site or a vendor-hosted site.

Be forewarned that vendors will generally not agree to this language in its entirety. In many cases, however, they will let you retain access to content published during the years you were actively paying for the content. For example, if you subscribed to a journal from 2007–2015 and received access to that journal's full run, you would still have access to the content published during 2007–2015 if you cancelled.

Good example language for this is: "On termination of this License, the Publisher shall provide continuing access for Authorized Users to that part of the Licensed Materials which was published and paid for within the Subscription Period, either from the Server or by supplying [electronic files] [CD-ROMS] [printed copies] to the Licensee."

Archival Access

This statement lists the options that exist for the licensee if the company stops being able to maintain electronic access (usually in the case of dissolution). This is a very nice clause to have in combination with perpetual access, as it gives you the peace of mind that you will be able to keep access to what you purchased no matter what happens to the original licensor.

There are three major programs for archival access online, called Portico, CLOCKSS, and LOCKSS. Try to get one or more of these programs listed in your license, especially for e-journals. Note that to use any of these programs, your library needs to be a member.

- Portico (www.portico.org/digital-preservation) works with publishers to archive their resources, but the archive is normally not available after cancellation. Instead, this material becomes available to the subscribing library only when the content is no longer available anywhere digitally.

- CLOCKSS (www.clockss.org/clockss/Home), which stands for Controlled LOCKSS, is similar to Portico, wherein material is preserved and then shared only once it is no longer available digitally anywhere else. However, unlike Portico, you do not need a subscription to access this shared content. Participating publishers have agreed to open their content to everyone, for free, under a Creative Commons license, in the event their content becomes unavailable elsewhere. Examples of such content can be found at clockss.org/clockss/Triggered_Content.

- For LOCKSS (www.lockss.org/about/how-it-works), being a member connects you to a network of publisher materials that have been crawled and extracted into a server. You maintain your own local version of this server, which only gathers the material to which you subscribe. Access automatically switches to the LOCKSS copy when the publisher's website is down for any reason.

E-Book Licenses

Most of the content in this chapter is relevant no matter what type of resource you are licensing, but e-books have their own set of special considerations: their licenses tend to be less consistent and more restrictive than e-journal licenses. This is due to the relative newness of the format and because books, unlike journals, tend to be read as a whole.

Initially, publishers were loath to sell e-book access to libraries. Whereas before a library might purchase hundreds of print copies of a bestseller to meet patron demand, the new technology threatened to change things.

Libraries fantasized about purchasing a grand total of one electronic copy. Everyone could read the same copy simultaneously, and it would never wear out.

This fantasy never came to pass. Publishers wanted to stay in business, and vendors understandably wanted to prevent unfettered access to popular e-books. Their solution took the form of artificial limits, restrictive guidelines, and strict controls over user access, often in the form of Digital Rights Management (DRM).

For librarians trying to negotiate licenses, these restrictions can lead to some challenges. E-books are much more likely to have programming built into their platform that stops readers from performing certain actions, such as printing more than 70 pages or downloading the entire book. They also tend to have DRM that controls how many people can access a book at once, often limiting use to only one or three users at a time.

It is very difficult to negotiate against DRM: these controls are often built directly into the software, and removing them would require an entire rewrite of the platform. Thus, in licenses, you must read carefully for a discussion of Digital Rights Management or Digital Locks. If the license is silent on this point, ask the publisher if this means there is no DRM. If there is DRM, make sure it is written explicitly in the license. You can try to strike DRM from licenses, but understand that it may be functionally impossible for the vendor to remove it.

If you don't want DRM, the best thing to do is to look for publishers who explicitly exclude it from their platform. This is a selling point for many vendors who sell to academic markets, including Project Muse, JSTOR, Springer, and Credo. For public libraries, DRM for e-books is all but unavoidable, though some platforms are less restrictive than others. The purchasing model for Hoopla, for instance, allows for unlimited simultaneous access to e-books.

Licenses for e-books generally include a clause that prohibits bypassing or removing DRM and that recognizes DRM tampering as a breach of contract. If you see language to this effect, be sure that the library is not held responsible for any DRM breaches and is not expected to police users. Use similar strategies as described in the Policing Users section earlier.

There are a few other things you will want to make sure are specified in e-book licenses:

- A list of the type of e-readers the e-books are compatible with
- A list of the file formats that are available for download
- The number of devices a patron may use to access the same book

- The conditions that trigger a purchase, in the case of demand-driven acquisitions (as discussed in Chapter 4)

Compared to e-journals, user rights for e-books tend to be much more restrictive at the beginning of negotiation. Very few companies allow full interlibrary loan, and few allow an entire book to be added as an e-reserve. Instead, vendors may permit ILL or e-reserve for discrete chapters, which are roughly equivalent in length to journal articles. When you get these clauses, feel free to insert language allowing ILL, such as:

"Licensee may fulfill a reasonable number of requests for Interlibrary Loan of the Licensed Materials from institutions not participating in this Agreement, provided such requests comply with Section 108 of the United States Copyright Law (17 USC §108) and clause 3 of the Guidelines for the Proviso of Subsection 108(g)(2) prepared by the National Commission on New Technological Uses of Copyrighted Works (CONTU)."

Finally, be aware that when you order e-books through book jobbers (for example, YBP or Ingram), you will need to negotiate a separate license for each vendor. This is due to the lack of standardization in licenses for e-books, especially around DRM restrictions of user privileges.

Streaming Media Licenses

Streaming media licensing is even newer than e-book licensing and therefore even murkier. As with printed books, physical multimedia such as audio and video are typically purchased on an individual basis and do not involve subscriptions. But the growing demand for online media, fueled by the development of commercial streaming services, has led to new methods of delivering content to patrons. Licensed on a subscription basis, these new methods most often take the form of platforms that offer package deals.

Some libraries have attempted to get permission to digitally reproduce their own physical holdings and then circulate the files to interested parties, but this approach requires a lot of individual negotiation and time. So, for now, the subscription license is the standard way to get access to streaming media.

As is the case with e-books, some special rules and trends surround the licensing of streaming media. The American Society of Composers and Producers, as well as a large number of movie studios, have a history of actively looking for violations of copyright and contract. Because of this, you need to make sure that online classroom use is explicitly permitted in the contract if you work at an academic institution. Scan the contract for language about support for the TEACH Act or fair use. This type of language generally will be found in the section detailing user rights, often next to statements about fair use.

The TEACH Act (Technology, Education, and Copyright Harmonization) is legislation that was developed to help interpret what counts as fair use for teachers in distance and online classrooms. The key part for streaming media is that instructors can show a film or play a track in an online classroom if access to it is controlled so that only those enrolled in the class can view it. Videos or movie links must also be removed after class is finished, and no permanent digital copy may be made.

In a similar vein, some streaming media licenses for academic libraries restrict use to onsite only. If you see language prohibiting off-campus use, try to replace it with language in your Authorized User section. Here are two variations you might use:

- The Licensor and Licensee define "Authorized Users" as the following: The Licensee's full-time and part-time students, regardless of their physical location.
- The Licensor and Licensee define "Authorized Users" as the following: All valid library ID holders, regardless of their physical location.

Another new area for negotiation is public performance rights (PPR). Per Section 101 of Title 17 of the U.S. Code, a performance or display is "public" if it is "at a place open to the public or at any place where a substantial number of persons outside of a normal circle of a family and its social acquaintances is gathered." Most contracts require a different set of permissions—and additional money—for public performances, and the inclusion of a statement about public performance rights is not a guarantee in a streaming media license.

If no such statement exists, you can try to add a phrase such as "This license grants the licensee the right to display the licensed material in a public setting without an additional fee or permissions." Similarly, you can attempt to remove language that forbids public performance. Often this is a very challenging thing to negotiate, as companies rely on this extra source of revenue.

PUBLIC LIBRARIES VS. ACADEMIC LIBRARIES: PPR

Well-intentioned but misinformed people often conflate public per-formance rights with fair use. They're not the same thing. In university settings, faculty and staff might blithely show a movie without PPR at an extracurricular lecture, mistakenly believing that it is permissible under fair use. In public libraries, librarians make the same mistake when they show clips as part of presentations to the community or when they play copyrighted songs as part of Story Hour.

If you cannot negotiate PPR, it is wise to mention this explicitly in any publicity for your new resource and on links to the content (such as a database A–Z page, a subject guide, or a MARC record). Indicate that the resource does not allow public performance rights, and direct users to the distributor of the film if they want to obtain these rights.

Tread carefully. Public performance rights are expensive, but not as expensive as lawsuits.

Another difference between streaming media and other types of elec-tronic resources is the short duration of their licenses. Often, streaming media licenses are only good for one to three years, after which the license needs to be renegotiated and the library needs to pay the leasing price again. This is due to the relationship between producers, such as music labels and movie studios, and distributors, such as Kanopy and Swank. Producers license their content to distributors for limited periods because they must juggle and renegotiate many licenses of their own with the many entities that create their content (stock footage, music used in films, etc.).

The conservative duration of the license on the producers' end passes to the distributor, which passes to the library. Libraries thus find them-selves forced to pay to relicense these resources as often as once per year. You may wish to negotiate for the longest allowable time for licenses, usually three to five years. This may be unsuccessful, though, as license duration is often out of the distributor's hands.

Finally, due to the streaming nature of this type of media, many ele-ments brought up in previous sections—like archival access, availability of ILL, and scholarly sharing—will either be omitted or prohibited. For archival access, this is because no systems like Portico or LOCKSS exist for streaming media. In addition, the very nature of streaming media means that it cannot be downloaded and then shared with another library or another researcher at a different institution. Including these elements in the license would simply be impractical.

Current Trends in Licensing

The rise of licensing for e-books and streaming media is currently the biggest change facing the licensing landscape. They are not the only movements in this field, though. Librarians and publishers have been working together to try to make the license process easier and more standard. In addition, scholars have begun implementing new ways to use licensed resources, such as data and text mining. Having at least a passing familiarity with these trends will allow you to more actively participate in the national conversations around licensing.

Discussed next are three new practices that are frequently discussed in the licensing world. There are not the only things happening in licensing now, of course, but they are some of the most visible trends and bear watching.

Shared Electronic Resource Understanding (SERU)

SERU (www.niso.org/workrooms/seru) is a standard developed by the National Information Standards Organization (NISO). It serves as an alternative to a license. Publishers and libraries can sign up with NISO to be a registered SERU partner, meaning they are willing to use SERU at their organization when feasible. SERU is not a contract and is not a legal document, and thus does not address issues like liability, indemnity, and warranties. Instead, it is a group of commonly agreed-upon terms concerning authorized users, accepted uses by users, inappropriate uses by users, confidentiality and privacy, archiving, perpetual use, and online service standards for vendors.

These terms are broadly defined and generally rely on copyright and fair use. Things that vary from agreement to agreement, such as renewal terms, price, title lists, and type of purchase (PDA, DDA) need to be added in a separate document, such as a purchase order.

Once your library is registered, having a publisher agree to use a SERU agreement can save a great deal of time that would otherwise be spent on negotiation. If a vendor does not initially offer a SERU agreement—especially if it is an agreement with a small publisher for a small, relatively standard collection of resources—it can be worth asking if they would be willing to use SERU. Many vendors say yes, as this also saves them time.

ONIX-PL

ONIX-PL (www.editeur.org/21/onix-pl) is an XML schema that encodes licenses in a machine-readable, standardized layout. Vendors are supposed to do the initial coding, and then library systems are supposed to be able to interpret this code and use it to push important end-user restrictions to public interfaces. It is also supposed to allow for easier comparison of terms across licenses.

Some systems, such as the open-source project KB+ in the UK, have begun to incorporate ONIX-PL. Most systems have not, however, and so the implementation rate has remained low. But there is hope for a future increase in adoption: in recent iterations, an easier editor called OPEL has been developed, and the complexity of the overall structure has been reduced.

Data and Text Mining

Especially for academic content, scholars have increasingly been interested in searching, via code, through a large amount of either text or data in order to find hitherto unknown patterns. This technique is especially popular within the digital humanities. However, due to concerns about the selling of content and illegal sharing, many publishers prohibit the downloading and subsequent searching of vast amounts of their resources. Scholars who perform text or data mining can be accused of violating the contract. Due to this, libraries have begun to insert clauses into the User Rights section that cover data and text mining. An example from the Liblicense model license would be:

"Authorized Users may use the Licensed Materials to perform and engage in text and/or data mining activities for academic research, scholarship, and other educational purposes, utilize and share the results of text and/or data mining in their scholarly work, and make the results available for use by others, so long as the purpose is not to create a product for use by third parties that would substitute for the Licensed Materials. Licensor will cooperate with Licensee and Authorized Users as reasonably necessary in making the Licensed Materials available in a manner and form most useful to the Authorized User."

Most public libraries do not use this type of clause. But for academic libraries, especially those serving large research institutions, this is something that will come up and, if not covered in a license this way, will cause a breach of contract. Securing permission for text and data mining is therefore an important preventative measure for academic libraries.

You Are Not Alone

Though this chapter provides examples of licensing language to help with your negotiations, it is certainly not comprehensive in scope.

Fortunately, librarians have already realized the need for more examples of language and have created numerous model licenses to assist in negotiation. A model license is a license developed by a group of librarians that includes example terminology that the creators recommend as advantageous to libraries. You are free to copy and modify any of the language in these licenses and use it in your own negotiation. Here are few good ones to check out:

- **Liblicense** (liblicense.crl.edu/licensing-information/model-license): Developed by the Center for Research Libraries, this license's language is written with the academic library as the primary audience. It was completely revised in 2014 to include more recent concerns such as Digital Rights Management and text and data mining. It not only contains example language for most terms a librarian would need, but also includes editorial commentary about why the authors decided to phrase the language the way they did.
- **California Digital Library Standard Licensing Agreement** (www.cdlib.org/services/collections/toolkit): This license is specifically written for a large public university system, but it can be adapted for many types and sizes of libraries. The license provides a lot of good language and features an example of a licensing checklist. The language concerning perpetual access and confidentiality is especially good.
- **NERL Model License** (nerl.org/nerl-documents/nerl-model-license): Updated in 2016, this is another academic-leaning model license. This license goes deeply into good business terms and terms of agreement.

PUBLIC VS. ACADEMIC LIBRARIES: LICENSES

Where are all the examples of public library licenses? They do exist, though they are not available online with the same purpose and scope as the examples of academic library licenses. This is presumably because there is less perceived need. Licenses are a do-it-yourself affair at most academic libraries, whereas in public libraries, it is much more common for third parties to handle negotiations.

Housekeeping

Because licenses are a binding legal document for each resource, they need to be managed and preserved. They serve as the main legal and historical record for an agreement and thus will be drawn upon frequently in the event of any questions regarding user access, price, title lists, or other legal questions. They also contain information that users should know regarding copying, sharing, and printing. Most vendors do not license resources in perpetuity, which means that the calendar for renegotiation needs to be tracked. These steps generally fall under the purview of the Electronic Resources Librarian.

Although methods of organization need to be guided by your own institution's workflows and practices, you may wish to incorporate some or all of these suggestions:

Save your final license electronically. Use a space that can be accessed by numerous parties. If you have an Electronic Resource Management (ERM) system, it may allow you to create records for licenses and then attach the actual license to the record. If you don't have an ERM, creating a folder on a shared drive works well. Use a straightforward, intuitive organizational structure, such as storing licenses based on the year they were signed, with the filename identifying the publisher and product.

Push terms to end-users. Some ERM systems let you record different terms of a license and then display selected terms to users via notifications in your journal A–Z list, catalog, or database A–Z list. This requires integration between your ERM and your front-end systems. Common terms pushed to users include information about copying, printing, ILL, and downloading. ERM systems that provide this functionality include stand-alone systems like Goldrush and CORAL, as well as systems integrated into broader integrated library management systems, like Alma, OCLC Worldshare, Sierra, and BLUEcloud.

Share generic terms with end-users. If you do not have an ERM but still want to share license information with end-users, one option is to create a generic page listing typical license details, such as adherence to copyright and fair use, and a warning to patrons that the library cannot be held responsible for their use or misuse.

Track negotiations and renewals. Minchew (2015) wrote an excellent piece about keeping track of license negotiation and renewals without an ERM and instead using the free piece of workflow management software called Trello. Her article describes using Trello, a software tool that allows the product administrator to create tasks or even checklists on cards and assign them to a user. As steps in the workflow are completed, the assigned person then moves the card through the corresponding column. Deadlines can also be set to remind the user that certain steps need to be completed soon. Minchew used this setup to assign users various negotiation and license processing tasks and to make sure licenses moved smoothly through the system. Some ERMs, like Alma and CORAL, also have workflow management components that can help a user through the steps of negotiation and even send an email reminder to the user when it is time to negotiate a license.

Conclusion

Though licensing can seem overwhelming and filled with a great many technicalities and pitfalls, it is an essential skill for Electronic Resources Librarians, be they academic or public. This chapter was designed to provide a broad overview of licensing. The goal here is not that you will become an expert license negotiator, but that you now have a better understanding of what some of the terms thrown around in licenses mean, that you now have some practical guidance on how to start to approach these terms, and that you can more easily understand conversations about licensing happening on a national level. Remember: you only get better with practice, so go out there and license!

Additional Readings

Algenio, Emilie, and Alexia Thompson-Young. 2005. "Licensing E-Books: The Good, the Bad, and the Ugly." *Journal of Library Administration* 42, no. 3–4: 113–128.

Barrett, Heather. 2016. "Building Your Licensing and Negotiation Skills Toolkit." *Serials Librarian* 70, no. 1: 333–342.

Bowen, Tim, et al. 2014. "Using Computing Power to Replace Lawyers: Advances in Licensing and Access." *Serials Librarian* 66, no. 1–4: 232–240.

Carrico, Jeffrey C., and Kathleen L. Smalldon. 2004. "Licensed to ILL: A Beginning Guide to Negotiating E-Resources Licenses to Permit Resource Sharing." *Journal of Library Administration* 40, no. 1–2: 41–54.

Chamberlain, Clint, Vida Damijonaitis, Selden Durgom Lamoureux, Brett Rubinstein, Lisa Sibert, and Micheline Westfall. 2010. "Informing Licensing Stakeholders: Toward a More Effective Negotiation." *Serials Librarian* 58, no. 1–4: 127–140.

Dygert, Claire, and Jeanne M. Langendorfer. 2014. "Fundamentals of E-Resource Licensing." *Serials Librarian* 66, no. 1–4: 289–297.

Dygert, Claire T., and Elizabeth Parang. 2013. "Honing Your Negotiation Skills." *Serials Librarian* 64, no. 1–4: 105–110.

Eschenfelder, Kristin R. 2008. "Every Library's Nightmare? Digital Rights Management, Use Restrictions, and Licensed Scholarly Digital Resources." *College & Research Libraries* 69, no. 3: 205–225.

Fowler, David C. 2005. "Licensing: An Historical Perspective." *Journal of Library Administration* 42, no. 3–4: 177–197.

Harris, Lesley Ellen. 2001. *Licensing Digital Content: A Practical Guide for Librarians.* Chicago: ALA Editions.

Hiatt, C. Derrik. 2013. "ONIX-PL: An Adaptable Standard for E-Resource Licenses." *Technicalities* 33, no. 5: 12–15.

Johnson, Peggy. 2014. *Developing and Managing Electronic Collections: The Essentials*. Chicago: ALA Editions.

Kaplan, Richard. 2012. *A How-To-Do-It Manual for Librarians: Building and Managing E-Book Collections*. Chicago: ALA Editions.

Lamoureux, Selden Durgom, Clint Chamberlain, and Jane Bethel. 2010. "Basics of E-Resource Licensing." *Serials Librarian* 58, no. 1–4: 20–31.

Lokhande, Amogh S. 2014. "Licensing of Electronic Periodicals in Academic Libraries." *International Journal of Information Dissemination & Technology* 4, no. 4: 275–277.

McElfresh, Laura Kane. 2006. "Licensing of E-Resources: Easing the Flow." *Technicalities* 26, no. 3: 1–14.

Regan, Shannon. 2015. "Lassoing the Licensing Beast: How Electronic Resources Librarians Can Build Competency and Advocate for Wrangling Electronic Content Licensing." *Serials Librarian* 68, no. 1–4: 318–324.

Rolnik, Zachary, Selden Lamoureux, and Kelly A. Smith. 2008. "Alternatives to Licensing of E-Resources." *Serials Librarian* 54, no. 3–4: 281–287.

Schiller, Kurt. 2010. "A Happy Medium: Ebooks, Licensing, and DRM." *Information Today* 27, no. 2: 1–44.

Taylor, Liane, and Eugenia Beh. 2014. "Model Licenses and License Templates: Present and Future." *Serials Librarian* 66, no. 1–4: 92–95.

References

Center for Research Libraries. 2017. "Model Licenses." *LIBLICENSE: Licensing Digital Content* http://liblicense.crl.edu/licensing-information/model-license.

Minchew, Tessa. 2015. "Who's on First?: License Team Workflow Tracking With Trello." *Serials Review* 41, no. 3: 165–172.

CHAPTER FOUR

Buy All the Things!

Acquisitions is collection development's ugly little sister. Collection development is the fun part of the equation: you get to read reviews and listen to requests and judge the needs of your library, and then you go forth and find what works best for your budget. I'll take this e-book bundle, please! And that package of journals and these databases!

Pity the acquisitions staff, who have to figure out how to make all that happen.

The role of acquiring resources for the library does not get enough love. Collection development is a mainstay of library school curricula, but the nuts and bolts of the acquisitions process rarely gets addressed. In an Amazon world, people shrug it off as an insignificant detail. What's so hard about clicking a button, right?

If only it were so easy.

The act of acquiring electronic resources may not be sexy, but it is essential work, and far more complicated than it would seem at first blush. This chapter takes some of the mystery out of acquisitions by exploring a few key concepts:

- **Traditional Purchasing Options**: These are the standard purchasing options that everyone expects you to magically know from day one on the job.
- **Emerging Purchasing Options**: Still very much in flux, these are alternatives to the traditional way of doing things.
- **Pricing Models**: Unfortunately, not nearly as straightforward as you might think.
- **Workflows for Acquisitions**: How to get your systems in place.
- **Open Access**: A new way of disseminating ideas, Open Access may be a dud . . . or it may be a game-changer.

Make no mistake: acquiring electronic resources is a complex undertaking. Even if you work in a small public library and have access only to what the state provides, you and your colleagues are still affected by the license, the terms of use, and the questions of access and ownership. All the various models and options can be intimidating, frankly, especially because they're changing so rapidly.

But do not despair. You do not need to be an expert in all the intricacies of electronic resources acquisitions. Read on to get a solid understanding of the fundamentals.

Traditional Purchasing Options

Although new options for acquiring electronic resources continue to emerge, the traditional purchasing options are by far the most prevalent. Emerging options typically complement the traditional options, rather than replacing them. Here, we take a look at some of the key concepts of traditional purchasing options.

Subscription Resources

As with print journals and magazines, you must pay a yearly cost to maintain access to the content of subscription resources. This is currently the most common purchasing option for databases and journal packages, though "purchasing option" is a misnomer: in most cases you are leasing the content, not purchasing it. In public libraries, digital magazines are often offered via a single browsing platform like Zinio or Flipster where users browse and read articles from many magazines in one digital environment. Compare subscribing to a car lease: as long as you keep paying your bills on time, you get to keep the content—but if you stop paying for the lease, the company will repossess it.

Although e-books are sometimes purchased with perpetual access rights, they can also be acquired as subscription resources. This model is more common in academic libraries. There is a plethora of vendors, some with big names, including ProQuest, Safari, EBSCO, and JSTOR, in addition to individual publishers. They provide a mix of subscription and perpetual access options.

Perpetual Access

In contrast to subscription resources, perpetual access is an outright purchase rather than a lease. Most commonly found with e-journal packages and individual e-book titles, this model allows for continued

---

PUBLIC VS. ACADEMIC LIBRARIES: JOURNAL SUBSCRIPTIONS

Books are the bread and butter of the public library collection. Whether in print, large print, e-book, CD, or downloadable audio, the humble monograph is the foundation of the public library collection. The bulk of money for collections goes toward print purchases, with the remainder going into databases and magazines, whether in print or online.

That proportion is flipped in academic libraries. Roughly one quarter of the budget goes toward monographs, be they electronic or print. The rest goes into databases and journals.

In this regard, public libraries get off lucky. The price of books is generally stable year to year and does not outpace inflation. But the cost of journals and databases—the lion's share of the academic library's collections budget—grows alarmingly each and every year.

---

access to purchased content, even if you allow your subscription to lapse. In other words, you get to retain access to all the content at the time of the lapsed subscription, though you will not acquire any new content (unless you decide to renew your subscription in the future). Check the details carefully. Perpetual access is the exception, not the norm, as most e-journal packages and databases are usually all-or-nothing subscriptions.

Aggregator Databases

Aggregator databases collect journal content from various publishers and bring that content together in one platform with a search interface. Aggregator databases are an all-or-nothing subscription and usually provide indexing, abstracting, and/or full text to articles from a vast collection of e-journals. The e-journals included in an aggregator database can and do change often, dropping in and out of the database. This can be a nightmare to manage. It creates headaches for Collection Development Librarians and frustrates library patrons who find that journals and magazines they used to enjoy are no longer available.

Access-Only

Titles that pass in and out of e-journal packages and databases are called access-only titles because the library really doesn't subscribe to them and the access can change at any time. They are the *bête noire* of journals.

Journal Packages

Usually purchased by academic rather than public libraries, subscriptions to e-journal packages are a double-edged sword. On one hand, they provide access to a large collection of e-journals for far less than what that same title list would cost if purchased individually. Astonishingly, any two individual subscriptions may cost more than a package of dozens of subscriptions. The drink and the fries, purchased *a la carte*, cost more than the value meal of drink, fries, and hamburger.

On the other hand, e-journal content is often "bundled," meaning it is sold as an all-or-nothing package. This is increasingly becoming a problem as the cost of e-journals, databases, and e-journal package subscriptions continues to outpace library budgets and inflation, leaving libraries with no choice but to cancel content. You may find much of your library's bundled e-journal content gets little or no use, but cancelling a package and buying the high-use titles individually is not always feasible due to the high cost per title. This leads many libraries to continue shelling out large sums of collection money on behemoth packages of e-journal titles, colloquially called "Big Deals."

And with these Big Deals, libraries are sometimes saddled with content they actively do not want. Sometimes the only way to get access to the *Journal of Desirable Content* is to subscribe to a package that also contains the *Journal of Embarrassing and Disreputable Content*.

More and more libraries are experimenting with newer acquisition models in an effort to escape the Big Deals and the large sums of money required to maintain access to them. But the majority of libraries are still trapped by the Big Deals and spend a large portion of their collections budget to maintain them. See Chapter 8 for more about the pros and cons of Big Deals and how and why libraries choose to keep or reject them.

One-Time Funds

Some electronic resources can be purchased with one-time funds, but still require the payment of a yearly maintenance fee or hosting fee for continued access. This one-time purchase model is most often available for databases that contain digitized collections, such as primary source materials, an archive journal package, or backfiles, which consolidate older journal content from a publisher into one package, with no new content to be added. The library pays for the collection of content and a maintenance or access fee.

One-time purchases can be very useful for building collections without getting locked into a never-ending subscription, but remember: those annual access fees can pile up, so be aware of how much you are really committing to spend to continue to "own" the content. This is not technically a subscription fee, but you still have to budget for it, forever and ever and ever.

Emerging Purchasing Options

Increasingly, as budgets are tightening and usage data becomes an even more important consideration for how to spend limited funds, newer forms of purchasing collectively known as usage-driven acquisition (UDA) aim to maximize collection budgets by providing "just-in-time" collections instead of "just-in-case" collections. These models include demand-driven acquisitions (DDA), patron-driven acquisitions (PDA), evidence-based acquisitions (EBA), ILL purchase on demand (ILL PoD), and pay-per-view (PPV).

JUST-IN-CASE v. JUST-IN-TIME

For years, the norm in collection development was to err on the side of just-in-case. Let's purchase this book, just in case someone, someday, might conceivably need it. We can't cancel this subscription, because it might have an article someone might want. This philosophy still has many adherents, for good reasons. You can't serendipitously discover a book if it's not on the shelf. And even if you already know what book or article you want, alternative means of access such as interlibrary loan (ILL) can take days or weeks. That's not really helpful if your homework is due tomorrow.

But with limited budgets and limited shelf space, the just-in-time model begins to look more attractive. Instead of purchasing books with potential appeal, wait to purchase them if, and only if, someone requests them—or better yet, borrow them through ILL. And with requests for articles from e-journals, you might not even need to wait that long, as loans from other libraries can sometimes appear in your inbox within hours. This model does have detractors, though. Patrons do not make selections with the same rigor and care that librarians do.

Demand-Driven Acquisitions (DDA) and Patron-Driven Acquisitions (PDA)

Demand-driven acquisitions and patron-driven acquisitions are essentially different terms for the same model. DDA/PDA models were the earliest form of UDA and are primarily used to purchase print books, e-books, and streaming video. In this model, the vendor opens up a collection of titles to your users at little or no upfront cost by loading MARC records directly into the library's catalog. The end-user has no idea that the library does not own the book.

Public vs. Academic Libraries: DDA/PDA

In public libraries, PDA is mainly used for print books, with patron demand indicated by holds. (PDA is also used for streaming videos, but is uncommonly used for e-books.) Holds are not a perfect indicator—some folks don't use the catalog, and even people who do use the catalog may not realize they want a book unless they stumble across it on the New Book shelf—but holds are nonetheless a useful tool for gauging demand. For a book that may or may not have an audience, load the records and see if anyone takes the bait. If someone places a hold, buy the book; if not, pat yourself on the back for saving that money.

In academic libraries, DDA is used for e-books rather than print books and also for streaming videos. Demand for e-books is indicated by triggers. The definition of "trigger" varies by publisher, but commonly includes metrics such as a fixed number of minutes of viewing a book, or printing or downloading a chapter. The library does not pay any money unless and until the book is triggered.

How does the vendor know which catalog records to send to the library? It's very similar to a traditional approval plan: the vendor works with the library to set up a profile, and only books that match those parameters make the cut. The library then places funds on deposit and, as titles are triggered by use, the funds are encumbered from the deposit account.

DDA and PDA models can be a great cost-saver, and these models can be very valuable to libraries. Another variation of the DDA/PDA model, the short-term loan (STL), can sometimes (but not always) save the library money. With STLs, the initial trigger results in a loan rather than a purchase. This loan is a fraction of the full cost of the book. Not until the second trigger (or third, or fourth; the library gets to decide) does the library purchase the book.

Depending on the specifics, the library saves money overall if a book only gets one or two triggers; after that, the cumulative price of the loans exceeds the price of the book. Publishers are increasingly setting more expensive prices for STLs, so a cost-saving strategy may be to reduce the purchase trigger limits and skip the short-term loan in favor of purchasing. Put it this way: if you know you're only going to watch a movie once, you should rent it—but if you suspect you're going to watch it again and again, you'll save money by buying it outright the first time.

PDA is an especially attractive collection option for public libraries and is becoming more of an established method for making collection development decisions. Academic libraries are very tolerant of books with little or no circulation, but in public libraries, a book with no circulation may only have a few years—or even a few months—to prove its value. This discourages librarians from buying niche and oddball titles; after all, who wants to buy a book if you're only going to toss it two years later? But this conservative approach to collection development, though necessary during lean budget years, stifles the breadth and diversity of the collection. As PDA vendors begin to offer more sophisticated profiles and better ways to control triggering purchases, public and academic libraries alike will be better able to control the offerings to their patrons and maintain budgetary control with deposit accounts and purchasing caps.

Evidence-Based Acquisitions (EBA)

Evidence-based acquisitions (EBA) is the new kid on the block and is a variation of the DDA/PDA model. It is used most commonly for e-books and streaming videos. As with DDA and PDA, collections are opened up to users via MARC records loaded into the catalog. Unlike DDA and PDA, however, librarians pledge to spend a set amount of money up front, and they mediate the purchase of all titles. At the end of a set time (often a year), librarians make their selections. They can refer to usage data from the preceding year to make their selections, but the purchases are not automatic.

Increasingly both EBA and PDA/DDA title pools can be built from guidelines set by the library rather than lists determined by the publisher or distributor. This allows more flexibility and the ability to set parameters for the subjects and other specifications desired. Many libraries are now reallocating firm order book funds and sometimes media funds to these kinds of programs with great success.

Interlibrary Loan Purchase-on-Demand (ILL PoD)

Another purchase model more and more libraries are enacting is interlibrary loan purchase-on-demand. As with the other UDA models we have discussed, ILL PoD is a just-in-time versus just-in-case acquisition model and fulfills interlibrary loan requests for books, e-books, and sometimes media and streaming media, but by purchasing the requested title rather than borrowing it via ILL. Sometimes the purchase is desirable because the title fits within certain library profile parameters; other times, the purchase is desirable because the format (as with streaming media, e-books, and certain physical media) cannot or may not be loaned by other libraries.

Additionally, libraries use ILL PoD to purchase items that are frequently requested via ILL, especially in cases where the number of requests for a particular title would be costly and/or bump up against copyright clearance limitations, as with a request of more than one or two chapters from a book or with a journal request in excess of The Rule of Five.

The Rule of Five is the de facto rule on quantitative limits on ILL borrowing. It states that, within a calendar year, a borrowing library should not borrow more than five articles from the same periodical published within five years of the request (Minow & Lipinski 2003, 51–52).

Pay-Per-View (PPV)

As the cost of e-journal content continues to rise, and although content bundling still reigns supreme in e-journal acquisitions, pay-per-view article services are becoming increasingly popular, especially in academic libraries. In the PPV model, the vendor provides the library with access to unsubscribed journal titles, and the library uses a token system to permit purchasing that is either mediated (by librarians) or unmediated (a Wild West free-for-all). PPV allows users to access articles from unsubscribed journals on demand.

The drawback to this model, of course, is that the article is only available to the user for whom it was purchased, and sometimes only for a limited time. The library does not grow its collection, but merely provides access. It's similar to a traditional ILL, though usually with a higher price tag than an ILL and without the traditional limits such as The Rule of Five.

Pricing Models

Electronic resources are often sold at different price tiers depending on the kind of institution (public, academic, or corporate/private) and the library or institution size. Different vendors have different ways of determining size. For public libraries, size may be measured in terms of population served, number of active card holders, or number of branches. For academic libraries, pricing is usually set by Full Time Equivalent enrollment (FTE) and/or Carnegie classification. An institution's Carnegie Enrollment Profile Classification is determined by enrollment mix and level of institution, with levels ranging from two-year undergraduate to exclusively graduate. Graduate-level institutions are usually charged a higher amount than predominantly undergraduate institutions, because they are research libraries.

Another pricing model involves limiting the number of users who can access a resource at one time. This is called the one copy/one user model, and it is extremely common for e-books, especially in public libraries. As with physical books, only one person at a time may check out a digital book. This is not intuitive and may require some explaining to frustrated readers who rightly assume that books in electronic format need not have the same inherent circulation limitations of their print counterparts. These limitations are publisher driven, not technological. Monitor the holds queue to see if you ought to purchase more copies.

In public libraries, OverDrive offers e-books and downloadable audiobooks. They offer a mixed subscription model: some books are only offered in the one copy/one user model; other books offer Simultaneous Use models, wherein titles can be borrowed simultaneously by an unlimited number of users; and other titles only trigger a purchase if they are ever checked out.

Like OverDrive, Recorded Books sells both e-books and downloadable audiobooks to the public library market, though it is best known for its audiobooks. Content is sold on the one copy/one user model and is made available on the RBdigital platform.

A relatively recent competitor to both OverDrive and Recorded Books is Midwest Tape's Hoopla, a platform for streaming and downloading movies, music, e-books, and audiobooks. The Hoopla model is noticeably different. Patrons never have to wait for content, and the library pays a fee for each circulation.

Some public libraries provide popular streaming music, usually through Hoopla (discussed earlier) or Freegal, a downloadable music service that provides access to the catalog of artists in Sony Music Entertainment. With Freegal, library cardholders can download a certain number of songs per

---

PUBLIC VS. ACADEMIC LIBRARIES: DOWNLOADABLE AUDIOBOOKS AND MUSIC

Although audiobooks and music are popular formats in public libraries, they are much less common in academic libraries. When academic libraries do collect audio content, it is usually in the form of original oral histories, such as those produced in Special Collections departments, or in the form of streaming audio music collections, such as those from Naxos Music Group, which provides subscription access to classical, jazz, and world music.

---

week. Freegal is a subscription model that works with any MP3 device, including iPods.

Databases and other electronic resources sometimes offer a limited-user pricing model. Libraries may find this attractive, as it enables them to subscribe to a resource or collection that would otherwise be unafford-able. Usually these limited subscriptions allow access to one, two, or three users, or "seats," at a time. In academic libraries especially, simultane-ous user limits can be a lifesaver for small departments where resources can be expensive relative to the number of students and faculty who will actually use a niche resource.

Vendors and publishers may agree to lift the user limit for a set time to allow librarians to demonstrate a resource in a class and enable the students in that class to practice searching the resource. If this is something that's important to you, bring it up with the vendor at the time of licensing.

If you do subscribe to a resource with limited seats, it's in your interest to keep track of turnaways. This measures the number of times people were denied access to a resource because someone else was already using it. If a limited-user resource is generating too many denials, it may be time to consider adding more user seats to your subscription.

Workflows for Acquisitions

Your library probably has a streamlined workflow for acquiring physi-cal books. That's a routine process that happens frequently, even at the smallest, most understaffed libraries. But what about electronic resources? Is there a documented, agreed-upon workflow for acquiring e-books and downloadable audiobooks? How about streaming media, databases, elec-tronic magazines, and journal bundles?

Don't be alarmed: in general, the workflow for acquiring electronic resources will be similar across all electronic formats, and you get to take a lot of shortcuts with the less expensive acquisitions. You definitely don't need to sign a license every time you buy an e-book. But as with all library functions, it's important to have clearly defined steps, whether you're building a workflow from scratch or tweaking an existing process.

With databases, media platforms, and sometimes journal or e-book bundles, the library will often begin by offering their users a trial, during which time the vendor provides courtesy access to its product. Libraries sometimes restrict trial access to employees because you don't want to get people's hopes up for a resource you decide not to buy; other times, libraries will decide to open the trial to anyone who visits the library or campus. This trial period gives users a chance to try out the resource before committing to a subscription or purchase.

Of course, content is king, but in addition to evaluating the need for the content, there are other considerations worth noting:

- Does the resource fill a collections gap?
- Does the resource serve a known need (for instance, homework assignments on campus or in the local schools)?
- How easy is the interface to use?
- Are there restrictions on copying, printing, and downloading information?
- Are there any required software plugins, like a special reader for e-books or Adobe Acrobat Reader for PDFs? Is this software free and easy to install, even on public computers within the library?
- Is the content easy to link to (permalinks, etc.) for use in online classes?
- What is the cost/benefit analysis—will the resource get enough use to justify the cost?

If your library decides to purchase the content, the vendor/publisher will send along a license to review. You should feel empowered to negotiate the license to include your "must haves" and be ready to walk away if these key needs cannot be met; see Chapters 2 and 3 for more on negotiation. Once you and the vendor have agreed to the license and both parties have signed it, you'll pay the invoice and register the resource to activate access. Finally, you'll want to check that access to the resource is working, both from the library and from remote locations.

In many cases, once you have signed a license with a particular publisher or vendor, you will not need to sign a new license when adding resources from that same publisher or vendor in the future. Regardless, be sure to keep meticulous records of every contract you sign. That way, if questions come up (such as whether you may lend the resource via ILL or put it on e-reserve), you can easily consult the terms.

Some Electronic Resource Management (ERM) products that libraries may have purchased, like EBSCONET ERM Essentials, ExLibris Alma, and Serials Solution 360 Resource Manager, have a mechanism for saving a license and setting up reminders for when a license is set to expire (Anderson 2014, 30–33). If you don't have an ERM system, you must devise a way to securely store the licenses, keep track of renewal dates, and monitor when new licenses must be amended or signed. Placing a simple reminder alert in an online calendar system is a low-tech way to achieve this goal.

Details will vary according to the needs of your library, but a workflow for electronic resources acquisitions will look something like this:

1. Conduct a trial of the resource (optional; usually applies to databases).
2. Request the license from the vendor.
3. Review and revise the license.
4. Return the signed version to the vendor (usually only necessary with large purchases such as databases and journal packages).
5. Pay the invoice.
6. Receive activation information from the vendor.
7. Set up access for the public: configure the proxy server; proxy the link; test the link; and add it to the public website, catalog, or list of journal holdings (as appropriate).

And remember, day-to-day acquisitions such as e-books and streaming films do not require this labor-intensive workflow. All of the hard work (trials, licenses, and setting up access) happens up front. After the details are in place, individual purchases of discrete resources like e-books and streaming media are much simpler, requiring only the downloading of MARC records to keep the catalog up to date.

Open Access

An open access (OA) e-journal is a scholarly journal that is online, free of charge to users, and free of most copyright and licensing restrictions. The costs associated with creating scholarship (including writing and research, peer review, editing, and platform fees) are not paid by the end-user, but by other parties, such as university departments, libraries, and the authors themselves.

There are two predominant open access models: Green and Gold. In the Green OA model, an article becomes openly available "at some point after formal publication . . . The publisher allows authors to self-archive a version of the published work for free public use in their institutional repository" (Warren 2015). In the Gold OA model, an article is freely available upon publication, without an embargo period, without access restrictions. In this model, authors often pay fees (sometimes thousands of dollars) to submit to a journal.

As the rate of serial inflation continues to outpace library budgets, open access becomes increasingly attractive. The goal of OA is to provide scholarly literature to all researchers, not just those affiliated with large, well-funded research libraries. Science journals in particular have taken up the OA challenge to more widely disseminate scientific literature. In fact, many government-funded agencies, including the National Science Foundation (NSF) and the National Institutes of Health (NIH), require researchers receiving grants to publish their findings as open access so that access to research doesn't create a barrier to scientists.

But science journals are also the most likely to charge high fees to scholars who hope to publish in their journals. Euphemistically called article processing charges (APCs), many scholars fulfill these publishing costs by requesting funds from university departments or by using a portion of their grant funding. Some (but nowhere near all) universities and/or university libraries have OA publishing funds to which scholars may apply.

In libraries, the hope has been that open access journals would alleviate budget woes by offsetting the high cost of journal subscriptions, which currently consume the bulk of academic libraries' collection budgets. Unfortunately, OA publishing may in fact just be redistributing publishing costs to authors and ultimately libraries, who are often asked by their universities to help fund OA scholarship so that authors can publish in OA journals.

In reality, as Bosch and Henderson describe in their yearly review of serials, libraries have still not seen any decrease in the cost of journals. The average e-journal package increased by 6 percent in 2016 from the previous year, which is twice the rate of inflation. The average journal cost per title is coming in at $1,486, and the science, technology, and medical (STM) serials remain the highest-priced journals (even though STM has the most OA journals due to NIH and NSF requirements). For example, chemistry journals came in at the highest price, with an average price per title at a whopping $5,105, whereas agriculture journals came in at the lowest among the STM journals at a price per title of $1,687, which is still above the average journal cost, if only by $201 (Bosch & Henderson 2016, 35–36).

So, before you jump onto the OA train, consider whether there really is a cost savings, and be aware that the environment is still very much in flux, with many problems still not resolved. In particular, there are serious concerns about the quality of some OA e-journals. There is a need to educate scholars and researchers about predatory journals. As with pay-to-publish models for popular press monographs, some publishers are ethical, and some are swindlers and thieves.

One resource that can help is the Directory of Open Access Journals (DOAJ), which is a clearinghouse for OA journals. In the past, the DOAJ was lax about the journals it included, but it now has strict criteria for including journals on its list (Berger & Cirasella 2015, 134). Journals that have a green check mark or an orange DOAJ seal of quality have undergone the new stricter application process.

Also, new tools are coming out that can assist authors in finding reputable journals to publish their work. Springer has developed a free tool called Springer Journal Suggester (https://journalsuggester.springer.com), where an author may enter their manuscript title and abstract text, choose a subject area (optional), and limit to either all journals, fully OA journals, or subscription journals. Then the journal suggester will bring back a list of authoritative journals in which the author might consider publishing. The journal list includes the journal's impact factor; the length of time until a publication decision is reached; the acceptance rate of the journal; whether the journal is Open Access, subscription based, or hybrid; a link for authors to directly submit their manuscript to the journal; and more details, such as the aim and scope of the journal and a link to the journal website.

Another new resource is Cabells Blacklist, a complement to Cabells Whitelist (formerly Cabells Directories of Publishing Opportunities). Both are subscription resources, though at the time of this writing, the Blacklist is so new that it is not clear if these products will be offered separately or only as a package. According to an announcement on the Blacklist website (2017), the product fights the rise of predatory publishers with "specialists [who] analyze over 60 behavioral indicators to keep the community aware of growing threats and keep academia protected from exploitative operations" (Cabells 2017). The search page allows you to search blacklisted journals by a known journal title or by keyword, publisher, country, ISSN, or e-ISSN and to toggle the OA switch on or off.

Finally, the SHERPA/RoMEO database is an excellent resource for scholarly authors and librarians. It tracks the copyright and self-archiving policies of OA journals, giving authors an easy way to look up the rights to the articles they have published or hope to publish. This is particularly useful for faculty wanting to know if they have permission to submit their articles and manuscripts to their university's institutional repository.

Conclusion

Electronic resources come in a dizzying number of products, formats, and purchasing and licensing models. Keeping track of the current options is a job unto itself, and staying abreast of trends and emerging resources adds another layer of complexity. But with an understanding of the concepts covered in this chapter, you are prepared to understand the different possibilities and make strong acquisitions choices for your library's needs.

Additional Readings

Anderson, Elsa K. 2014. "Electronic Resource Management Systems and Related Products." *Library Technology Reports* 50, no. 3: 30–42.

Carrico, Steven, Michelle Leonard, Erin Gallagher, and Trey Shelton. 2016. *Implementing and Assessing Use-Driven Acquisitions: A Practical Guide for Librarians.* Vol. 23. Practical Guides for Librarians. Lanham, MD: Rowman & Littlefield Publishers.

Minow, Mary, and Tomas Lipinski. 2003. *The Library's Legal Answer Book.* Chicago: American Library Association.

Singley, Emily, and Jane Natches. 2017. "Finding the Gaps: A Survey of Electronic Resource Management in Alma, Sierra, and WMS." *Journal of Electronic Resources Librarianship* 29, no. 2: 71–83.

Wilkinson, Frances C., Linda K. Lewis, and Rebecca L. Lubas. 2015. *The Complete Guide to Acquisitions Management.* Westport, CT: Libraries Unlimited.

References

Anderson, Elsa K. 2014. "Electronic Resource Management Systems and Related Products." *Library Technology Reports* 50, no. 3: 30–42.

Berger, Monica, and Jill Cirasella. 2015. "Beyond Beall's List." *College & Research Libraries News* 76, no. 3: 132–135.

Bosch, Stephen, and Kittie Henderson. 2016. "Fracking the Ecosystem: Periodicals Price Survey 2016." *Library Journal* 141.7: 32–38.

Cabell's International. 2017. "Cabells Blacklist to Launch June 15th." www.cabells .com/newsletter-blacklist.

Minow, Mary, and Tomas Lipinski. 2003. *The Library's Legal Answer Book.* Chicago: American Library Association.

Warren, John W. 2015. "Scholarly Communication Basics." Mason Publishing Group. http://publishing.gmu.edu/communication/scholarly-communication-basics/.

CHAPTER FIVE

Creating Access in All the Right Places

One of the most vital roles of the Electronic Resources Librarian is providing optimal access to your library's electronic resources. This is undoubtedly the most visible aspect of the job, because if access is down, you will hear about it from your users. Our patrons don't understand and don't care about the intricacies involved in setting up and maintaining access to resources. For that matter, your library colleagues probably don't understand the intricacies, either. Unless they've worked closely with electronic resources, they probably don't appreciate the work it takes. As Lawson and Janyk note, electronic resource management tends to be learned on the job, not taught in library school (2014, 155–156).

Even seemingly simple problems can have complex answers. Davis, Malinowski, Davis, MacIver, and Currado demonstrate this by examining a straightforward problem, in which a library paid the invoice for a new electronic journal, but still had no access. Possible clues were scattered across the ILS, the ERM, various emails, and handwritten pieces of paper, and possible causes included title transfers, incorrect IPs, and bad data in the link resolver (2012, 25). This is a typical problem for an Electronic Resources Librarian, with a solution involving far more than making a quick phone call or dashing off an email.

Here's the kicker: if you're doing a good job of creating and maintaining access to resources, it probably does seem easy to people on the outside looking in. They can be forgiven for assuming that access is an automatic, low-effort process. When things are going well, all your hard work and effort are invisible to the end-user.

This chapter makes that work visible by examining a few key topics:

- **Definitions:** Because no one bothers to tell you this stuff.
- **IP Authentication:** How vendors identify libraries and their patrons.
- **Proxy Servers:** The tools of the access trade.
- **Access to Databases:** The quintessential job duty of the Electronic Resources Librarian.
- **Access to Journals:** The thorniest access of all.
- **Access to Streaming Media:** Perhaps the easiest type of access to manage.
- **Access to E-books and Audiobooks:** Sometimes simple, sometimes not so much.
- **Access to Discovery Services:** Another wrinkle in providing access.
- **Publicity:** The final step for access.

Fair warning: this is the most technical chapter in this entire book. Depending on your organization's structure, the information might not even apply to you; it's possible you can foist this off on your IT people or your Systems Librarian. But even if the fidgety technical parts aren't your direct responsibility, this chapter is worth at least skimming through so you can be aware of what's going on behind the scenes.

But if it does fall to you to fuss over the technical details, fear not: we'll walk you through the basics.

Definitions

If librarianship is a jargon-happy profession (and it most certainly is), the area of electronic resources is particularly guilty. The language of access is rife with specialized words. What is a knowledge base? An OpenURL link resolver? An A-Z list? (That last one is fairly intuitive, at least.)

- **A-Z list:** This is the public view of the library's holdings of a given type of electronic resource. This list is commonly used for databases (in public and academic libraries) and for journals (in academic libraries). For maximum accessibility, maintain one master list of all the resources, along with shorter, subject-specific lists, such as "Business Databases, A-Z."
- **URL:** Uniform Resource Locator. Often called a web address, a link, or (less commonly) a hyperlink.
- **OpenURL:** A framework that uses metadata, extracted from a citation, to describe a resource within a URL. It is used chiefly by libraries to facilitate access to subscription content.

- **OpenURL link resolver:** The tool that parses, or deciphers, the metadata in an OpenURL. The link resolver first runs the OpenURL for a bibliographic citation through an OpenURL knowledge base and then provides the ultimate goal: full text at the article level. Examples include EBSCO's Full Text Finder, ExLibris's SFX, and ProQuest's 360 Link.

- **Knowledge Base (KB):** An OpenURL knowledge base is a collection of electronic resources holdings. It goes beyond offering only the bibliographic information and metadata description of a library's electronic journal holdings (and sometimes e-book holdings). The knowledge base delivers linking to those holdings in full text via OpenURL standards.

- **Electronic Resource Management (ERM) tools:** More sophisticated than simple knowledge bases, ERM tools allow tracking of electronic resources through their entire life cycle, from ordering and licensing through access setup and ongoing maintenance. Common features include custom alerts, linking licenses to resource records, and usage statistics retrieval, all in one integrated system. Examples of ERM tools include ProQuest's 360 Resource Manager, CORAL, and EBSCO's ERM Essentials.

- **ILS:** Also known as a Library Management System, the Integrated Library System comprises, at a minimum, the public catalog and the back-end catalog. It is the software that allows for acquisitions, cataloging, circulation, and reporting. Some ILS platforms have ERM systems, usually offered as an optional add-on purchase. The ERM add-ons provide functionality such as the ability to manage licenses and to track administration information and customer service contacts.

- **APIs:** Application Programming Interfaces are sophisticated tools for customizing or improving existing software so that data can be shared across software applications. APIs fall outside the scope of this introductory text and usually work best with significant in-house technical support from a Systems Librarian or IT department. Though the learning curve can be steep, they are fairly common in library-land.

- **DOI:** The digital object identifier is a unique string of letters and numbers that identifies an article or book chapter. They are increasingly found in both traditional citations and OpenURLs.

Important! Sometimes people get sloppy with their language. Librarians, patrons, customer service reps, and vendors are all occasionally guilty of this. Someone might say "the catalog" when they really mean "the ILS," or they might say "library website" when what they really are referring to is a database. Be mindful that precision and accuracy sometimes suffer in lingo-land, and know that sometimes people don't quite mean what they think they mean.

IP Authentication

When you subscribe to a new electronic resource, the vendor will send you a welcome email that will likely contain a username and password for the administrative portal, a common (though not quite universal) feature for databases, journal packages, and media platforms. Most portals allow you to customize the look and feel of your resource, add your logo, add your proxy information, update IP addresses, and collect usage statistics.

> Save early, save often! Keep the emails you receive from vendors and customer service reps. If inbox space is at a premium, use a storage service such as Microsoft OneDrive or Dropbox. Also consider saving administrative portal usernames, passwords, and vendor contact information in a simple Excel spreadsheet for future access.

Whether you communicate via portal or email, you will need to send the vendor the IP address, or range of IP addresses, of your library branches (for public libraries) or for your campus (for academic libraries). The IP address, short for internet protocol address, is a string of characters, usually numbers and periods. It looks something like this:

192.168.0.10

An IP range is a sequence of IP addresses belonging to a single organization and is typically written as 192.168.0.0-192.0.255; it is what you will submit to vendors.

If a dentist's office subscribes to *The New Yorker*, anyone who visits the waiting room can read the magazine; if a library subscribes to *Heritage-Quest*, anyone who visits the library or academic campus can use the database.

The use of an IP address to verify that an end-user has the right to access an electronic resource is called IP authentication. Most vendors who work with libraries know this very well, but sometimes vendors prefer a different form of authentication, such as an individual username and password for each user. Vendors who deviate from the standard are usually niche mom-and-pop operations, or else large companies more accustomed to selling to private businesses. Whether you accommodate a vendor's preference for something other than IP authentication is your choice, but for many libraries, it is a deal-breaker: asking patrons to keep track of a bunch of different usernames and passwords is poor customer service at best, and a major security risk at worst.

Proxy Servers

The proxy server operates behind the scenes to authenticate end-users and connect them to electronic resources. It has lots of fussy parts, including configuration files, patron group settings, message files, and log files. Managing the systems side of proxy servers commonly falls to the Systems Librarian or IT support, but don't be surprised if you have some role in the process. Or perhaps you *want* a bigger role: it can be faster to fix problems yourself, instead of depending on a different department to step in.

Proxy servers are standard tools in libraries, and this chapter assumes that your library has one. It is possible, however, to authenticate without proxies. Some libraries, especially public libraries with small populations, find it simpler and cheaper to have vendors handle authentication. The libraries use their ILS to maintain the information that verifies their patrons, such as patron name, barcode, and/or PIN. They communicate this information to the vendors for authentication by using a tool such as SIP2 (Standard Interchange Protocol).

Authentication Methods

When an end-user attempts to access an electronic resource, the proxy server checks their IP address. Most commonly, the proxy server is configured to automatically grant access to anyone inside the library building (for public libraries) or on campus (for academic libraries), though the server may be configured to challenge in-house users for credentials.

All users outside of the library, or off campus, must verify their affiliation with the library. When they attempt to access a resource, the proxy server challenges them to authenticate—and like the Sphinx asking riddles, it grants access only to those people who answer the challenge correctly. Patrons of public libraries supply the correct answer by typing in their library barcode number and perhaps a PIN; for those affiliated with academic libraries, the correct answer is usually their .edu email address and password.

The precise details vary by library, but the basic concept of authentication is simple:

1. A patron clicks on the link to a resource.
2. The proxy server prompts the patron to enter credentials.

The vast majority of a library's electronic resources will be offered to both local and remote patrons. Occasionally a library might subscribe to an electronic resource that does not offer remote access, reasoning that limited access is better than no access at all, but this scenario is uncommon: libraries are loath to subscribe to electronic resources that can only be used onsite. Resources without remote use are inconvenient at best and completely inaccessible to homebound patrons or distance-education students.

3. The proxy server checks those credentials against the library's records.
4. If those credentials match, the patron is authenticated. If not, the patron is denied access.

Once the patron is authenticated, the proxy server processes the URL and "resolves"—that is, changes—the link to include the proxy server address. You'll hear this frequently in verb form: the server *proxied* the address.

PUBLIC VS. ACADEMIC LIBRARIES: FLUCTUATING POPULATIONS

In most public libraries, patrons lose their circulation privileges if they accumulate excessive fines, but (with some exceptions) they're allowed to keep using electronic resources. Licenses are written to accommodate patrons with active barcodes. As long as a library card number has not expired, it is still active, no matter how many overdue books and lost fees a person has.

In academic libraries, sophisticated authentication methods are needed to keep up with the ever-changing enrollment status of the students. Known as identity and access management systems or identity management systems, these methods are chosen by the campus IT department rather than the library. Popular implementations include the LDAP Active Directory, Shibboleth, OpenAthens, and SAML. They synchronize with university registration systems like Banner or PeopleSoft to ensure that access is provided only to current students, faculty, and staff.

Setting up remote authentication will require some knowledge of library systems; if you're at an academic library, it will also involve work with other campus systems such as the Banner or PeopleSoft system. Be sure to consult with your IT support and your Systems Librarian, and determine early on which people are responsible for the different parts of setting up and maintaining access to electronic resources.

Some libraries will have support in the form of local consortium, so if you lack local experts, consider contacting people in your consortium who may be able to offer you their expertise, answer questions, and help with local setup.

Choosing a Proxy Server

Your library should already have a proxy server in place, so as long as it's working well—or well enough—you don't need to rush any decisions. But as with any ongoing expense, the proxy server should be assessed periodically to make sure that it is still the best choice for the library.

Libraries may pay a vendor to handle proxy services, or they may use their own personnel, systems, and servers to run their proxies in-house. Outsourcing to a vendor means that the library must pay a recurring annual cost, but many libraries are glad to pay for the support and customer service that a commercial vendor provides. Outsourcing is clearly the better choice if local staff are lacking in either the expertise or the time to manage their own proxy servers.

On the other hand, the customer support from the vendor may not be as thorough, prompt, and effective as the library's own staff. Running a proxy server in-house gives libraries a level of independence and control they could never get from a third party.

The biggest player among library proxy servers is EZproxy, which can be hosted by OCLC or on the library's own servers; it is discussed in more detail later. Another common option is to use the proxy software that is sold with, or in addition to, the ILS, such as Innovative's WAM server. Open-source proxy servers can also be an attractive choice, especially when there's strong in-house support from the Systems Administrator.

Using a niche or do-it-yourself proxy server may feel like a lonely endeavor. EZproxy is certainly not the only choice out there, but it is the one with the biggest user community and the most name recognition. All of the major vendors of electronic resources are conversant in EZproxy, but they are less able to support other types of proxy servers. When you subscribe to a new resource, for instance, the vendor might supply you with an EZproxy stanza. This stanza will contain valuable information, but you'll have to tinker with it to make it work for your server.

Security certificates provide an encrypted connection between a user's browser and a secure website. As more and more library resources move to an https:// secure site, security certificates are required to create a secure connection to the library resources. Most modern certificates and browsers support Wildcard Certificates and Subject Alternative Name (SAN) Certificates, which allow for a single certificate to apply to multiple domains. Both work with EZproxy.

For proxy servers like WAM that do not generate prefixed proxy URLs, however, neither Wildcard nor SAN certificates will work. With WAM, each electronic resource requires a separate certificate. You may need to request these certificates from your IT department or Systems Librarian.

EZproxy

EZproxy is not the only fish in the proxy-server sea—but it is the *biggest* fish. Because it is the proxy server you are most likely to work with, this section will take a close look at the details of adding EZproxy content stanzas to your EZproxy server. This is the process that allows the database (or e-journal package, or individual e-journal title) to work remotely by passing through your EZproxy server.

When setting up EZproxy access to a new resource, the first step is to ask the vendor if they have proxy configurations. Luckily, most library vendors are quite familiar with EZproxy and can readily support its use. If the vendor can supply a configuration for your EZproxy, you can add the content stanza to a portal site. If the vendor cannot provide you with a working stanza, consult OCLC's EZproxy list, which provides content stanzas for many common databases and journal publishers.

But if you can't nab an existing content stanza, you'll need to follow the basic format to build one from scratch. The content stanza will contain directives, which are instructions for the proxy server. There are several common directives, including:

T: Title
U: URL
D: Domain
DJ: Domainjavascript
H: Host
HJ: Hostjavascript

Not all basic stanzas will contain all of these directives, but at a minimum they will contain title and URL, and most will be followed by at least one Host/HostJavascript and one Domain/DomainJavascript. Here's a content stanza with four directives:

T: AAUP Journal of Academic Freedom

U: http://www.academicfreedomjournal.org

H: www.academicfreedomjournal.org

DJ: academicfreedomjournal.org

Rendered through a proxy server, this example yields a link that looks something like this:

http://proxy195.nclive.org/login?url=http://www.academicfreedomjournal .org/index.html

A great resource for assistance is the EZproxy listserv at ezproxy@ls.suny .edu. The members of this community can help with stanzas, and they are experts in troubleshooting EZproxy problems, including EZproxy setup and log errors. Again, EZproxy system maintenance should be the purview of the Systems Librarian or IT department, but if you find yourself in need of this kind of expertise, the EZproxy listserv at SUNY is a lifesaver.

Access to Databases

"I just need three articles for my homework!" If you've ever worked in public services, you've heard countless variations of that question—and it is thanks to the fearless Electronic Resources Librarian that the library can provide answers.

Setting up database access is one of the most fundamental roles of the Electronic Resources Librarian. Discovery layers may replace traditional database searching in some libraries, but databases are still the entry point for most library users conducting a research project. Creating and maintaining proper database access is essential.

Fortunately, databases require little maintenance after the initial setup. Once the vendor sends you the access link, you arrange for local and remote IP authentication, as discussed in the previous section. Then, after you publicize your new database, you don't have to do anything to keep it running . . . unless there are problems.

We discuss troubleshooting in depth in Chapter 10, but one of the most common database problem bears mentioning here. Library users often contact public service staff with session links, confused as to why the link they previously copied and pasted no longer works. The reason is simple: the link they saved came from a temporary database session. What they needed was a permalink, which, as the name implies, is made to last.

A permalink is the permanent, static hyperlink to a specific webpage. It is the link you should be using when creating proxy links to your library resources. In contrast, a query string link is a temporary link that shows in the address bar during a particular web session. It may or may not contain search terms and other information unique to that session within the link.

Here's an example of a query string, or session, link:

http://web.b.ebscohost.com.proxy195.nclive.org/ehost/results?sid
=f2cbd399-4f31-43ca-9157-2eece0988393%40sessionmgr105&vid
=4&hid=123&bquery=(presidential+AND+election)+AND+2016&bdata=J
mRiPWE5aCZ0eXBlPTAmc2l0ZT1laG9zdC1saXZlJnNjb3BlPXNpdGU%3d

Note that the words "session" and "query" can be found in the link. This is an immediate tip-off that this link is not stable and should not be used for linking.

With a session link like the one in this example, a skilled eye can sometimes discern clues, such as which database the user was searching in and what search terms they were using. Other times, the expired session link may not reveal much at all; for instance, it might indicate that the search took place in an EBSCO database, which is not terribly helpful if your library subscribes to 30 EBSCO resources.

Just say no to session links! Encourage the public services staff at your library to explain permalinks to their patrons in interactions at the reference desk or in more formal instructional settings. Don't click on the address bar, but look for icons in that database that provide the permalink. Alternatively, use the database's email feature to send a copy of the article directly to the end-user's inbox.

Your colleagues may sometimes ask you for help with creating links to a specific part of a database, a particular search screen, a collection of articles, and so on. Understanding permalinks is essential for fulfilling these requests and troubleshooting secondhand links.

Of particular note is the trend in some newer database interfaces toward multiple permalinks: one for remote access and one for local access. This can lead to headaches, because the local-access permalink does not always include the proxy prefix, and thereby renders it unusable offsite. Be aware of this quirk, and when assisting others with permalink creation, always ensure the link is proxy-formatted to work remotely.

Here's an example of a proxy-formatted database permalink: http://proxy195.nclive.org/login?url=http://search.ebscohost.com/login.aspx?authtype=ip,uid&profile=ehost&defaultdb=a9h

Notice how it appears to be two links smooshed together: first the proxy part of the link, followed by the destination link. The proxy prefix is your clue that this link will work remotely.

Once you have the link, you can add it to your A-Z list. Some libraries host their own browsable A-Z list of databases on their library website, whereas others use a tool such as Springshare LibGuides to set up, manage, and populate the list to their library website.

Access to Journals

Electronic journals are the one area where public libraries truly diverge from academic libraries. In academic libraries, access to journals (which increasingly is understood to mean access to *electronic* journals) is vital. Academic publishing and scholarly inquiry would not exist without journals.

The mission of the public library is much different. Patrons still need journals to meet their research needs, but databases (including journal aggregators) are usually sufficient to answer those needs. Public libraries spend only a sliver of their collection development dollars on journals, and most of those are print subscriptions for browsing. And, as with e-books in public libraries, e-journals in public libraries are platform specific.

Journals in Public Libraries

Public libraries provide most of their access to electronic journals with databases. A database like Newsbank provides access to various newspapers, chosen *a la carte* or purchased in bundles; an aggregator like ProQuest Central brings together many resources that are chosen by the vendor; and, less commonly, individual journals are available in database form, as with ConsumerReports.org, hosted by EBSCO as a database.

A second means of providing access is through platforms like Zinio and Flipster. As with e-book platforms, these magazine platforms can be loaded in computer browsers or downloaded as apps. The library selects journals to subscribe to, and patrons check out issues using their library card numbers.

Because journal access in public libraries is handled through databases and magazine platforms, the remainder of this section speaks to the concerns of academic libraries.

Knowledge Bases

The most important e-journal management tool for the academic librarian is the knowledge base. Sometimes called a KB, the knowledge base allows you to maintain an A-Z list of all of your library's electronic journals holdings, including their coverage dates. Because of the fluid nature of journal package content and subscriptions, journal access is the most demanding access to maintain. Electronic Resources Librarians are responsible for managing potentially thousands and thousands of journals and for providing access to these journals to users.

Knowledge bases are essential because journals are always changing. The library adds new subscriptions, publishers change, titles change names, titles stop publishing, and new titles spring into existence. And access-only journals drop in and out of packages all the time; these are journals that are bundled in journal packages but which your library doesn't subscribe to. Knowledge bases, or their more robust cousins, ERM (Electronic Resource Management) tools, help Electronic Resources Librarians keep track of all of these changes while maintaining access to full text.

Most knowledge bases are commercial products; popular examples include EBSCOAdmin, 360 Core, and SFX KnowledgeBase. There was an open-source knowledge base called CUFTS knowledgebase, but it was decommissioned in August 2017. In conjunction with subscription management services like EBSCONET, knowledge bases allow Electronic Resources Librarians to manage their journal resources. With a knowledge base, you can:

- Monitor new subscriptions.
- Discover new access-only titles that have been added as part of subscribed packages.
- Discover which access-only titles have been dropped as part of subscribed packages.

- Set holdings: that is, identify subscriptions and coverage dates at the journal package and title level that will show up on your public A-Z journal list.
- Set up OpenURL linking to provide full-text access to users.

Depending on the knowledge base, other features may be standard or may be purchased as add-ons. These additional features include license management and various types of statistics tracking: for journals at the package and journal title level, for databases at the platform level, and for e-books at the package and title level.

OpenURLs

Let's say you're searching in a database aggregator and come across this citation:

Whitney, Wanda, Alla Keselman, and Betsy Humphreys. 2017. "Libraries and librarians: Key partners for progress in health literacy research and practice." *Information Services & Use* 37, no. 1: 85–100. doi:10.3233/ISU-170821.

The format of this citation is familiar to anyone who's ever written a research paper, but it needs to be further processed before it can deliver the full text of the article onto your screen. That processing happens behind the scenes with the OpenURL resolver, which assigns each piece of information to a metatag, also known as an element or field. The resulting link is a long string of seeming gibberish:

http://resolver.EBSCOhost.com/OpenURL?ID=doi:10.3233/ISU
-170821&genre=article&atitle=Libraries%20and%20librarians%3A%20
Key%20partners%20for%20progress%20in%20health%20literacy%20
research%20and%20practice&title=Information%20Services%20
%26%20Use&issn=01675265&isbn=&volume=37&issue=1&date
=20170401&aulast=Whitney,%20Wanda&spage=85&pages=85-100&sid
=EBSCO:Education%20Source:121676495

Broken into its constituent parts, that same string of gibberish begins to look decipherable:

http://resolver.EBSCOhost.com/OpenURL?ID=doi:10.3233/ISU-170821
&genre=article

```
&atitle=Libraries%20and%20librarians%3A%20Key%20partners%20
for%20progress%20in%20health%20literacy%20research%20and%20
practice
&title=Information%20Services%20%26%20Use
&issn=01675265
&isbn=
&volume=37
&issue=1
&date=20170401
&aulast=Whitney,%20Wanda
&spage=85
&pages=85–100
&sid=EBSCO:Education%20Source:121676495
```

Each element indicator begins with the ampersand and ends with the equal sign and is directly followed by the citation information. In this example, you can see this article is from the journal *Information Services and Use*, volume 37, issue 1, 2017, pages 85–100, and you can tell that the link was from an abstract found in the EBSCO Education Source database.

Depending on which version of OpenURL you're using, the metatags may follow a slightly different notation system, as seen in this fragment of a link:

```
&rft.jtitle=Science&rft.aulast=Bergelson
```

Regardless, the format employs the ampersand and the equal sign to show where metatags begin and end.

The OpenURL link resolver searches for a match in the volume, issue, and year fields. If it finds a match—that is, if the library has access to that resource—the link resolver will pull up the full text of the article. If the OpenURL link resolver doesn't find a match in the volume, issue, and year fields indicated, then it can be set to provide the user with an alternative link, such as a link to request an interlibrary loan.

Journals and EZproxy

As with databases, journals and journal packages need to be configured for proxy access. With EZproxy, the most common proxy server in libraries, certain journal packages require minimal effort on your part to get the proxy working: you just add a stanza for a package and you're done. But in some packages, you must add a line to the stanza for *each new title* in order for access to the title to be granted. This is every bit as tedious as it sounds.

If you miss a title, the end-user who is trying to access the journal will see an error screen that looks something like this:

To allow http://cebp.aacrjournals.org.cgi/content/abstract/8/6/489 to be used in a starting point URL, your EZproxy administrator must first authorize the hostname of this URL in the config.txt file.

Within this database's section of config.txt, either the following line must be added:

Host cebp.aacrjournals.org

Or, alternatively, a RedirectSafe for this host or domain may be appropriate.

After editing config.txt, the EZproxy server must be restarted for the changes to take effect.

The patron trying to use the resource will likely be flummoxed, because this error message makes no sense to anyone other than an Electronic Resources Librarian. You will come to despise this loathsome error screen, but it's really not a big deal: it just means you have to go in and add the resource to an existing EZproxy stanza (or create a new EZproxy stanza) and restart the server.

If you are using a proxy server other than EZproxy, the error message and the solution will be different. With the WAM proxy server, for instance, the error message is "The address you are trying to access is invalid." This indicates that you need to go into the WAM proxy table in your ILS, add the WAM proxy string (for example, *aacrjounrals.org) for each journal title, and reboot your server.

Access to Streaming Media

Activating access to streaming media is often no different than setting up access to a database, because many academic and public library streaming media resources come in collections that are accessed and activated like databases. Some major streaming media library providers that are licensed as databases include Hoopla, Films on Demand, Alexander Street Press, Docuseek2, Ambrose Digital, Swank Digital Campus, and Kanopy. With these resources, setting up the proxy prefix and other customizations can often be done through direct communication with the vendor, or you may need to enter data in the database administration portal.

The exceptions come in the form of physical DVDs that are purchased individually. Often when contacted by well-meaning libraries who are trying to follow copyright, distributors will offer to sell a library streaming rights, but without offering to host or even digitize the film. This is an unworkable solution for most libraries. If the distributor tries to sell you streaming rights but does not offer to digitize and host the film, you should only proceed if you're equipped to do that work yourself.

Access to E-books and Audiobooks

Providing access to e-books and audiobooks on the title-by-title level is usually straightforward. In public libraries, these formats are made accessible through one or more platforms like OverDrive, Hoopla, and RBdigital. After you originally sign up with a vendor and provide IP ranges, access is easy: you make your title selections, much as if you were shopping in Amazon, and then the vendor does all the hard work of making the title available to patrons, sometimes within a matter of minutes.

The process is similar for academic libraries. Instead of purchasing through one or two platform interfaces, however, you make your acquisitions through book jobbers such as GOBI or directly from publishers like Credo or SAGE.

But for academic libraries, things get more complicated if you purchase e-book bundles, a process that can and does vary by vendor. It's similar to a database activation in that you submit your IP address or IP ranges to the vendor and ask the vendor if they have a working stanza for your proxy. Where it differs is that some e-book vendors add the proxy to their e-book titles at licensing for you; some require you to go into the administrative portal and submit the proxy prefix to activate the proxy; and still others require that the proxy be added to the vendor's MARC records each time new records for the e-book packages are downloaded.

So, when purchasing or subscribing to a new e-book package, there are several key questions to ask the vendor: What is the method for adding the proxy? When, where, and how often should MARC records be downloaded to keep the package up to date? How many simultaneous users are you entitled to per title?

When you publicize your e-books, in the public catalog or elsewhere, it's a good practice to include the simultaneous user limit. Obviously, this lets end-users and library staff know what the user-limit information for a particular e-book or e-book package is, but there's another good reason for it: if you don't make note of the user limits right away, you risk losing track of that information in the future.

Access to Discovery Services

Discovery services are interfaces designed to replace the public catalog. They provide an improved search interface and offer features such as relevancy-ranked search results; faceted searching; metadata and full text from local collections, open access repositories, and subscription resources; and bibliographic and holdings information from the library's catalog. The four main products are ProQuest's Summon, EBSCO's Discovery Service, OCLC's WorldCat Discovery Service, and ExLibris' Primo Central.

Not all libraries have embraced discovery services. Public libraries have adopted them sparingly, and though they are more common in academic libraries, they are by no means universal; the use of discovery tools is about 29 percent in the United States (Lee & Chung 2016, 530). Sometimes libraries forego discovery services for financial reasons, but even at an affordable price, discovery services are not always desirable: none of them offer a truly unified search of a library's entire collection, and the results they do return are sometimes ranked in problematic ways.

To be fair, early federated search tools were notoriously ineffective compared to native library database interfaces, and may have left a lingering mistrust of all meta-search tools among librarians who lived through them. Modern web discovery services have vastly improved upon the old federated searches, though relevancy ranking is still a sticky problem that deters some libraries from going down the web discovery road.

Several studies of web discovery tools have looked at differences in relevancy ranking and student use behaviors between the EBSCO Discovery Service (EDS) and the ProQuest discovery service Summon. Asher, Duke, and Wilson found that EDS *may* provide better relevancy ranking than Summon. Specifically, there is some evidence that Summon's search algorithm may rank newspaper and perhaps magazine results too highly (Asher et al. 2013, 471). Another study at Grand Valley State University showed a similar pattern of significant increase in newspaper usage following the implementation of Summon, though they also saw an overall increase in scholarly journals (Way 2010, 219). It appears that although Summon and EDS both weight articles by content type, EDS also weights content by article length, which in turn favors the higher ranking of peer-reviewed journal articles (Asher et al. 2013, 472).

This ranking is a disadvantage for researchers seeking peer-reviewed articles and books, especially as we have come to realize that most end users have a limited understanding of the search results produced by web discovery tools. Many users fail to understand where the results came from and what the results are and can't discern a newspaper article from a journal article. They may even get a book record and a book review confused.

The single search box of a web discovery tool can make this distinction even murkier (Lee & Chung 2016, 530). Additionally, recent studies suggest that even the "good" web discovery tools are not as precise as discipline-specific databases (Lee & Chung 2016, 533).

Regardless of the merits of one tool over another, probably the most important finding of these studies are that students (especially undergraduate students) generally only use the default ranking provided by a given discovery tool (Asher et al. 2013, 471–472). Badke proposed that only 5 percent of users facet their searches, though a recent study found that most students *do* sometimes use the peer-reviewed (41 percent) and date limiter (28 percent) filters, and they do seem aware of the other limiters (Badke 2013, 66; Dempsey & Valenti 2016, 202). Still, because users often ignore the limiters and fail to understand the results they get, the default ranking of results is very important.

If your library does implement a discovery service, you'll start by working with the vendor to create a base index consisting of subscription content, catalog records, and digital repository content. This process is fairly easy if the provider of your discovery service is also the provider of your other electronic resources tools. If you already use EBSCOAdmin to manage your journal packages and you subscribe to many EBSCO databases, it won't be too hard to build a base index to work with the EBSCO Discovery Service (EDS). Signing on with ProQuest's Summon discovery service, however, may lead to problems. Complications are common when the link resolver and the discovery service pull from different indexes, and you may need to manage two knowledge bases or migrate to a new knowledge base (Jantzi, Richard, & Wong 2016, 188).

Publicity

The final step in creating access to electronic resources is to update the catalog—or, to sticklers, the OPAC ("Online Public Access Catalog"), which is the public interface of the library catalog. This is not an essential step, provided that you've made your electronic resources accessible elsewhere, and some libraries may decide to skip the catalog records, with the optimistic hope that a discovery tool or A-Z database list will be adequate for their users' searching needs. For many libraries, however, including catalog records is a worthy use of staff time.

For the most part, the cataloging librarians will be in charge of adding resources to the catalog, but if you are the librarian in charge of setting up and maintaining access to electronic resources, you will want to learn a little bit about catalog records. This will facilitate collaboration and communication with your cataloging and/or metadata librarians as you seek to keep the catalog clean and up to date.

Even if you're not a cataloger, there are a few key MARC fields every Electronic Resources Librarian should know:

- 245 field: Title
- 246 field: Varying form of title
- 856 field: This is the field for all links to electronic resources; you may have to edit it to fix broken links

In some cases, you may need to ask the cataloging/metadata librarian to do a global update to your catalog if a large number of fields in a package need updating; this would be necessary, for instance, after a big change to a new proxy server. But most of the time, you can and will update individual links yourself by going into the MARC 856 field. This field has a great number of possible indicators and subfields, among them:

- The first indicator is for the access method. A value of 4 indicates an HTTP resource.
- Subfield |u is the Uniform Resource Identifier (the URL).
- Subfield |z is a public note, which, if added, will show in the public catalog view. This is where you can choose to put the simultaneous user limit information.

Finally, once you have made your resource accessible and tested that it works locally and remotely, don't forget to publicize it beyond the A-Z database list, the A-Z journal list, and the catalog. Publicize the resource to your library users and other library staff on the new resources section of your website, send out an email with an annotation and link to the resource, and post on your library's blog or newsletter. See Chapters 6 and 7 for a more in-depth discussion of marketing.

Conclusion

Creating and maintaining access to electronic resources are absolutely essential tasks. Each format has its own quirks and frustrations, and a resource that works beautifully one day will go belly-up the next. Although this part of the job never gets easy, it does get *easier*, and the concepts and walk-throughs in this chapter will help smooth the way.

Additional Readings

Anderson, Elsa K. 2014. "Electronic Resource Management Systems and Related Products." *Library Technology Reports* 50, no. 3: 30–42.

Breeding, Marshall. 2015. "The Future of Library Resource Discovery." A white paper commissioned by the NISO Discovery to Delivery (D2D) Topic Committee. www.niso.org/apps/group_public/download.php/14487/future_library_resource_discovery.pdf.

Davis, Robin Camille. 2016. "APIs and Libraries." *Behavioral & Social Sciences Librarian* 35, no. 4: 192–195.

Shadle, Steve. 2013. "How Libraries Use Publisher Metadata." *Insights: The UKSG Journal* 26, no. 3: 290–297.

Thompson, Jolinda L., Kathe S. Obrig, and Laura E. Abate. 2013. "Web-Scale Discovery in an Academic Health Sciences Library: Development and Implementation of the EBSCO Discovery Service." *Medical Reference Services Quarterly* 32, no. 1: 26–41.

White, Heather Tones. 2010. "Electronic Resources Security: A Look at Unauthorized Users." *Code4lib Journal* no. 12: 1–10.

References

Asher, Andrew D., Lynda M. Duke, and Suzanne Wilson. 2013. "Paths of Discovery: Comparing the Search Effectiveness of EBSCO Discovery Service, Summon, Google Scholar, and Conventional Library Resources." *College & Research Libraries* 74, no. 5: 464–488.

Badke, William. 2013. "The Path of Least Resistance." *Online Searcher* 37, no. 1: 65–67.

Davis, Susan, Teresa Malinowski, Eve Davis, Dustin MacIver, and Tina Currado. 2012. "Who Ya Gonna Call? Troubleshooting Strategies for E-Resources Access Problems." *Serials Librarian* 62, no. 1–4: 24–32.

Dempsey, Megan, and Alyssa M. Valenti. 2016. "Student Use of Keywords and Limiters in Web-Scale Discovery Searching." *Journal of Academic Librarianship* 42, no. 3: 200–206.

Jantzi, Leanna, Jennifer Richard, and Sandra Wong. 2016. "Managing Discovery and Linking Services." *Serials Librarian* 70, no. 1–4: 184–197.

Lawson, Emma, and Roën Janyk. 2014. "Getting to the Core of the Matter: Competencies for New E-Resources Librarians." *Serials Librarian* 66, no. 1–4: 153–160.

Lee, Boram, and EunKyung Chung. 2016. "An Analysis of Web-Scale Discovery Services from the Perspective of User's Relevance Judgment." *Journal of Academic Librarianship* 42, no. 5: 529–534.

Way, Doug. 2010. "The Impact of Web-Scale Discovery on the Use of a Library Collection." *Serials Review* 36, no. 4: 214–220.

CHAPTER SIX

Marketing, Part I: Planning

I had just started my current job at the University of North Carolina at Greensboro and was looking through the prescribed goals for the person in this position. As I scanned through the document, I ran across goal number five:

    "Improve the marketing and promotion of Electronic Resources at UNCG."

    My heart sank. The dreaded M-word stared me in the face. I didn't know how to market, I couldn't make something look graphically well designed to save my life, and even the thought of marketing felt wrong to me, as if it would sully the pure altruistic world of libraries with business. But yet, here I was.

    Two years on from that experience, I am here to tell you that you can and should market and that it will not cost you or your library its soul.

—Kate Hill

The Association of Research Libraries (ARL) defines marketing as the "organized process of planning and executing the conception, pricing, promotion, and distribution of ideas, goods, and services to create exchanges that will, if applicable, satisfy individual and organizational objectives" (Smykla 1999, 3). Let's unpack this a little.

First: marketing is organized, and it is a process. This means marketing needs to be planned for; just throwing promotional materials around the library and hoping for the best is not, in fact, marketing.

Second: marketing needs to work towards sharing your library's organizational objectives: the values, goals, and mission of the institution.

Finally, marketing satisfies individual objectives by connecting the things we create with a library user's goals and needs in a way that demonstrates the value to them. Put more simply, marketing is a disciplined way of "communicating with users what the library has to offer to the community" (Duke & Tucker 2007, 52).

When you look at marketing from this perspective, as an organized method of communicating what libraries provide in a way that demonstrates to patrons the benefits of using library resources, it becomes more obviously beneficial instead of evil. Marketing does not have to be a method of manipulation. It does not necessarily involve selling out to The Man. Marketing electronic resources promotes the library's mission, assists with users' information needs, and helps stakeholders and patrons appreciate why we spend the money we do on these resources.

Marketing also helps us move beyond elementary questions ("What resources get a lot of usage?") to more sophisticated questions: How do we reach an audience that is not using these resources but could be? What is our competition, and how do we differentiate ourselves from them in our resources? How can we proactively get resources to customers, rather than hoping they will just stumble on them via our catalog?

Being able to explore and attempt to answer these questions will work towards improving not just our marketing, but also the general user experience of searching for electronic resources at the library. As an added benefit, the more users know about the resources we provide and the more we clearly mark the resources we provide as coming from the library, the more they will realize the value of the library. Marketing makes sure that what we purchase is used, appreciated, and recommended to others.

This is the first of two chapters that focus on marketing. Whereas Chapter 7 focuses on the nitty-gritty of promotional strategies, this chapter emphasizes the planning stages:

- **The Rules of Marketing:** Kind of loose, but still good to know.
- **The Marketing Plan:** Ten steps, described in detail.
- **Conducting Market Research:** Surveys and focus groups.

Like every chapter in this book, this is meant to provide an introduction to basic practical concepts without going deeply into any one area. For those interested in exploring any of the areas discussed, a list of useful resources for further reading can be found at the end of this chapter.

The Rules of Marketing

The first rule of marketing electronic resources is, there are no rules. Or at least, they haven't been studied very much.

You probably want to know which techniques have been proven over and over again to work wonderfully for marketing electronic resources, but there's not a lot of research out there. In fact, two surveys—one conducted by JISC (2008) in the UK and one conducted by Linda Ashcroft (2002)—found that although libraries knew marketing in general was important, they had not gone about it in a systematic way.

Kennedy and LaGuardia (2013, xv–xxi) found that, although marketers of electronic resources were good at identifying their target market (that is, who they wanted to market to), only a few stated specific goals that could be measured, and very few had assessments of their practices. Their research is backed up by a finding by the ARL (1999) that only 30 percent of libraries that conducted marketing actually assessed that marketing.

Because of the ad hoc nature of most efforts in libraries, and especially because of the lack of measurable goals, it is very hard to say what actually does work. With that caveat in mind, this chapter is based on the authors' experiences, the findings of marketing assessments, and the successes that have been published in the library literature. The content herein is valuable, but remember that there is no magic wand that will solve all your marketing problems.

The Marketing Plan

If you think back to the ARL definition at the start of this chapter, one of the defining features of marketing is that it is an organized, planned activity. Before you begin creating beautiful flyers and launching a Twitter account, it is important to take some time to gather your thoughts, take a look at your current situation, and think about not only what you want to do, but why you want to do it.

A common type of marketing document, the marketing plan, is extremely helpful for this process. This plan does not need to be lengthy or even very detailed, but having a few pages can help your marketing efforts succeed. Not only will you organize your thoughts, you will be forced to write goals and think about ways to measure those goals. You will have a document that you can share with the rest of your library staff, who will understand what your plans are and who can actively engage in future marketing efforts. Finally, you'll have a document that you can revise and adapt for different resources and different audiences.

The rest of this section will describe how to develop a basic e-resources marketing plan. The following structure is deeply inspired by Marie Kennedy and Cheryl LaGuardia's invaluable book, *Marketing Your Library's Electronic Resources* (2013), with additional influences drawn from Dowd,

Evangeliste, and Silberman (2010, 38–41); Duke and Tucker (2007); and Walters (2012). It may be that some of these suggestions are not appropriate for your library. Most libraries, however, will be well served by adhering to all 10 steps as discussed next.

Step 1: Research What Has Already Been Done

Before you create a broad and exciting new marketing vision, it can be fruitful to consider past actions, both in terms of mistakes and successes. If people who formerly worked with electronic resources are at your library, set up a meeting with them. Ask them about the types of promotion that have previously been conducted. Sometimes the answer will be "nothing," and that is okay. But if they do mention previous efforts, ask them to elaborate on why those efforts were or were not successful. Also find out if anyone conducted an assessment of those efforts.

Kate's Experience: Before I created my marketing plan, I set up a meeting with the three librarians who had previously participated in managing electronic resources. All three still worked at my university, UNCG. Before we met, I let them know that I was going to ask about past marketing and promotion efforts related to electronic resources, which gave them some time to think.

When we got into the meeting, I simply asked them what they could remember. For each example they brought up, I then wanted to know if there were any materials left from that effort that I could see and why (or why not) they considered the event a success. I found out that most of the efforts had been very ad hoc and had centered around attending various outreach events across campus. These events had good attendance and got a lot of feedback from professors, but we had not really tracked whether the events were successful in any meaningful way. I also discovered that events on campus were much more successful with food. I wrote down the lessons learned so I could build upon these and not repeat mistakes and missteps.

Step 2: Perform an Environmental Scan

Performing an environmental scan involves looking at the cultural, technological, and marketing milieu of your library. The scan creates a snapshot of where you are in terms of community served, resources available, and current library usage and indicates where you should focus your efforts.

When scanning the environment of electronic resources, there are many different questions you can ask; following are four of the most useful questions (from Kennedy & LaGuardia 2013, 20–23):

What Questions Are Patrons Asking?

Strategy: Talk to your public service librarians and ask them what trends in questions they notice. If your library keeps statistics related to questions asked at the public services desks, look through a few months' worth. Do the same with chat reference logs if available. Look especially for questions about needing a particular type of resource or not finding a particular type of material. These questions will give you clues about which types of resources your patrons value.

How Do We Currently Help Patrons Find Electronic Resources?

Strategy: Go through your website, and make note of all of the places where patrons can go to find electronic resources. In addition to this, browse through any kind of help pages, tutorials, and guides, and see if any of these are aimed at helping patrons find electronic resources. Write these down as well.

Then think about all the services the library offers. Do any of these work towards helping patrons find electronic resources? Finally, examine your reference area for any print materials, handouts, etc., that advertise or guide patrons towards using electronic resources. When done, you should have a solid list of all the ways you are currently helping your patrons locate and use these resources.

What Exactly Are We Trying to Market?

Strategy: To begin tackling this question, pull together a list of all your electronic resources. If your library has a large number of electronic resources, it might not be feasible to consider them at a granular level. In that case, look only at databases (found on your A-Z list) and—if you're in an academic library—at journal collections; if you don't have a browsable list of your journals or collections of journals, you can grab them from your knowledge base.

Once you have a list of your resources, look at their usage statistics for the last year. (The process of gathering usage stats is further described in Chapter 8.) Make a spreadsheet with the name of the resource and total annual usage as the only columns for better comparison. Sort by highest to lowest use. What are the trends you see in terms of lower usage? Are they correlated with a particular subject or type of resource? Areas with surprisingly low usage, when you had expected high usage based on patrons' needs (as gleaned from the first question), give you a good hint about gaps that exist in your marketing.

Whom Do We Want to Focus On?

Strategy: Look for previous library survey information, if any exists. If not, look for demographic information about your community. If you're at an academic library, this will likely be mentioned on the college's website, often on the admissions pages. If you're at a public library, you can consult United States census records, though you might get more information from your chamber of commerce or your local tourism bureau, if applicable.

You should also draw on your own knowledge of the place where you live. Write down a list of different categories of population that could exist. You can segment them in numerous ways: by age, gender, year in school, role at your campus, college major, jobs, hobbies, or interests (such as consumer health, genealogy, or reading). Once you have your big list, choose a population that you want to target in this first marketing plan. Your marketing plan can be broad, but don't try to target the entire local population all at one time. The good news is that once you have developed one plan, you usually can reuse it for a different population.

Step 3: Develop a Marketing Group

If you can get the institutional support, it is best to have more than one person working on developing the marketing plan, especially after the first three steps are completed. This helps you not have to do everything, for one, but it also ensures that different perspectives and different areas of expertise are brought to bear. It also has the potential to engage different parts of the library in the process, which can lead to increased awareness and buy-in of the plan among staff.

At a minimum, have one representative from public services and another from technical services. If you have a marketing librarian or a marketing committee, be sure to include them, too. This allows for the marketing plan to be shaped by a wide variety of perspectives, reflecting the many parts of the library. Be sure everyone has permission from their supervisor to be on your marketing team. Also be sure everyone agrees to the length of time that members will serve on the team. Your group might prefer fixed terms, indefinite terms, or as-needed terms.

Step 4: Conduct Market Research

This stage consists of detailed, in-depth work that you perform to discover new information about the population you chose to target in your environmental scan. The goal of this research is twofold: to determine your target population's need for electronic resources and to learn how they currently prefer to fulfill those needs. Two tools commonly used to investigate a population's information-consuming habits are surveys and focus groups, which are described in detail in the next section of this chapter, "Conducting Market Research."

Step 5: Write a SWOT

Performing a SWOT (Strengths, Weaknesses, Opportunities, Threats) analysis is a classic marketing technique (Kennedy & LaGuardia 2013, 23–27). A SWOT is simply a two-by-two grid, with one square for each of the four categories, like so:

Strengths	Weaknesses
Opportunities	**Threats**

Figure 6.1   A SWOT grid

To fill in the SWOT grid, you and your marketing group will look over the environmental scan and then brainstorm responses for the categories of Strengths, Weaknesses, Opportunities, and Threats. As you do this, make sure to think not just in terms of your own librarian perspective, but to consider how your patrons might perceive these categories as they relate to electronic resources. This is where the marketing research you conducted in the previous step can help. All of the answers on the grid should relate specifically to electronic resources marketing.

Strengths/Weaknesses

These are internal factors that exist within the library's culture and practices. There are several questions you might consider:

- How knowledgeable is your reference staff in terms of promoting and recommending electronic resources?
- How well supported is electronic resource management in the organizational structure of the library?
- How easy is it for patrons to find electronic resources?
- What perceptions do patrons have of your electronic resources collection?
- Is there resistance to change or technology within the organizational culture?
- Are political factors involved in requesting resources and funds for different areas of the population?

Opportunities/Threats

These are the external factors that influence the library's ability to market electronic resources. They include broader factors in the library's community, factors with the publishing market, and the behavior of members of your target population. Here's a sampling of questions to consider:

- How well does your community deal with technological change?
- How flexible and technology savvy are your patrons when it comes to electronic resources? Do they embrace new trends?
- Who currently are your competitors in this market? How strong are they?
- Do you keep up with trends in library services?
- With which vendors and publishers do you have the strongest relationship? How are they considered by the rest of the market? Stable? Troubled? Innovative?
- How is your relationship with your target community? Are there barriers to reaching them? Are other factors helping or hurting that relationship?

Come up with five to six ideas in each category as you brainstorm. As you do this, resist the temptation to rank one as more important than the other. The SWOT creation process should be neutral.

Step 6: Develop Goals

Now it is finally time to figure out your goals for this plan. When developing goals for your marketing efforts, it is good to look at your library's current strategic plan, if you have one, so that you are promoting things that are important to the library. Also look to frame your goals in terms of the library's mission statement: How are your efforts going to work towards that mission?

Creating three goals to begin with is usually ideal. They can be big or ambitious, but eventually you'll need to be able to break them down into discrete, measurable milestones. These steps create your library's roadmap, showing you the way towards achieving your goals.

Step 7: Create an Action Plan

In this stage of the planning process, you start to develop actual marketing components, examining both promotional strategies and core project management issues such as budgeting and the time to completion. This step itself can be broken down into four parts.

Part One: Develop Your Messaging Strategy

This is where you figure out which tools, techniques, and language to use when promoting your selected resources to your target market. How your target audience prefers to receive information should be the biggest influence on this section. You need to consider what your message will say, where you will place it in the community, and which other organizations and media outlets you can work with to help spread your message.

Before you plunge into this step, take a look at Chapter 7, which provides an in-depth discussion of various promotion tools.

Part Two: Create a Timeline

Look at the steps you need to take to accomplish your goal and the milestones that you developed. Make your best guess as to how much time each of those steps will take. The timeline you create will go in your planning document, of course, but it should also go into a shared calendar so that all members of the team receive reminders as due dates approach.

Part Three: Assign Staff to Different Tasks

Reconvene your marketing team to review the steps for promotion and marketing that you laid out in your strategy and goals. Go through each milestone and step, and then determine which person from the marketing team would be ideal for each role. Make assignments in this way, and then assess how much time each step requires (based on the estimates in your timeline). If the workload appears uneven, redistribute things so that no one is taking on more than they can reasonably fit in their work schedule. If you still have unassigned tasks, you can also ask for volunteers outside of the marketing team.

Part Four: Plan the Budget

Often libraries do not have a separate marketing budget, so it is especially important to describe how much everything will cost before you begin. This will help you accurately ask for the amount of money that you will need and to plan for future years. Try not to overlook any possible expenditures so you don't unexpectedly have to pay for something out of pocket. In order to help with future planning, even include costs for something you can get for free now in case that goes away in later years.

Step 8: Develop an Assessment Plan

Assessment is one of the most important things you can do, as it lets you know if your efforts were successful in changing user habits. This is why it is so essential to write goals that can be measured, like "increase the use of streaming media by faculty over the next year" or "increase the in-house use of the NoveList readers' advisory database." These goals are clearly measurable.

Depending on the goals you write, your assessments can be different, but there are a few common ways to assess electronic resources marketing. Probably the most obvious way is to look at usage of targeted resources before and after you put your marketing plan into place. Although, of course, many factors can contribute to an increase in usage, a positive trend is evidence of behavior moving in the right direction.

Another, more direct, method would be to add a survey that pops up, either when users click on a targeted resource or when they exit a targeted resource. The survey would consist of one simple question: "How did you find out about this resource?" Answers can be used to see how many people going to targeted resources did so because of your marketing campaign (Fagan 2009, 51; Potter 2012, 20–21). Alternatively, if you want to promote the use of a specific website, advertisement, or electronic resources portal, you can use web analytics to measure the number of times a page has been selected and to learn where people went after leaving that page.

In addition to measuring goals, it is important to assess individual promotion components. If you create a handout, count how many actually get taken. If you have a poster or flyer, create a separate, direct URL to a website that is tied to that promotion. You can then use web analytics of that specific page to see how many people followed through on the physical promotion. Similar URL tricks can also be created for featured electronic resources on your website (Matthews 2009, 133–134). If you are marketing through events or instructional sessions, make sure to not only get attendance, but to provide an assessment at the end of class for attendees to fill out.

All of these ways are valid, and thinking about how you will accomplish assessment before you even begin will greatly help you achieve success.

Step 9: Evaluate

Once you finish planning your marketing campaign, plan how you'll evaluate it. To begin with, you can come up with some questions to ask afterwards, such as these:

- What went well with this campaign? What didn't? Why did it not go well?
- Did our assessment and measurement demonstrate that we met our goals? What should we do differently next time?
- What story do the measurements tell?

When your campaign is over, use these questions and any others you think of to document how it went. People often do not take time for this step, but it is essential so you know what you did well and how you can move forward.

You'll also want to evaluate how well you did on the marketing plan itself, not just the marketing campaign, so that you can rewrite and revise future plans. Kennedy and LaGuardia (2013) suggest developing a rubric to evaluate your plan after it has fully been implemented. If you would prefer a less formal evaluation, these are some good questions to ask:

- How well did you paint a picture of your target market? Did you find unexpected information during the campaign that threw off your promotional strategy?
- Did you discover unexpected populations and needs that you did not catch during your environmental scan? How could you better account for these populations and needs?

- Did your marketing strategy match and reach your target audience? This does not mean that they worked, but simply that they seemed well targeted.

- Do you know enough from your measurements that you can judge the success or failure of different aspects?

Step 10: Revise

Finally—after you have completed your plan, implemented it, evaluated the success of your goals, and scrutinized the quality of the actual plan itself—it is time to do some more planning. No good deed goes unpunished.

You need to revise and rewrite the plan for future use. Taking what you discovered during your implementation and what you reflected on during your evaluation, address the problems that arose and the changes that need to be made. For example, you might have realized that something you listed in your SWOT as a threat actually was an opportunity, or you might have gone over budget or stretched your staff too thin. This is where you can fix those issues.

Conducting Market Research

We already briefly mentioned market research, back in the fourth step of the planning stage, but it deserves some additional examination, due to the specific methods used and its importance to everything you develop later on in your plan. Discovering your target audience's information needs, wants, and current information-seeking behaviors are key pieces of information that can guide how, where, and when you promote a resource.

Before we dive into the methods you can use to conduct market research, there are a few things that everyone should think about before delving into question construction or setting up focus groups.

First of all, think about the main question that you need to answer (Potter 2012, 17–19); for target markets, you might want to know about the informational needs of your users and how they are currently filling those needs. From there, you might decide you need to create questions that explore the reasoning behind current product preference and usage, how patrons make the decisions on what to use, and what technologies they are comfortable with. Once you have these different areas of exploration figured out, then you can think about what methods might work best to get you to the answers you want.

Notice that none of these sample questions mention the library. This is because you are not trying to figure out how users use the library. Rather, you are trying to figure out what users actually do and need. Framing questions around the user instead of the library lets the responder answer in a way that is unconstrained by what librarians think they might need.

Once you have thought about your main questions(s) and have framed them in a non–library-centric way, you can decide which methodology you want to implement for gathering your information. This section covers two major methods: surveys and focus groups. They can be used separately or in conjunction with one another. Both are perfectly valid and excellent ways to better inform yourself about your target market.

Focus groups are better for when you want to dig deeper into questions that you could not explore in a survey (often controversial ones) or if you want a group to come to consensus about potential marketing strategies.

Surveys

Surveys are good for generating a broad overview of the behavior of an entire target population. They are a great way to scan what your target population is thinking. Bad surveys, however, are a waste of everyone's time. Make the effort to prepare them carefully: you'll gather quality information and save the library from embarrassment.

Methods of Distribution

There are two ways to administer a survey: either directly, with an actual person asking questions and recording answers, or self-administered, where a person receives a survey and fills it out in their own time, without guidance from an administrator. The most common methods used in direct administration are in person and by phone. The most common ways to distribute self-administered surveys are by mail and email.

When deciding what method you want to use, you need to consider some things about your targeted population:

- How many of them have email addresses, or even regular access to a computer? If the answer is not near 100 percent, you should not conduct a survey via email or a website.

- How stable is your target group's living situation? If you have a transient population, you probably do not want to rely on going door to door with surveys in person or using mail. Instead, you may want to go to where that population gathers or use phone survey techniques.

- Do you want to only reach people who come into the library? Do you want to reach people who actively use the library's resources without visiting the physical building? Do you want to reach nonlibrary users? In that case, you might want to go in person to places that you know to be gathering spots for your target population and either hand out or conduct in-person surveys there. For a public library, for example, you could go to a local community center, a bookstore, a movie theater, or other places that meet the same needs that a library meets. On campus, you might want to go to the faculty center, into departmental meetings, or to the student union, depending on your population (Dowd et al. 2010, 6–9; Potter 2012, 22–26).

Eliminating Bias

Although most target market surveys do not undergo rigorous scientific testing, it is best if you can to avoid only having volunteers take surveys. There are many methods of randomizing a sample, but probably one of the simplest ways is to draw up a list of all the people you want to include (a list of all faculty, or a list of all house numbers in your community, or a list of all patrons who have library cards), number that list, and use a random number generator to pick samples. Another method, a bit more complicated, is called the stratified sample. This is where you first divide your list into categories (like age or class rank) and then choose equal amounts from each section (Fowler 2009, 23–26). Both work well.

Another way to try to make your survey more accurate is to try to minimize nonresponse rates. The more people who don't respond, the more likely your survey will inaccurately reflect the wider community. The following are a few good ways to encourage people to respond:

- Keep it short and tell participants how long you expect it to take in the beginning.
- Make it look professional. Some ways to do this include branding and clean, open designs.
- Keep the survey all on one page for electronic surveys. Clicking to other pages has been shown to cause people to drop out (Fowler 2009, 79–81).
- Give people rewards they would actually want. Do a drawing for something relatively big, not just a five-dollar gift card (Potter 2012, 20).
- If people don't respond, send nonrespondents a follow-up a few weeks later and then another final follow-up a few weeks after that. For the last one, be sure to send a new link to the survey or a new mail version (Fowler 2009, 58–62).

Writing Good Survey Questions

Once you know how and to whom you are going to distribute your survey, you are ready to get down to writing. There are a few good rules to keep in mind when writing questions, but by far the most important is this: know what you want to find out when you write questions. Start by jotting down a few words or sentences that describe why you're doing the survey and what you hope it will show you. Then, every time you write a survey question, look back at that paragraph and ask: "Is this question going to get at what I want to know?" For example, if you want to know about a professor's use of electronic information, it might be useful to ask their discipline, but you probably don't need to know their gender or race.

You can see samples of surveys in the appendix. Beyond that, you can find many books on how to write good questions for surveys. The following ones (mostly inspired by Fowler 2009, 86–112) are some of the most useful points to keep in mind:

- Avoid incomplete wording. Write out entire phrases. Don't write "Age." Write "How old were you on your last birthday?"

- Although you can use parentheses to add optional wording (you/he/she/them), don't use it to suggest answers. If you feel like you need this, you need to write a clearer question.

- Never use the "other" possible answer. Instead ask things like "is there anything else you would like to tell us about X?"

- If you think a word could be misinterpreted, add in a definition. If you absolutely must use jargon, be extremely clear. Define what you mean by a database if you ask about one!

- Particularly with self-administered surveys, don't ask many open-ended questions. Try to limit yourself to multiple choice, ranking, and scale ("On a scale of 1 to 5") questions (Matthews 2009, 47–50).

When you have finished writing your survey, it is a good practice to recruit some guinea pigs to test it. Administer the survey to them and be sure to note down any feedback they provide or areas where they get confused. After this, you can go back, revise the survey, and present it to your general survey population.

The surveying process takes a while to complete, especially when the surveys are self-administered. You want to allow for at least a month, if not longer, for this process. Often you need to send out the survey, then remind people a few weeks later, and then remind them again a few weeks after that. You generally won't get everyone, but you do want to make sure you allow enough time for those who perhaps are out on vacation or in a very busy period of their work.

Focus Groups

Focus groups are simply a research technique in which a researcher gathers a group of people and then facilitates a guided conversation among them. Focus groups for marketing can certainly stand on their own, especially in terms of receiving feedback to a proposed marketing campaign. They are also excellent follow-ups to surveys. Whereas surveys give you a broad exploration of a customer base, focus groups allow you to more deeply answer questions or trends raised in the survey.

If you decide a focus group would be useful for your purpose, the first step is to create criteria for who will be in each group. You generally want at least three groups, and everyone in each group should have something in common. Apart from that one common factor, however, you want to try to get diversity in the composition of the group.

> You can achieve a diverse composition in a variety of ways. If you're surveying distance-education faculty, for example, you might first arrange groups based on their discipline (humanities, social sciences, health sciences, etc.) but then select participants to ensure variety in terms of years teaching, experience teaching online, age, gender, etc.

After deciding what types of participants you want for each group, you then want to recruit these participants through methods you discovered (probably via your survey) that they respond to well. A technique suggested by Brian Matthews (2009) is to ask a survey taker to come to a focus group and then invite them to bring a friend. This increases your size and also lets you reach people who might not be regular library users.

Once you have your participants, there are a few guidelines to keep in mind when it comes to actually running an event. First of all, a group size of between 8 and 12 people is ideal, and a time of between an hour to hour and a half allows all of those people to engage and delve deeply into an activity or series of questions without running out of conversation. Providing food is also a good idea (Barbour 2007, 75). It not only helps with recruitment, but the sharing of food seems to break down barriers and open up conversation.

Limit yourself to 8 to 10 prepared questions. Fewer can be fine, but more is too diffuse. In the beginning, questions should be broader and should ease your participants into the correct frame of mind (Matthews 2009, 55–56). For example, you might ask patrons to "Think back to a time when you were trying to find good information about a news story you read" to get them to consider their information-finding processes.

From that broad question, you can move into discussing specifics of the information-finding process, such as why they decided to use that method, what they look for when they choose a method of finding information, and what would convince them to use one method over another.

As the focus group runs, it is your job as facilitator to keep the conversation moving, to ask additional questions or to ask for clarifications when needed, and to take notes or (with the members' consent) record the conversation. After the focus group finishes, you then should type up the notes and write your impressions of what the focus group's conversation means for your own questions and research (Barbour 2007, 76–79). Combined with survey results, or on their own, the information you gathered from these methods should now help you move on to figuring out how to best create a message and a promotional campaign that will speak to your target audience.

Conclusion

The mere mention of marketing strikes fear into the hearts of many a librarian, but it is essential for connecting your library patrons with your electronic resources. We can buy resources, make them accessible, and fix them when they break, but if no one knows they exist, our other roles become meaningless. This chapter presents marketing as an achievable goal by detailing a 10-step marketing plan and discussing how to conduct market research. After you're comfortable with the ideas in this chapter, turn to Chapter 7 to put your plan into action.

Additional Readings

Barber, Peggy, and Linda K. Wallace. 2010. *Building a Buzz: Libraries & Word-of-MouthMarketing.* Chicago: American Library Association.

Connaway, Lynn Silipigni, and Ronald R. Powell. 2016. *Basic Research Methods for Librarians.* Santa Barbara, CA: ABC-CLIO.

Gupta, Dinesh, and Rejean Savard. 2011. *IFLA Publications: Marketing Libraries in a Web 2.0 World.* IFLA Publication Series 145. Berlin: De Gruyter.

Hair, Joseph F., Robert P. Bush, and David J. Ortinau. 2000. *Marketing Research: A Practical Approach for the New Millennium.* Boston: Irwin/McGraw-Hill.

Kennedy, Marie. 2011. "What Are We Really Doing to Market Electronic Resources?" *Library Management* 32, no. 3: 144–158.

Krueger, Richard. 1998. *Developing Questions for Focus Groups.* Thousand Oaks, CA: SAGE Publications, Inc. http://sk.sagepub.com/books/developing-questions-for-focus-groups.

Lee, Deborah. 2003. "Marketing Research: Laying the Marketing Foundation." *Library Administration & Management* 17, no. 4: 186–188.

Richardson, Hillary A., and Marie R. Kennedy. 2014. "How to Market Your Library's Electronic Resources." *Serials Librarian* 67, no. 1: 42–47.

Woods, Shelley L. 2007. "A Three-Step Approach to Marketing Electronic Resources at Brock University." *Serials Librarian* 53, no. 3: 107–124.

References

Ashcroft, L. 2002. "The Marketing and Management of Electronic Journals in Academic Libraries: A Need for Change." In Savard, J. ed. *Education and Research for Marketing and Quality Management in Libraries*, Munich: K. G. Saur. 173–189.

Barbour, Rosalind. 2007. *Doing Focus Groups*. London: SAGE Publications.

Dowd, Nancy, Mary Evangeliste, and Jonathan Silberman. 2010. *Bite-Sized Marketing: Realistic Solutions for the Overworked Librarian*. Chicago: ALA Editions.

Duke, Lynda M. and Toni Tucker. 2007. "How to Develop a Marketing Plan for an Academic Library." *Technical Services Quarterly* 25, no. 1: 51–68.

Fagan, Jody Condit. 2009. "Marketing the Virtual Library." *Computers in Libraries* 29, no. 7: 25–30.

Fowler, Floyd. 2009. *Survey Research Methods* (4th ed.). California: SAGE Publications, Inc.

JISC. 2008. "JISC Attitudinal Survey: Head of Senior Learning and Librarian Staff." www.webarchive.org.uk/wayback/archive/20140616001827/http://www.jisc.ac.uk/media/documents/publications/attitudinalsurvey2008librariansreport.pdf.

Kennedy, Marie and Cheryl LaGuardia. 2013. *Marketing Your Library's Electronic Resources*. Chicago: ALA Editions.

Matthews, Brian. 2009. *Marketing Today's Academic Library: A Bold New Approach to Communicating with Students*. Chicago: ALA Publications.

Potter, Ned. 2012. *Library Marketing Toolkit*. London: Facet Publishing.

Smykla, Evelyn O. 1999. *Marketing and Public Relations Activities in ARL Libraries*. Washington, D.C.: Association of Research Libraries.

Walters, Suzanne. 2004. *Library Marketing That Works*. New York: Neal-Schuman Publishers.

CHAPTER SEVEN

Marketing, Part II: Promotional Strategies

In Chapter 6, we discussed the various steps involved in planning a successful marketing campaign. We cannot overstate the importance of planning (and if you haven't read that chapter yet, go ahead and do that now), but we recognize that planning is not what you'd call thrilling.

But promotion? Actually going out there and selling your stuff? This is where the fun begins.

Before we plunge in, though, two important lessons from Chapter 6 must be restated. First of all, your marketing strategies must all have a way to be measured for impact and effectiveness. No matter what you do, you must think about how to measure whether your strategy is actually reaching people.

Second, there is no perfect promotional strategy that will work for every target group. Promotional strategies need to be tailored and targeted to your particular audience, using the market research that you conducted. Although this chapter does provide plentiful examples of promotional strategies that have worked for librarians, it does not contain a list called "Do This Exactly and You Will Succeed."

That being said, there are some general guidelines and common methods of promotion that should be in a librarian's toolbox. These tips have been used successfully in libraries across the country:

- Don't use jargon. A survey that Potter (2012, 51–52) did for his book *Library Marketing Toolkit* found that the least understood words in libraries are "periodical" and "reference resource." Instead use words like "journal" or "encyclopedias and dictionaries."

- Make it relevant, but don't try too hard to be cool. People can tell.
- Be humorous and be brief.
- Remember: Marketing studies have found that it takes up to seven times viewing something for it to sink in, so don't feel scared about overdoing it (Duke & Tucker 2007, 58).
- Focus on the benefits of using a product, not how to use it or that it exists. It needs to seem relevant to the user.
- Never insult the user or their intelligence. Don't try to get people to use the library's resources by acting superior to things they might currently use (like Google or YouTube). This makes them feel stupid for having used the products they choose. Instead focus on how we can best get them from point A to point B in a friendly manner (Potter 2012, 5).
- If you are unsure about the product's ability to work well or consistently, don't market it. A way to get people to lose trust in your library is to market something as great and then have it not work.
- What you market should be easy to use, or at least easy to follow through on, so the value does not go below the cost in terms of user time.

This chapter will focus on six promotional strategies you can use in your library:

- **Word-of-Mouth Marketing:** In which you convince other people to do your marketing for you.
- **Web Marketing:** If you choose only one strategy for promoting your electronic resources, make it this one.
- **Print Marketing:** Pretty little flyers.
- **Outreach Marketing:** A legitimate reason to get out of your office.
- **Branding:** Express yourself.
- **Social Media:** Like it or not, social media is unavoidable for the library marketer.

Each section offers suggestions for effectively creating and executing the various promotional strategies.

Word-of-Mouth Marketing

Word-of-mouth marketing can incorporate a variety of marketing strategies, most notably social media, and it can be transmitted via any of the types of formats discussed in this chapter. It attempts to narrow in on certain members of a target audience who have influence on that community. Specifically, the main people you're trying to reach are influencers (the people who are connected to many communities and spread a lot of information to others) and adopters (those who quickly sign up for new services and help others learn them).

As a strategy, word-of-mouth marketing requires building lots of relationships with gatekeepers and other important members of your target community. You can reach out to influencers and adopters through social media or sometimes even directly, inviting them to be the first to know about services or new offers and asking them to help spread the word (Buczynski 2007, 198–200; Dowd, Evangeliste, & Silberman 2010, 13–17; Mathews 2009, 70–73).

For this strategy to work, you need to tell a story that will appeal to people, especially influencers and adopters, who will then share it with others. In this type of marketing, it is the human story you tell—the emotional, memorable story told about how a user employs electronic resources from the library to solve their challenge and move forward in life—that is the main feature (Dowd et al. 2010, 27–32). Different types of challenges appeal to different users, which is another place to draw on your marketing research.

Public vs. Academic Libraries: Word-of-Mouth Marketing

In academic libraries, the biggest influencers of student use of electronic resources are faculty. Students regard their professors as authoritative sources who know what the best resources to use would be, so a good deal of your marketing should be aimed at faculty. Seek to tell the story of how using our electronic resources can help them teach their classes and do their own research. Once a professor uses and likes a particular product for their own work, they recommend it to their students.

For public libraries, you want to target more official channels of marketing, like newspaper reporters, and develop a relationship with them so they know they can come to you on a slow news day. You also want to locate the important community organizations, business leaders and politicians, and even teachers at your local schools. All of these are people who could be influencers in your community. Target your marketing towards them.

Word-of-mouth marketing is all about building relationships with influencers and adopters and then using those relationships to expand your reach outwards. Often it can be a challenge to even know who to reach out to and how, especially for a profession with more than its fair share of introverts, but the secret is simple: participate in the life of your community. Show up for games, events, and lectures; strike up conversations at the dog park and the farmers' market; and attend faculty trainings and get-togethers and award ceremonies. And when you don't have it in you to be social, read the local news.

Keep an eye out for the people who seem to be actively involved in different areas of the community, including faculty and students who are highly engaged in campus life. Talk with the ones who support causes similarly aligned with the library, such as education, job readiness, and computer skills. Bring the library into your conversation and see if they are interested in talking about how electronic resources can help them. If they're interested, invite them out to coffee or lunch, and go from there.

Although external relationships are very important, you should not forget building internal relationships. All of the people who work in your library, especially your public service librarians and staff, can be excellent influencers of patrons. The key here is to make sure that your public service staff both believes in the importance of your marketing effort and that they are aware of what you are attempting to promote.

Make sure that your marketing plan is distributed around the library and that it has buy-in from public services, and regularly inform all public service staff about what you are trying to promote. When you get new resources, send an email to all the frontline staff and ask them to promote these resources to faculty and students. You can also provide regular internal trainings to public staff about specific resources so they know when to introduce them to patrons during reference encounters.

Web Marketing

Web marketing is any type of marketing that is on your library's website. It can take the form of a wide variety of specific promotions, such as banners across the top of a website's home page, home page spotlights concerning specific resources, or special pages detailing new or featured resources. It also entails the placement of links that patrons use to access electronic resources on library webpages such as the Database A-Z list or subject-specific research guides.

The Value of Web Marketing

The library website is prime real estate. For many patrons, it is the main way—sometimes the *only* way—they interact with the library. It makes sense to focus marketing efforts on the website, especially for electronic resources, because that's where patrons go for access. Indeed, in a survey done by the University of Liverpool, the most common ways libraries in North America advertise electronic resources is on their websites (Ashcroft 2002, 151).

Tips for Web Marketing

Pay Attention to the Patron's Experience

You might not think that the patron's user experience in accessing and finding electronic resources is part of marketing and promotion, but it really is vital. If it takes people more than a few clicks to get to their destination, or if navigating your website and locating resources is confusing for them, they will move to something easier. More about making sure your tools provide a good user experience can be found in Chapter 11.

Include MARC Records

People use the catalog as a one-stop shop. They don't want to have to hunt through guides or lists to get what they want. They expect to find everything in the library in one place, so you need to include as many MARC records for electronic resources as possible.

Create User-Friendly Categories

We just mentioned that you should load MARC records for electronic resources wherever possible, but you still need to maintain other access points, and you'll want to organize them with user-friendly categories. For instance, an A-Z list of your databases is great if you know the name of the database you want, but it can be bewildering if you don't know what resources to use. Supplement the master A-Z list with thematic groups, such as "Health and Medicine" or "Technology and Engineering."

Avoid Boilerplate Descriptions

When writing descriptions of electronic resources for access points or in marketing, think about tailoring it for your target population. Do not just copy what the vendors say about the resource. These descriptions tend to be written with librarians in mind. Instead write about how your patrons could use the resource.

For example, this is the blurb used at the University of North Carolina Greensboro to describe the database Social Explorer: "Easily explore and compare US Demographic data through side by side visualizations of different parts of the country or the same area across time. You can also create your own visualizations and custom data sets."

Once you have a brand (which we will discuss later on), be sure to feature it on as many electronic resources as possible. Branding these resources helps the patron understand that, no matter how they make their way there, they are using a resource provided by the library. Most vendors allow you to upload your logo to their platform via their back-end administration portal.

Some libraries go one step further. The University of Oregon created a custom EZproxy link, which showed the user a splash page indicating that the University of Oregon was providing access to their resource (Frumkin & Reese 2011). You can also do this at your library, provided that you have local control over your link resolver and proxy server.

Print Marketing

Print marketing encompasses any promotions that are physical. These are items that can be put up on walls, handed out to people, and integrated into displays. They can be placed most anywhere, including in the library or around your community. They also can be mailed to your target audience.

Varieties of Print Marketing

Print promotion can take any number of forms, from low-tech printouts to elaborate displays. These are just a few possible ideas:

- Flyers that include lists of resources for specific disciplines or topics.
- Bookmarks from vendors advertising specific resources.
- Posters advertising streaming media resources posted near your DVDs.
- Posters advertising the popular magazine service Flipster posted near your popular magazines.

Other options include creating physical displays for electronic resources, especially in high-traffic areas, creating dummy books or magazines to draw attention to collections while people are browsing the physical stacks, or sending postcards discussing specific resources to the target population's mailboxes (Fagan 2009).

Tips for Print Marketing

Location, Location, Location

When marketing with printed materials, pay close attention to their location. The key here is to look back at your market research and recognize where people are most likely to look at print information. Where do their routines take them where they might be able to read something? Be strategic about the placement and put information in easy-to-locate, highly visible spots that catch people when they actually have time to read something.

On a college campus, if you were targeting faculty, you could send them something their campus mail or put up flyers on bulletin boards outside faculty lounges. For students, you could work with resident advisors in dorms to hang up flyers, partner with dining services to put information on table tents in the cafeteria, and have your writing center and peer tutor services stock handouts to pass along to students. In a public library, you could stock subject-specific bookmarks on the endcaps of the relevant Dewey range, and you could advertise a Database of the Month on table tents at your public computers.

Graphic Design

The graphic design of your printed marketing materials does not need to be intricate, but it does need to look professional. Making a sign using clipart from Microsoft Publisher is not the best choice if you want to stand out.

Luckily, you have alternatives. At any library, you can reach out to other librarians who have design skills and ask for their assistance or opinions. At a public library, you might be able to hire a design firm to make templates or concepts that you could then take and use over and over again, for a signature look (Dowd et al. 2010, 111–114). You could also partner with a local college with a graphic design program, providing students a chance to build their portfolio while also receiving assistance for a lower cost.

If you work at an academic library, you could extend this partnership, making designing library materials a regular internship or part of a final class assignment (Mathews 2009, 77–83). And if budget allows, you could hire art or design students to work on your marketing campaign. They get to earn money and build their portfolios, and you get to lure in patrons with attractive marketing materials.

Ease the Transition

You need to have a well-designed product displayed at well-chosen locations, but there's one more thing to consider: users need to be able to easily get from the print material to the electronic resource advertised.

One way to handle this is with link renamers and link shorteners such as tinyurl, a popular, freely available tool. Link shorteners make links easier to remember, write down, or even take a photograph of for later. If you cannot include a direct URL, make sure to include clear directions on how to find the resource.

Some libraries use QR codes, which are barcodes designed to be scanned by apps on smartphones. The idea is that you scan the QR code on a poster for a database, and then your phone opens the link to the resource. It sounds great, but in reality, QR codes have limited value in marketing electronic resources, due to the extra step of downloading an app, the need for a person to have a smartphone with a good camera, and the high error rates.

Outreach Marketing

Although all of the types of marketing previously discussed touch on outreach, this section is concerned with efforts to go out into the community in person to promote the library, efforts to bring the target market into the library, or efforts to partner with other organizations in your community to have them share that information.

If this seems like a catchall, well, it kind of is. The thread that ties all of these types of techniques together is the act of reaching out into your community and making direct contact with them. This differentiates it from word-of-mouth marketing, print marketing, and web marketing, in which the library can take a more passive role.

Examples of Outreach Marketing

- Sending out press releases about new resources to the local newspaper or campus newsletter.
- Attending new teacher orientation at local schools to introduce the library's resources and register new library members.
- Reminding faculty of library resources at faculty meetings, orientations, trainings, and resource fairs.
- Introducing students to library resources at new student orientation.

- Working with the librarians who offer instruction to make sure they highlight resources on their LibGuides and mention them in class.

- Having vendors come to the library to offer training for librarians, faculty, or the public.

- Emailing targeted groups, such as public service librarians or faculty, about new or interesting resources.

- In an academic setting, working with campus IT to set up a system to allow professors to easily bring in links to library guides or even automatically populate a course based on its subject designation with a subject guide. This takes your links and guides to where the students and faculty actually are (Vasileiou & Rowley 2011).

- Reaching out to your Friends of the Library group or student advocacy group with your marketing ideas and using them as an early focus group. Once they like the campaign, have them work to promote the campaign and products throughout their own networks (Mathews 2009, 73–74).

- Holding a vendor expo fair. Invite vendors that you feel (based on your market research!) should be promoted and let the vendors directly market to your participants. Allow them to set up booths where they can talk to users and hold demonstrations of their product. Make sure to include a survey for participants to fill out to judge the effectiveness and what you could do differently in the future. This technique was discussed by Janosko (2014) at Indiana University of Pennsylvania, and they discovered they had an increase of usage afterwards.

Tips for Outreach Marketing

Provide Incentives

If you are holding a voluntary event, like a vendor fair or an in-house library demonstration, be sure to provide an incentive for participation. Janosko (2014, 255) provided cards for attendees in which they had to gather evidence of having visited at least four vendors. Once they did, they could turn in their card to be entered for a large drawing.

Make Sure They're Good Incentives

Make incentives actually worth something. Don't just hold a drawing for a five-dollar gift certificate, but make it something that the population that you are trying to reach would actually want.

Bribe Them with Food

Everyone loves food. Increase attendance at your events by advertising snacks, hors d'oeuvres, or pizza. And if your local regulations permit the serving of alcohol, you will find that free wine engenders an enthusiastic interest in the library's electronic resources.

Use Email Wisely

No one likes spam. Follow these tips to make sure your email outreach is effective:

- Email is best used to encourage people to follow up or explore a different marketing thing (like your website).
- Don't bury the lede! Emails need to be read, so make your headline punchy, and start right away with the most important part of the message. People will not read a long email (Potter 2012, 88–90).
- Remember your target audience. Do they use email? On campuses, almost everyone has email so it works, though people get email fatigue (Leong 2007, 89–91).
- Emails that correspond to specific needs and times of the year are more effective than generic emails. On campus, this might mean that you send emails earlier in the semester about fun resources (like audiobooks and streaming films) and as people get closer to midterms, send emails about citation management products or more research-oriented resources (Mathews 2009, 123–127). In public libraries, this might mean highlighting your downloadable audiobooks during summer, when families take long trips in cars.

Branding

A brand is a recognizable visual style that expresses, in a general way, what your library considers its mission, goals, or ethos. Branding includes a color palette, specific fonts, and logos. Often these components are documented in what is called a style guide so that all librarians can reference guidelines when designing documents and materials (Dowd et al. 2010, 122–123).

Developing Your Brand

Brands are often developed by the entire library, as are their corresponding style guides. When branding your electronic resources, you should work with the style guide that is already in place for your campus or library.

If a style guide does not yet exist—which may be the case at smaller public libraries—you'll want to create one, though not all by yourself. Be sure
to include the rest of the library in the process.

Branding can also take the form of logos that you create specifically for
electronic resources, though again, you should get approval from the rest
of your library. Going rogue with your own logos dilutes the library's brand.

Once you have a logo or brand, you can use it on your websites, print
materials, and other physical and digital artifacts created for promotion.
Many publisher and vendor platforms offer the ability to upload a logo of
your own creation to be displayed on their site. Take advantage of this feature, because it reinforces the link between the library and its electronic
resources in the mind of the end-user.

Tips for Branding

As mentioned earlier, the brand is a library-wide initiative that falls outside the purview of strictly electronic resources marketing. That said, this
section discusses a few good things to keep in mind when implementing
a brand in your own marketing initiative.

Mind the Curlicues

Use serif fonts in your logo when using print and sans serif when using
fonts online.

Go Easy on the Colors

Stick with two to three colors when designing any kind of promotional
materials. Use these colors over and over again, which will give your material cohesiveness and visual interest without being too busy.

Make It Accessible

When designing any kind of marketing templates or logos, think about
accessibility. Avoid colors with high contrast, for example, to accommodate users with color blindness. Putting text over images and using italics
and cursive also makes materials harder to read.

Social Media

Social media can take a great deal of work and generally delivers tepid
results. People who work in libraries know this already—or if they don't,

they're going to be disappointed when they start a Facebook page and their database usage does not magically double.

But social media makes up a large part of what people think of as marketing, promotion, and outreach. Libraries are practically obliged to maintain a social media presence, even if doing so yields only modest returns. If you are responsible for marketing electronic resources, you will need to address it in your marketing plans.

What follows is a brief overview of how some of the most common tools—Twitter, Facebook, and blogging—can be used to market electronic resources, along with tips for creating a good general social media presence. This section will not go into detail about the technical ins and outs of these platforms. Turn to the end of this chapter for additional readings if you want to dig deeply into tracking use of your platforms, optimizing your settings, and setting up accounts.

Social media is any type of media that allows for users to create and share content with others and then allow others to comment on this content. Through the exchange of user-created content and ideas, a relationship and a free exchange of ideas can occur (Thomsett-Scott 2014, 1–4). Social media can also help libraries get feedback quickly from users and respond in an organic fashion. This in turn helps users feel more invested, engaged, and connected.

Tips for Social Media

Electronic resources can be marketed a variety of ways through social media. You may wish to piggyback off of your library's existing social media accounts; for instance, you can post to the library's general news blog when you acquire new electronic resources. If you'd rather, you can set up separate accounts that are dedicated to information about electronic resources promotion, though you might struggle to get followers for such a niche topic.

No matter which way you decide to go, there are some general rules that apply to most forms of social media that authors who have written extensively on this topic for libraries agree on (Gupta & Savard 2011; Harrington 2010; Koontz & Mon 2014; Steiner 2012; Thomsett-Scott 2014).

Set Goals

As with all types of marketing, you need to create goals: Why is this strategy important for promotion? What do you want to accomplish by starting this blog or creating this account? Definitely write this down *before* you start posting.

Ease Yourself In

Don't jump into all the social media forms at once. Look at them and pick a few that you feel will appeal most to your target users and will serve your purpose. Getting into too many just leads to overwork and diffusion.

Don't Forget Your Branding

Make sure that all your social media accounts have a unified look and are clearly identified with your library. If you're maintaining a social media account specific to electronic resources, make sure it mimics the look and feel of your library's main social media account. And if you're at a university, make sure that any library accounts fit the aesthetic of the rest of the school.

Embrace the Vernacular

Don't use stiff, formal language. The language of social media is casual.

It's Not All About You

You know how people who always prattle on about themselves are annoying? Don't be that person. Don't just post about things you created or things your library is doing. Share information about interesting things that publishers, libraries, and community partners are doing. And if you post the occasional meme or kitten video? That's okay. We won't judge.

Read the Comments

Do not let a direct interaction with you (such as a post on your Facebook, a tweet directed at you, or a comment on your blog) go unanswered. You need to keep the conversation going and let people know they are being heard. It keeps them more engaged.

Mix It Up

Don't just post text, but branch out. Do a Facebook poll about what your favorite humanities resource is, for example. Show a picture of people using your resources.

Facebook

With over 1.86 billion active users, Facebook is the most popular of all of the social media services. For electronic resources marketing and library marketing in general, the best way to use Facebook is to create what is known as a page. A page is a public entity that users can follow and like. Users can control how often they see posts from it (including being notified every time something is posted to the page).

A page allows for easy customization and the purchasing of ads, which you can use to push information to people who are in certain communities or use a specific term frequently (Tomlin 2014, 28–29). Libraries typically run just one library-wide Facebook page, so you'll want to work with the person or people who run it to get your content posted.

At first you might be uncertain about which type of content to post on Facebook, but soon enough you'll learn which posts generate likes and which ones go unnoticed. For starters, you might repost an older advertisement (maybe something you spotlighted on your website) that has gone overlooked, and you can draw attention to a social media post from another platform (Potter 2012, 108). Facebook also works really well for quick polls to try to engage with users ("What is your favorite online art resource?") and is especially excellent for promotion of one-time events (Mathews 2009, 111–112).

You can create an event from a page and make sure that everyone who follows that page is invited to the event. Events tend to be promoted heavily by Facebook and allow attendees to not only mark their attendance, but also have a conversation about the event on its page. You can post regularly on the event page with updates to increase anticipation and keep the event regularly appearing on people's Facebook feeds (Tomlin 2014, 31–34).

GAME THE FACEBOOK SYSTEM

When posting on Facebook, there are a few basic rules that can help you reach more people (besides, as mentioned earlier, paying for ads). Facebook has a hidden algorithm that controls what content it shows you in your feed. The details are cloaked in secrecy, but there are some things known to improve the visibility of a post. Adding a photo or video increases visibility, and the more likes and shares a post gets, the more it will be seen. Other hacks include posting before nine in the morning and after five in the evening, making shorter posts, and avoiding the use of link shorteners (Potter 2012, 108–113). Use as many of these tips as possible to improve your visibility.

Finally, when posting in Facebook, it is good to establish a regular rhythm to your updates, especially at the beginning. The entire library should be posting three to four times a week on their page to make sure people are frequently getting new content and being reminded of the existence of the library's page. If you are running your own electronic resources page, three times weekly would be ideal. If you are posting your content on a main library page, you will need to post less often, perhaps once per week (Tomlin 2014, 30–31).

Twitter

As social media platforms go, Twitter is one of the easiest to set up but one of the hardest to use correctly. Twitter has a very active group of users, but is more niche than Facebook. Twitter's whole concept is quick updates about whatever you want, using no more than 140 characters. You can also respond to other people's tweets, tag people in your tweets by their username, and follow specific users.

Quite a few books (Potter 2012, 99; Solomon 2011, 1961; Thomsett-Scott 2014, 148) have suggested that Twitter is a good place to begin experimenting with social media, as it is so easy to set up. You simply go to Twitter, create a username, select a picture, and write a brief description about your account, perhaps mentioning the types of information you'll share. Then you can start putting out your initial tweets and following others. Understanding how best to use Twitter, however, is not as simple.

When you start your Twitter account, it is good to do initial tweets that will be indicative of the content you'll be tweeting in the future. Make sure you develop a messaging strategy around what you want to use Twitter for, and then stay focused on that strategy. After these initial tweets, you can begin to follow others (Potter 2012, 100–101). You want to follow people who are important to your community or whose mission interacts with yours (Carscaddon & Chapman 2014, 152–153).

Setting up your own Twitter account is simple, and it is probably a more realistic method of promoting electronic resources on their own than attempting it with a dedicated electronic resources Facebook page. That said, you do need to be able to regularly post content, about once a day, in order to keep followers engaged.

This can often be a challenge for electronic resources, which is why you might want to instead post tweets on a library-wide Twitter account. Remember, however, that all of the content does not need to be created by you—and in fact, *should* not be created by you. Posting interesting content for your readers from other sources and retweeting people you follow

---

Public vs. Academic Libraries: Who to Follow

In a public library, you might follow the local school system (especially their library), museums, community centers, and important social nonprofits, as well as local newspapers, news stations, and radio stations. Throw in some fun stuff, too. SUE the T. rex (@SUEtheTrex), tweeting from their home in Chicago's Field Museum, has an unreasonable fear of asteroids, and Merriam-Webster (@MerriamWebster) is unexpectedly sassy for a dictionary.

Academic libraries can follow other departments and services on campus, as well as other academic libraries in their geographic area or serving a similar demographic. You might also want to follow publishers, vendors, librarians, and academics writing about scholarly communication and new trends in academic publishing. And yes, you can follow dinosaurs and dictionaries, too.

---

make you a good Twitter citizen and add variety to the content you post. Twitter also is great for asking questions and responding to other's comments or questions. Posting questions allows people to engage quickly (Carscaddon & Chapman 2014, 154–155).

In terms of creating original content, Twitter, due to its short nature, often works best as a means to link to other sources. If you can describe electronic resources in pithy, funny posts of 280 characters, great! If not, rather than posting an inscrutable link to Medline Plus or ProQuest Central, post a link to another form of social media or a website where the user can explore the information about that particular resource in more depth.

In addition, Twitter lets you discover who is talking about the library. Not only can people directly tag the library's Twitter account in their post, but you can also set up your account to search through Twitter for any mentions of your library, even when people don't tag you directly. This can allow you to both see how people are talking about your library and to respond quickly to concerns or questions (Potter 2012, 102–103).

Blogging

Blogging is a long-form method of social media and probably the most time-consuming form as well. Its goal is to lay out information in a more in-depth way and generate conversation based on that information through the comments (Moore, Stringfellow, Vecchione, & Cordova 2014). Blogs work best when they raise questions that can be discussed, debated, and mulled over, but they can also be used for discussing topics that require greater explanation (Gupta & Sarvard 2011, 104). Blogging tends to be an excellent format for discussing very specialized topics, such as new or interesting electronic resources. People who are interested in your topic can subscribe to your blog and receive automatic updates when you post new information (Buczynski 2007, 206).

A blog post is in many ways well suited to discussing new or featured electronic resources. You have more room to go into detail than you could in an ad, and you can include screenshots and other images of the resource. You can also explain how the resource can be used for research or class assignments and then link other, shorter ads to this post.

According to the advice given in literature about social media marketing, the general recommendation is to write once a week to keep people engaged and not let them forget about your blog (Dowd et al. 2010, 82; Moore et al. 2014, 125; Potter 2012, 115). If you write on a shared blog, you personally can get away with posting less often.

If you are sharing blog responsibilities with numerous people at your library, it is also recommended that you make a calendar with dates for each person to post new content (Potter 2012, 114–115). Without reminders to add fresh content, people tend to let their blogs fall into disrepair, even if they have good intentions of creating new posts. But if you can find a good mixture of interesting questions and content and reach out to a specific audience, blogs can really allow for a much deeper interaction and sharing than is available on most other forms of social media.

Conclusion

Your electronic resources are no good if no one uses them. This chapter, in conjunction with the planning and researching stages discussed in Chapter 6, will help you spread the message to the people in your community. Not only will you bring awareness to your electronic resources, you'll promote the library's brand and encourage patrons to engage with the library.

Additional Readings

Barber, Peggy, and Linda K. Wallace. 2010. *Building a Buzz: Libraries & Word-of-Mouth Marketing.* Chicago: American Library Association.

Betz, Brie, et al. 2009. "Marketing Library Database Services to End Users: Peer-to-Peer Outreach Using the Student Ambassador Program (SAm)." *Serials Librarian* 56 no. 1–4: 250–254.

Clark, Wendy. 2013. "Having What You Want, Wanting What You Have: Making the Library Relevant from the Patron Perspective." *Alki* 29, no. 11: 7–9.

Fisher, Patricia, Marseille Pride, and Ellen Miller. 2006. *Blueprint for Your Library Marketing Plan: A Guide to Help You Survive and Thrive.* Chicago: American Library Association.

Grays, Lateka and James Cory Tucker. 2013. "Vendor of the Month: A Marketing Collaboration." *Collaborative Librarianship* 5, no. 2: 137–144.

Harmon, Charles, and Michael Messina. 2013. *Using Social Media in Libraries: Best Practices.* Lanham, MD: The Scarecrow Press.

James-Gilboe, Lynda. 2010. "Raising the Library Profile to Fight Budget Challenges." *Serials Librarian* 59, no. 3–4: 360–369.

Kennedy, Marie R. 2011. "Collaborative Marketing for Electronic Resources." *Library Hi Tech News* 28, no. 6: 22–24.

Kennedy, Marie R., and Cheryl LaGuardia. 2018. *Marketing Your Library's Electronic Resources* (2nd ed.). Chicago: Neal-Schuman Publishers.

Lackie, Robert J., and M. Sandra Wood. 2015. *Creative Library Marketing and Publicity: Best Practices.* Lanham, MD: Rowan & Littlefield.

Lai, Katie. 2015. "A Roadshow of Library Resources: Familiarize Students with What You Have." *Reference Services Review* 43, no. 2: 280–291.

Lindsay, Anita Rothwell. 2004. *Marketing and Public Relations Practices in College Libraries.* Chicago: Association of College and Research Libraries.

Millet, Michelle S., and Clint Chamberlain. 2007. "Word-of-Mouth Marketing Using Peer Tutors." *Serials Librarian* 53, no. 33: 95–105.

Solomon, Laura. 2016. *The Librarian's Nitty-Gritty Guide to Content Marketing.* Chicago: ALA Editions.

Thompson, Mark S., and Lynn Schott. 2007. "Marketing to Community College Users." *Serials Librarian* 53, no. 3: 57–76.

Watson-Lakamp, Paula. 2015. *Marketing Moxie for Librarians: Fresh Ideas, Proven Techniques, and Innovative Approaches.* Santa Barbara, CA: Libraries Unlimited.

References

Ashcroft, Linda. 2002. "Issues in Developing, Managing and Marketing Electronic Journals Collections." *Collection Building* 21, no. 4: 147–154.

Buczynski, James. 2007. "Referral Marketing Campaigns." *Serials Librarian* 53, no. 3: 193–209.

Carscaddon, Laura, and Kimberly Chapman. 2014. "Twitter as a Marketing Tool for Libraries." In *Marketing with Social Media: A LITA Guide* edited by Beth Thomsett-Scott. Chicago: ALA TechSource. 147–163.

Dowd, Nancy, Mary Evangeliste, and Jonathan Silberman. 2010. *Bite-Sized Marketing: Realistic Solutions for the Overworked Librarian.* Chicago: ALA Editions.

Duke, Lynda M. and Toni Tucker. 2007. "How to Develop a Marketing Plan for an Academic Library." *Technical Services Quarterly* 25, no. 1: 51–68.

Fagan, Jody Condit. 2009. "Marketing the Virtual Library." *Computers in Libraries* 29, no. 7: 25–30.

Frumkin, Jeremy, and Terry Reese. 2011. "Provision Recognition: Increasing Awareness of the Library's Value in Delivering Electronic Information Resources." *Journal of Library Administration* 51, no. 7–8: 810–819.

Gupta, Dinesh, and Rejean Savard. 2011. *IFLA Publications: Marketing Libraries in a Web 2.0 World.* IFLA Publication Series 145. Berlin: De Gruyter.

Harrington, Ryan. 2010. "Making Your Wallflowers Blossom: How to Implement the Best Social Media Strategy for Your Library." *AALL Spectrum* 15, no. 3: 16–17.

Janosko, Joann. 2014. "EXPO-Nential Success Redux, or, If You Plan It They Will Come." *Serials Librarian* 66 no. 1–4: 253–261.

Koontz, Christie, and Lorri M. Mon. 2014. *Marketing and Social Media: A Guide for Libraries, Archives, and Museums.* Lanham, MD: Rowman & Littlefield.

Leong, Julia. 2007. "Marketing Electronic Resources to Distance Students." *Serials Librarian* 53, no. 3: 77–93.

Mathews, Brian. 2009. *Marketing Today's Academic Library: A Bold New Approach to Communicating with Students.* Chicago: ALA Editions.

Moore, Carrie, Julia Stringfellow, Amy Vecchione, and Memo Cordova. 2014. "Using Blogs to Market Library Services and Resources." In *Marketing with Social Media: A LITA Guide* edited by Beth Thomsett-Scott. Chicago: ALA TechSource. 115–130.

Potter, Ned. 2012. *Library Marketing Toolkit.* London: Facet Publishing.

Solomon, Laura. 2011. *Doing Social Media So It Matters: A Librarian's Guide.* Chicago: American Library Association.

Steiner, Sarah. 2012. *Strategic Planning for Social Media in Libraries.* The Tech Set 15. Chicago: ALA TechSource.

Thomsett-Scott, Beth, ed. 2014. *Marketing with Social Media: A LITA Guide.* Chicago: ALA TechSource.

Tomlin, Mindy. 2014. "Using Facebook to Market Libraries." In *Marketing with Social Media: A LITA Guide* edited by Beth Thomsett-Scott. Chicago: ALA TechSource. 115–130.

Vasileiou, Magdalini, and Jennifer Rowley. 2011. "Marketing and Promotion of Ebooks in Academic Libraries." *Journal of Documentation* 67, no. 4: 624–643.

CHAPTER EIGHT

Assessment, Part I: Subscription Resources

In their oft-cited definition of the culture of assessment, Amos Lakos and Shelley Phipps describe an environment where "decisions are based on facts, research, and analysis, and where services are planned and delivered in ways that maximize positive outcomes and impacts for customers and stakeholders. A Culture of Assessment exists in organizations where staff care to know what results they produce and how those results relate to customers' expectations" (2004, 352).

For anyone involved with the assessment of library collections, this description should sound accurate and familiar—but not, we should hope, revolutionary. Of course, we use facts and research and analysis to make our collection decisions. Of course, we care about collecting resources that serve our customers' expectations. It goes without saying, doesn't it?

Well, sort of. Collection assessment has been a part of library operations since at least Classical antiquity, when Ptolemy II Philadelphus assessed the collections at the Library of Alexandria and found them too small. But the tools of modern collection assessment—spreadsheets and charts and usage reports—are quite recent developments. Peggy Johnson notes that collection assessment in libraries has been receiving increasing attention since the late 1990s (2014, 299), which begs the question of what, precisely, was going on prior to that.

Some of what has changed is perception. Assessment has become a buzzword in public and private spheres alike. Whereas before librarians may have quietly assessed their collections and gone about their work, certain other parties—supervisors, library board members, and even the general public—are now inclined to ask for proof that library dollars are being spent wisely.

Measures of quality have changed, too. In the first half of the 20th century, public librarians collected books of literary value. If patrons wanted to read those books, wonderful! If they didn't, well, it was hardly the library's job to provide recreational reading. And in academic libraries, at least through the 1970s, the driving impetus in collection development was collection size. Bigger was better, the thinking went. Ptolemy would have approved.

Vestiges of those assessment models remain. Public libraries still maintain works of enduring literary value, even if they don't circulate very often, and large research universities naturally endeavor to provide their scholars with abundant resources. But smaller schools now focus on quality rather than quantity, and public libraries happily circulate books of dubious literary worth.

In other words, we now assess our library collections not so much on whether they are "good"—which is difficult to assess in any objective way—but on whether they are satisfying patrons' expectations.

The advent of the Integrated Library System (ILS) has facilitated this new model of assessment. Librarians now have easy access to statistics for the books in their collections, including number of circulations, number of renewals, date of the most recent circulation, and performance of one section of the collection compared to another. And in recent decades, of course, there has been one other significant change to library collections and how we assess them: we have added electronic resources.

In this chapter, we discuss how to assess subscription electronic resources, which beg for assessment in ways that one-time purchases do not. A one-time purchase is exactly that: a single, discrete expenditure of funds. You might make a purchase that you later regret, but the damage is already done. With subscription electronic resources, you must recommit money every single year.

To help make sense of what can be an overwhelming task, this chapter breaks down assessment into several parts:

- **Data-Driven Decisions:** How to make sound judgments.
- **Measuring Usage:** How to gather and understand statistics.
- **Determining Value:** Special considerations for databases, journal packages and Big Deals, and media platforms.
- **Budgeting and Financial Sustainability:** Paying for subscription resources when budgets are flat.
- **Public Relations:** Working with the public when you lose access to a resource.

Some of the concepts discussed here are applicable to one-time purchases such as e-books and downloadable audiobooks, but these resources are discussed separately in Chapter 9.

Data-Driven Decisions

We hope this is obvious, but let us state it plainly: decisions about maintaining subscriptions to electronic resources should be grounded in data. No one would dream of canceling or starting a subscription on a lark, but the decision to renew is sometimes made without due diligence. "Well, we've always had it" is not a sufficient justification for renewal. Running out of time before a deadline and then rubber-stamping the renewal is not a winning strategy, either.

Data-driven decision making, as a concept, is popular in libraries, with applications for everything from strategic planning to outreach to reference and instruction. With regard to electronic resources, good data provides evidence that the library is spending collection monies wisely. It also serves as a shield when difficult decisions must be made. Bruce Massis (2016, 131) warns that data will not magically dispel contrary opinions, but it will at least make the discussion easier.

Any discussion of data and data-driven decision making conjures up images of statistics and spreadsheets. This is the quantitative side of the data equation, and it is discussed in detail in the next section. But qualitative data is part of the equation, too. Qualitative data encompasses factors related to electronic resources proper, as well as other, external considerations.

Qualitative Assessments of Electronic Resources

Qualitative assessments of electronic resources begin during the trial period. Quantitative assessments aren't really an option during these early stages. Some vendors will offer usage statistics at the trial stage and use them to persuade you of the product's worth, but it is difficult to draw any meaningful conclusions from such a short window—usually a month, give or take.

Not every electronic resource comes with a trial period; in academic libraries in particular, it is rare to trial journals or journal packages. Trials for databases and media platforms are standard, however. If the vendor offers a trial, take it. Even if you're certain that you want to subscribe, go ahead and take advantage of the free month of access.

> **The cost of a free trial.** Trials that range from two weeks to two months are standard business practice. Sometimes, though, a vendor will offer you free trial access for a longer duration, perhaps six months to a year. This free product may be a completely new resource, or it may be an add-on to a resource you already subscribe to.
>
> Proceed with caution. If the trial is successful—if your patrons use the product a lot and grow accustomed to it—you'll either have to pony up the money to subscribe or you'll have to answer to your patrons about why you took away the resource they liked.

Some libraries limit trial access to staff—or, in academic settings, to library staff and teaching faculty. Other libraries open trials to their entire user community, though this approach risks causing confusion among patrons who might not realize that the product is a trial.

When conducting the trial, collect feedback. Whether you use a survey instrument or ask for an email response, it is best to ask specific questions rather than offering a vague request for people's thoughts. In an academic library, you can and should ask faculty to comment on whether the resource serves a need and fills a gap. In both academic and public libraries, you should solicit feedback on the content and usability.

Content

Content is king. Librarians and end-users are willing to put up with a lot (bad interfaces, high price tags, limited functionality) for the right content. More than any other factor, it is the content of an electronic resource that will dictate your decisions about starting and maintaining subscriptions. Consider these aspects when judging a resource's content:

- **Uniqueness.** Does this content fill a collection gap?
- **Collection Need.** Does this content serve a collection need? (This is not necessarily the same as a collection gap.) Is the content urgently needed? Is it optional? Somewhere in between?
- **Print Alternatives.** Print is hardly, if ever, an acceptable alternative for databases, but it may be a tolerable alternative for some journals.
- **Free Alternatives.** We're not suggesting that Wikipedia replace your database aggregator, but some paid subscription databases are hardly better than freely available websites that cover the same content.

- **Size and Scope.** Though quality is usually more important than quantity, databases that draw from larger data sets are sometimes advantageous. This is particularly true with database aggregators that serve broad, multidisciplinary research needs.
- **Currency.** How current is the information contained within the resource? How frequently is it updated?

Usability

The best content in the world is worthless if people can't get to it. We have moved beyond text-based, command-line interfaces, but certain electronic resources still leave something to be desired. If patrons get frustrated and give up before they find what they're looking for, it doesn't matter how amazing the content is. Keep these ideas in mind when deciding whether a resource is usable:

- **Learning Curve.** Does the typical end-user need help using the product?
- **Bells and Whistles.** What features come with the product? Predictive searching? Faceted searching? Help screens? Controlled vocabulary?
- **Accessibility.** What accessibility features does the product offer? Language translation? Audio transcription? Closed captioning?
- **Glitchiness.** Does the product freeze every time you try to download an audiobook? Does it crash when you load its interactive visual models? Does it revert to date-sorted results after you've changed it to title-sorted?
- **Remote Access.** Can remote patrons realistically use the product? This is especially relevant with streaming media in communities where high-speed internet connections are unreliable or unavailable.
- **Tech Toys.** For media platforms, do movies, books, and music download seamlessly to cell phones, tablets, and e-readers? Do they work well with laptops and desktops?
- **Design of Interface.** Is the interface easy to navigate? Does it have a clean, easy-to-read design? Can someone accustomed to searching Google and Amazon easily adapt to this interface?
- **Mobile Friendliness.** Is the product mobile friendly?

During your trial period, be sure that typical end-users test the resource. If your trial is limited to teaching faculty and library staff, you may need to rope in some patrons to help you out. Chapter 11 discusses usability testing in great detail, but if you don't have the time or means to conduct a proper test, you can still gather valuable feedback.

Qualitative Assessments beyond the Products Themselves

In a perfect world, you would subscribe to all of the electronic resources that met the needs of your community. You wouldn't trouble yourself with worldly concerns about money, or whether the administrative portal for a media platform worked well, or whether you got along with your database rep. You would care only about content and usability.

But we do not make decisions in a vacuum. Other factors come into play with electronic resources, most notably with price. In data-driven decision making, it is the final, incontrovertible criterion for starting, maintaining, or cancelling a subscription. Price may be negotiable, depending on how much leniency sales reps have. And it is funny how often a supposedly inflexible price tag will suddenly be up for discussion if you threaten to cancel a subscription.

There are other factors to consider, too, even if the price is right. If you're looking to buy a home and you find the perfect house in your budget, that's wonderful—but you shouldn't buy it if the neighborhood is too dangerous, or if the power company doesn't provide service, or if the house is located by a river of toxic sludge. And with electronic resources, you don't want to start or maintain a subscription without considering issues of workability, perks, and politics.

Workability

Even if an electronic resource works beautifully on the front end, it may be a flaming pile of garbage on the back end. Developers put most of their energy into the main product. This is understandable, but a bad experience behind the scenes can be a deal-breaker, especially for products that are borderline purchases. When deciding whether to add or maintain a subscription, these are some factors to bear in mind:

- **Customer Service.** How quickly does the vendor get back to you? When there are problems, how good are the answers? Are the salespeople pushy? How often do they visit you at your library?
- **Invoicing.** Does the vendor provide timely, reliable invoicing?
- **Discovery Integration.** If you use a discovery service, will it be able to integrate with your resource? If not, is the resource still worthwhile?
- **Stats.** Are the statistics COUNTER compliant? Are they granular enough for your library's needs?
- **Size and Reputation of the Vendor.** Is the vendor a small startup, an established behemoth, or somewhere in between? Is their reputation good, bad, or unknown?

- **Admin Portal.** Does the product come with an admin portal? Is it user friendly? Is it a valuable tool?
- **Library Savvy.** Is the vendor accustomed to working with your type of library? If they more commonly serve businesses, the government sector, or special libraries, they might not be familiar with your needs.
- **MARC Records.** Does the vendor supply MARC records? Are those records in good shape? Will they require excessive in-house editing to bring them up to the standards of your catalog?
- **Reps.** Are you comfortable with your reps? Larger operations may be able to assign you a different rep if you're unhappy with your current one. With smaller vendors, you're probably stuck with whomever you've got.

Perks

When you subscribe to a resource, you're not just getting the product: you're getting the perks that come with it, too. If you buy a car, you can negotiate not just the price but the warranty and service; if you subscribe to a new electronic resource, you can negotiate the finer points of the deal. Chapters 2 and 3 discuss negotiations in detail, but some of the perks to consider negotiating are listed here:

- **DRM.** How permissive is the product's Digital Rights Management? Are the restrictions acceptable to you and your user community?
- **Financial Forecasting.** Can you negotiate an inflation cap? If not, what price increase can you expect to see in subsequent years?
- **Hidden Fees.** Does the price of the resource include access fees, platform fees, or maintenance fees? Can these be waived?

Politics

Sometimes the decision to add or maintain a resource has more to do with subjective value than objective value. This is not necessarily a bad thing. A library might commission a sculpture for the front lawn, which has nothing to do with information literacy—but if that sculpture builds the library's brand and makes the community a more beautiful place, then it may well be worth the money. Likewise, an investment in a shiny new electronic resource may pay dividends, even if it means cancelling a subscription to an existing resource.

And, as with all things political, sometimes things are beyond your control. If your library director schmoozes with a vendor at a conference and promises to subscribe to a product called Sparkly New Database, guess what? You better make room in your budget for Sparkly New Database.

Listed here are a few of the many possible political angles you might want to, or *have* to, consider:

Historical Context. Consider the decisions that have been made in recent times. If your Performing Arts resources took a shellacking last year, it might come across as mean-spirited if you further chip away at their resources this year.

Vocal Constituents. Did the local population of homeschooling parents write to your library director, asking for a kid-friendly database? Did the dean of the business school complain to the provost that the library isn't supporting her scholarly needs? Patrons sometimes lobby for their particular interests, and though you may have had other plans in mind, you may need to adjust your spending priorities. Sometimes the squeaky wheel gets the grease.

Accreditation and Program Development. In academic libraries, you may need to subscribe to certain resources to satisfy various disciplines' accreditation requirements. You may also need to subscribe to resources to support the curricula of new programs, with the understanding that resource use in new disciplines is likely to underperform the first few years.

Good PR. New electronic resources can generate good publicity for the library. Streaming media is popular with, basically, everybody. If you can introduce a crowd-pleasing resource, even at the expense of another worthy resource, you'll make a lot of people happy.

Measuring Usage

"Gathering usage statistics may be the least glamorous part of my job," says Electronic Resources and Systems Librarian Nancy Bennett in an opinion piece, "Could We Ever Get Rid of Usage Statistics?" (2015, 83). Her answer to that question, by the way, is no.

Collecting stats is a tedious, fussy, time-drain of a chore. Fons and Jewell refer to it, alternately, as "overwhelming" and "typically quite time-consuming" (2007, 156). And in reading "Practitioner Responses on the Collection and Use of Usage Statistics," the overarching sentiment of the responding librarians is one of exasperation (Fleming-May & Grogg 2010).

And yet statistics collection is essential. In the previous section, we discussed the importance of data-driven decision making, as well as qualitative means of assessing electronic resources, but that was only part of the equation. Now we'll look at how to gather numbers, which are crucial data for your decision about whether to renew electronic resources.

Or rather, they are crucial data for *most* resources. For some resources, the decision to renew is out of your hands. This is true for resources that are provided by state consortia, and in academic libraries, it is true for resources that are required for accreditation. Usage statistics can still tell you whether a resource is performing well or if you need to market it better, but when annual renewals are a given, it may not be worth your time and labor to gather stats.

In libraries with small budgets for electronic resources, statistics gathering might not seem onerous. It's not much of a pain to grab numbers for one or two databases. But if your library subscribes to hundreds of databases and thousands of journals, you might spend a week out of every month collecting and storing stats (and that doesn't even include analyzing them!).

There are three main ways to gather usage statistics:

- Receive an email from the vendor.
- Log in to the admin portal.
- Use a product that supports SUSHI to harvest COUNTER-compliant stats (discussed in detail later).

Much of the tedium of the process comes from visiting many different sites, supplying many different usernames and passwords, and then remembering which links to follow and drop-down menus to select once you've logged in. Then, once you've found the statistics, you need to store them in a central location.

Many libraries commonly gather statistics monthly—45 percent of them, according to one survey (Fleming-May & Grogg 2010, 28). In the opinion of the authors, this is inefficient and unnecessary unless someone is monitoring the performance of electronic resources every single month. A more reasonable frequency would be quarterly, biannually, or even annually. You would always be able to gather statistics on an as-needed basis to support your routine collections decisions, of course.

If you have a discovery service, however, a monthly review of statistics should be standard, particularly if the discovery service was recently implemented. By analyzing usage statistics, you can notice if resources experienced an unexpected drop in use. This is a strong indicator that the discovery service is for some reason failing to include these resources in search results. Indeed, this kind of eagle-eyed analysis may be your *only* indication that your discovery service is neglecting to show these resources.

COUNTER and SUSHI

If you're reading this and wondering why someone hasn't automated this process already, for crying out loud, the answer is that someone *has* automated it, sort of.

First introduced in 2002, COUNTER (Counting Online Usage of Networked Electronic Resources) sought to introduce standards to statistics. It publishes and periodically updates a Code of Practice, in its fourth iteration at the time of this writing. The purpose of COUNTER is to give libraries an apples-to-apples comparison across products so that vendors provide the same metrics and use a common language. COUNTER statistics are also valuable to libraries in that they are trustworthy: vendors who supply COUNTER statistics undergo an annual external audit for credibility.

Then along came SUSHI (Standardized Usage Statistics Harvesting Initiative), a NISO (National Information Standards Organization) standard first released in 2007. Designed to facilitate the automatic retrieval of COUNTER statistics, SUSHI is not a piece of software but is rather a protocol. You use a computer program with SUSHI functionality to gather all of your stats for you.

If this sounds too good to be true, that's because it is.

The first problem is that not every vendor uses COUNTER. If you subscribe to resources that are not COUNTER-compliant, you will still have to gather those statistics manually. Moreover, not every COUNTER-compliant resource is harvestable by SUSHI.

The second problem is that not every library uses SUSHI. In some cases, this is due to cost; in some cases it is due to frustrations with setting up or using SUSHI; and in some cases, it is because libraries are not convinced of the utility of SUSHI. If your library does not use SUSHI and has not recently evaluated its merits, it may be time to revisit that decision. In "Implementing SUSHI and COUNTER: A Primer for Librarians" (2015), Oliver Pesch of EBSCO explains why SUSHI may be a good choice for your library and provides detailed instructions for setting up the mechanics of SUSHI harvesting.

In that same article, Pesch addresses a common concern of academic libraries: Why are there no COUNTER reports for journal packages? The reason is that COUNTER counts usage for platforms and titles, but not for bundled packages. However, you can take COUNTER numbers and create your own report by identifying which packages the titles belong to. As Pesch explains, this does not need to be a laborious process if you use the VLOOKUP function in Excel (123).

Tools and Resources

Several tools can make your usage-gathering process less painful. If you're looking to implement SUSHI, it may be that there is a SUSHI feature in your ERM (Electronic Resources Management) software, if you use one. You may be able to subscribe to a usage consolidation product such as 360 COUNTER (from ProQuest) or Usage Consolidation (from EBSCO). Commercial tools such as these can offer sophisticated analyses and reports, in addition to gathering the raw numbers. But if raw numbers are all you need, or if the commercial products are cost prohibitive, you might consider an open-source tool like MISO (also from ProQuest).

Additionally, three free web-based resources can help you with COUNTER, SUSHI, and anything else related to gathering statistics. First is the Lib Stats listserv; sign up at www.jiscmail.ac.uk/cgi-bin/webadmin ?A0=LIB-STATS. Members can ask questions and read through the archives. Then there's the SUSHI Registry at www.niso.org/workrooms /sushi/registry_server, where you can find out of a vendor is SUSHI compliant and get instructions for setting up a SUSHI harvest. And USUS (www .usus.org.uk), a community website on library usage, has a wealth of resources, including guides to understanding journal, book, and database COUNTER reports and Excel templates for analyzing data.

Determining Value

You've gathered your data, qualitative and quantitative. This information can be used for a few different purposes: maybe an administrator wants some numbers for a report, or perhaps you need to fill out a survey, or maybe your Readers' Services Librarian wants granular information about your readers' advisory database.

But the biggest reason to gather data about electronic resources is to assess them for the purposes of making renewal decisions. It is the library's job to consider the data for subscription resources and each year make an informed decision about whether to renew or cancel.

This is not as simple as running a few reports and looking at the numbers. The qualitative data we discussed earlier does not lend itself to spreadsheet formulas, and even the quantitative data needs to be interpreted with context. As Geoffrey Timms observes, "usage data and statistics can only tell us *what* happened with regard to e-resource usage as logged by the vendor, not why it happened" (2012, 108).

For starters, one year's worth of statistics is acceptable but not ideal. One year isn't long enough to speak to trends over time. In an academic library, a certain journal or database may be *extremely* valuable to a class that is only taught in alternating years. In a public library, demand can be driven by external, often unpredictable, factors: economic recessions, wars, epidemics, natural disasters, and presidential elections.

When interpreting usage numbers, bear in mind that internal factors can make a difference, too:

- **Access.** Were all of your resources accessible via all the same channels (catalog, A-Z database list, etc.)? Did resources from certain providers experience intermittent access errors?
- **Promotion.** Did you market some resources more than others?
- **Functionality.** Can you attribute a resource's increased usage to improved functionality, such as better searching capabilities or a more intuitive interface? Alternatively, did a resource receive enhancements *without* seeing an increase in searches?
- **Competition.** Did you recently add a second resource in the same subject area? If so, the competing product might account for decreased usage in the first resource.
- **Discovery.** Did you recently add a discovery service? This often results in "decreases in the use of traditional abstracting and indexing databases and an equally dramatic increase in the use of full-text resources from full-text database and online journal collections" (Dunkley 2016, 4).

Keep those factors in mind as you look at usage numbers. It is possible to perform sophisticated analyses on those numbers to draw conclusions, and you certainly may wish to do so if you have the time and knowledge; if you are going to justify your decisions to a general audience, however, it is wise to keep your numbers and statistics simple for maximum impact. Some of the most common metrics used by libraries are simple but powerful:

- **Cost.** This is the universal metric. Everyone understands dollar signs.
- **Inflation.** If you're renewing a resource, look at the percentage of its price increase, and compare it to the percentage increase of your other electronic resources in the same year.
- **Use.** This one can be a little tricky. Of course, you should think twice about renewing resources that get comparatively low usage, but neither do you want to eliminate all of your niche resources. Also, a high number of searches may be a function of poor interface design.
- **Cost per use.** This is the price of a product divided by the number of uses it receives. It's a great metric for comparing similar resources—for instance, one journal package to another. It does have limitations, though. If you're defining "use" as "article download," then it's an irrelevant measure for a database consisting only of indexes and abstracts. Alternatively, if you're defining "use" as "article search," the metric disadvantages any databases that are not automatically searched in a unified search.

We'll look now at specific concerns in databases, journals and Big Deals, and media platforms.

Databases

Comparing one database to another can be tricky. It's easy enough if you're comparing one general-purpose journal aggregator to another, but how do you compare a general-purpose journal aggregator to a database of stock and market information? To a database of prescription drug information? To a database for learning foreign languages?

Again, context is crucial. A basic topical search in a journal aggregator may result in a flurry of record views and article downloads, whereas an intensive language-learning session will show only the rather unimpressive statistic of a single patron login.

To supplement the numbers-based metrics, gather input from frontline staff. Present them with a list of all of your databases, and ask them to rank the resources into three or four tiers. This will give you a sense of how to assess the various resources in comparison to one another. Another idea is to look at the top-performing resources and use the mean average of their metrics as a baseline measure for judging all of the other resources (Sutton 2013, 247–249).

**PUBLIC LIBRARIES VS. ACADEMIC LIBRARIES:
DEEP RESEARCH AND IMMEDIATE RESEARCH**

A common (though not universal) difference between public and academic libraries is the need for indexing and abstracting content. In academic settings, scholars perform research that is deeper and broader than is typical in public libraries. If you're weighing whether to keep a full-text database or an abstracting/indexing database, it may be more important to keep the latter. Academic researchers need to know that relevant resources do exist, somewhere, even if they're not available at their home institutions.

In public libraries, there is less of a need to know about every bit of scholarship ever written about a particular topic. This is why abstracting and indexing, though of some importance, is less vital to the public library's mission. This is also why public libraries care more about current resources and less about historical resources. If a database only covers content that goes back a few years, that's often perfectly acceptable for public libraries.

Journals and Big Deals

In public libraries, electronic journals constitute a small part of budgetary spending, and decisions about them are usually made at the platform level, described later. In academic libraries, however, journal subscriptions can be as costly as databases, and librarians must consider them both at the title and package level.

Bundled packages of journals, or "Big Deals," are controversial. Some libraries find that Big Deals save them money overall; some find them to be an expensive habit that's hard to quit; and quite a few libraries, frankly, have not scrutinized the value of their journal packages. Properly studying the benefits, drawbacks, and possible costs of dropping a Big Deal can take months or even years (Enoch & Harker 2015), especially because serials management and analysis must often be done manually (Carroll & Cummings 2010, 227).

Big Deals are, almost always, an all-or-nothing proposition. They are extremely expensive, but they are staggeringly less expensive than individual subscriptions would be. Even subscriptions to the top two or three most-used journals in a package could easily cost more than subscribing to the entire package.

But neither does it seem sensible to spend money for journal titles that nobody wants. In fact, some of those journal titles may be actively unwelcome at your library, but you don't get any say in the matter. Libraries do not get to pick and choose titles when they get bundled deals. And it is particularly irksome to pay for content twice (or three times, or more), which often happens when libraries subscribe to multiple bundles.

Even if you do not have time right now to conduct a thorough analysis of your bundled journal packages, you can run a content overlap report to see if there are any easy places to cut. If you're paying for a package that consists mostly of titles that are available in other bundles or through your databases, you may be able to drop your subscription. Content overlap reports are available through commercial serials analysis tools. You can also create them yourself if you have strong Excel skills.

You may also wish to explore the one-time purchase of journal backfiles of popular titles. Having permanent access to older content makes the prospect of dismantling bundled packages somewhat less scary. This can be a good avenue to pursue if you receive one-time, end-of-budget-year funds.

Media Platforms

Media platforms are the easiest of all electronic resources to assess. Because of public demand, there is no ambiguity about whether you need to acquire them or whether you need to keep them, even if their functionality is less than ideal. In the years after Amazon released its first Kindle in 2007, for instance, patrons were vocal—*very* vocal—about their desire to borrow e-books from the public library. Libraries that did not sign on with an e-book service began to look hopelessly out of touch—even though, at first, library e-books and Kindles were completely incompatible. Libraries felt pressured to get e-books, even though they couldn't circulate on the world's most popular reading device.

In all but the poorest public libraries, it is standard to subscribe to a platform, or platforms, to provide e-books and downloadable audiobooks. It is becoming increasingly common for public libraries to also provide platforms for streaming movies and reading magazines. Platforms for downloading music are also popular, though not as prevalent.

In academic libraries, the demand for e-book platforms is less intense, because e-books are usually purchased from book jobbers or publishers and distributors. The provision of platforms for popular music and popular magazines is fairly uncommon, because these are not core resources at most academic libraries. Platforms for streaming movies, however—including feature films, documentaries, and shorter educational pieces—are widely seen as desirable, if not essential, particularly for serving the needs of distance-education students.

Subscribing to platforms is often free. At most, platforms come with a relatively low annual maintenance fee. The vendors make their money from the individual title purchases—or, in some models, from the number of patron views.

For those platforms wherein the library purchases content rather than leasing it, access to the platform must be maintained or else all that content vanishes (never mind that it was "purchased"). If you've been buying downloadable audiobooks for the RBdigital platform but then decide you'd rather acquire downloadable audiobooks from Hoopla, you must maintain access to both platforms or else you kiss your original collection goodbye.

Unless your library is facing dire financial circumstances, it is unwise to withdraw from a popular lending platform unless you replace it with an alternative. Moving from one e-book platform to another may or may not be a good decision, but taking away e-book access entirely would cause the patrons to revolt.

Budgeting and Financial Sustainability

Sometimes, after you've made your careful assessments and judged the comparative worth of all of your electronic resources, you receive your budget for the year and realize there's not enough money. You might be able to trim some fat here and there, but even so: you have more resources than capital. Something's got to give.

This is not, by the way, an unlikely scenario. Like any other institution, libraries are subject to economic forces. There may be a national recession—or perhaps economic times are good and the local population is booming, but their tax dollars (or tuition dollars) haven't trickled down to the library budget yet.

Even in the extraordinarily unlikely scenario that your collections budget is always fully funded, with 3 percent more money each year than the year before to account for inflation, it's still not going to be enough. This is because database and journal subscriptions, in general, outpace the rate of inflation, to the tune of 6 percent on average (Bosch & Henderson 2017, 45). We who work in libraries have been conditioned to believe that a 5 percent increase is fair and desirable—and the sad thing is, 5 percent really does sound reasonable, when compared to other electronic resources that increase by 20 percent or more *per year.*

In public libraries, where monographs command the bulk of the collections budget, these price increases are unpleasant but usually bearable. In academic libraries, where databases and journals can easily eat up 75 percent or more of the collections budget (Phan, Hardesty, & Hug 2014, 24), the entire world of scholarly communication is endangered. We can make do with cuts and come up with creative financial solutions for a time, but we cannot sustain such dramatic price increases forever.

On that cheerful note, let's look at some ways to make cuts to electronic resources.

Talk to Your Reps

You do not want to cancel resources, and your sales reps do not want to lose your business. Speak with them. Explain your budgetary situation. Ask what allowances they can make. If possible, present them with a dollar amount you can afford or a percentage increase that is within your budget.

Speak to the reps of the resources you do *not* intend to cancel. We do not advocate lying, but you can absolutely inform your rep that, although you intend to maintain the subscription, you're in a bad budget situation and you need all the relief you can get.

Distributing the Misery

When you've got an unpopular, underperforming electronic resource, dropping it is easy—satisfying, even—but cancelling subscriptions to good resources is one of the unpleasant parts of a librarian's job. Trying to judge between them is like deciding whether to fund the fire station or the public schools.

Your task is to figure out how to distribute the pain. Should you cancel an all-purpose research database? Assuming you have another all-purpose database, a cancellation like that would hurt everyone a little bit, but no one in particular.

Alternatively, you could make cuts to niche resources with low usage. This spares more people overall, but you might cause real hardship to a small group—for instance, the one scholar on your campus who studies that particular subdiscipline.

If your budget cuts are severe enough, you'll have the distinct misfortune of applying both approaches.

Cancellation Band-Aids

In most cases, there are ways to ease the sting of cancellations. It is even possible that the outcry you expect will fail to materialize. It may be that the high-usage resource you cut was popular because it was available, not because it was specifically sought out. In academic and public libraries both, there will always be students who don't care about databases or journals as long as they can get three to five library resources for their paper.

For those cancellations that do cause noticeable pain, you have a few options:

- **ILL.** Not every database lends itself to ILL, and DRM forbids the loan of most e-books, downloadable audiobooks, and movies. With journal articles, however, ILL may be a cost-effective alternative. Take the mean average of the number of uses of a particular journal from the past few years and multiply that number by the cost of the typical ILL. If that figure is less than the cost of a subscription—and if you don't butt up against annual lending limits— then you may be able to save some money.

- **On-Demand Access.** Some articles may be purchased by the library for temporary use by individual patrons, usually somewhere in the neighborhood of $25 to $50 a pop. It can be an accounting headache, and the process needs to be mediated by a librarian, but it may save the library from paying expensive subscription fees. As with items borrowed through ILL, these articles are not added to the library collection.

- **Print.** Occasionally, there may be a viable print alternative to a subscription electronic resource, but don't get your hopes up too high. This is pretty uncommon. Also, if you take away a downloadable audiobook service and then recommend your patrons revert to physical audiobook CDs, expect to get some serious stink-eye.

- **Alternative Funders.** Sometimes other groups will be willing to fund a subscription or take it over from the library. The provost's office might pick up a grants database, for instance, or the chamber of commerce might pick up a business database.
- **Remaining Resources.** Cutting existing resources gives you the opportunity to showcase your remaining resources, both in print and online.

Public Relations

When you have to recommend which resources to cancel, present your data clearly. Whether the audience is your boss, your dean, your board of directors, or a town hall, make your report visually appealing. People respond well to graphs and charts; they respond to large data sets of numbers with vacant stares. And Morrisey (2010) stresses the importance of providing a narrative to go with your report: "Presenting just the numbers will often lead to people ignoring the numbers because they don't have time to interpret them themselves" (289).

After cuts have been made, you probably do not want to draw attention to every resource that is no longer available. In some cases, people won't notice that anything's changed, so why point it out? But for very popular resources, own it. Post a notice on your website. Don't point fingers ("Those jerks in city hall!") but explain that, because of budget cuts, the library can no longer offer access to the resource.

People need to be reminded that underfunding the library has consequences. Librarians as a whole are service-oriented people who want to shield their patrons from the ill effects of budget problems. We go to great lengths to provide the same level of service, even when we have less money. But this rewards the people who underfunded the library in the first place: they take away resources, and the patrons don't even notice! Those librarians sure are good sports, aren't they, to make do with scraps! There is an argument for transferring the pain of the cuts directly to the patrons. It gives them incentive to lean on funding bodies to fully fund the library.

Conclusion

Assessing subscription resources can be one of the most fun parts of your job, especially when you're looking at new products and your budget is healthy. It can also be one of the more unpleasant parts of the job: no one enjoys collecting usage statistics, and the occasional budgetary mandate to cancel valuable resources is one of the more disagreeable parts of librarianship. In good budgetary times and bad, however, data-driven analysis is crucial to ensure that the library is spending its money to best meet the needs of its patrons.

Additional Readings

Garza, Lanette. 2017. "The E-Resources Playbook: A Guide for Establishing Routine Assessment of E-Resources." *Technical Services Quarterly* 34, no. 3: 243–256.

Lemley, Trey, and Jie Li. 2015. "'Big Deal' Journal Subscription Packages: Are They Worth the Cost?" *Journal of Electronic Resources in Medical Libraries* 12, no. 1: 1–10.

Pesch, Oliver. 2015. "Implementing SUSHI and COUNTER: A Primer for Librarians." *Serials Librarian* 69, no. 2: 107–125.

Smith, Kelly, and Jens Arneson. 2017. "Determining Usage When Vendors Do Not Provide Data." *Serials Review* 43, no. 1: 46–50.

Sutton, Sarah. 2013. "A Model for Electronic Resources Value Assessment." *Serials Librarian* 64, no. 1–4: 245–253.

Timms, Geoffrey. 2012. "Gathering, Evaluating, and Communicating Statistical Usage Information for Electronic Resources." In *Managing Electronic Resources,* edited by Ryan O. Weir. Chicago: ALA Techsource. 87–120.

USUS: "A Community Website on Usage." www.usus.org.uk.

Wilde, Michelle, and Allison Level. 2011. "How to Drink from a Fire Hose without Drowning: Collection Assessment in a Numbers-Driven Environment." *Collection Management* 36, no. 4: 217–236.

References

Bennett, Nancy. 2015. "Could We Ever Get Rid of Usage Statistics?" *Insights* 28, no. 1: 83–84.

Bosch, Stephen, and Kittie Henderson. 2017. "New World, Same Model." *Library Journal* 142, no. 7: 40–45.

Carroll, Diane, and Joel Cummings. 2010. "Data Driven Collection Assessment Using a Serial Decision Database." *Serials Review* 36, no. 4: 227–239.

Dunkley, Mitchell. 2016. "Friendly Guide to COUNTER Database Reports." COUNTER. www.projectcounter.org/wp-content/uploads/2016/03/Database-pdf.pdf.

Enoch, Todd, and Karen R. Harker. 2015. "Planning for the Budget-ocalypse: The Evolution of a Serials/ER Cancellation Methodology." *Serials Librarian* 68, no. 1–4: 282–289.

Fleming-May, Rachel A., and Jill E. Grogg. 2010. "Practitioner Responses on the Collection and Use of Usage Statistics." *Library Technology Reports* 46, no. 6: 28–34.

Fons, Theodore A., and Timothy D. Jewell. 2007. "Envisioning the Future of ERM Systems." *Serials Librarian* 52, no. 1–2: 151–166.

Johnson, Peggy. 2014. *Fundamentals of Collection Development and Management* (3rd ed.). Chicago: ALA Editions.

Lakos, Amos, and Shelley Phipps. 2004. "Creating a Culture of Assessment: A Catalyst for Organizational Change." *Portal: Libraries & the Academy* 4, no. 3: 345–361.

Massis, Bruce. 2016. "Data-Driven Decision-Making in the Library." *New Library World* 117, no. 1: 131–134.

Morrisey, Locke. 2010. "Data-Driven Decision Making in Electronic Collection Development." *Journal of Library Administration* 50, no. 3: 283–290.

Pesch, Oliver. 2015. "Implementing SUSHI and COUNTER: A Primer for Librarians." *Serials Librarian* 69, no. 2: 107–125.

Phan, Tai, Laura Hardesty, and Jamie Hug. 2014. *Academic Libraries: 2012 (NCES 2014-038)*. Report. https://nces.ed.gov/pubs2014/2014038.pdf.

Sutton, Sarah. 2013. "A Model for Electronic Resources Value Assessment." *Serials Librarian* 64, no. 1–4: 245–253.

Timms, Geoffrey. 2012. "Gathering, Evaluating, and Communicating Statistical Usage Information for Electronic Resources." In *Managing Electronic Resources*, edited by Ryan O. Weir. Chicago: ALA Techsource. 87–120.

CHAPTER NINE

Assessment, Part II: One-Time Purchases and Leases

In the overarching conversation about assessing library collections, electronic resources that were purchased or leased are almost an afterthought. In library schools, at conferences, and in the professional literature, the bulk of the assessment discussion concerns two main areas: traditional print monographs and subscription electronic resources. Little attention goes toward assessing e-books, downloadable audiobooks, and digital movies.

The lack of conversation is understandable. In terms of intellectual content, these resources are identical to their physical counterparts. If you know how to select traditional print books for your collection, you theoretically know how to select e-books, too. The formats have changed, but the principles of collection development have not. And if hardly anyone ever talks about weeding e-books, well, so what? It's not like they're taking up room.

But what seems straightforward in theory is messy in practice. Electronic resources are not identical to print resources, and they do sometimes need to be weeded. This chapter helps bring clarity to the topic of assessing one-time purchases (or leases) by considering several aspects:

- **Collection Development of Electronic Resources:** Deciding what to select.
- **The Case for Weeding Electronic Resources:** The importance of cleaning your virtual shelves.
- **Identifying What to Weed:** Deciding what to deselect.

- **The Self-Weeding Collection:** Resources that vanish, whether you want them to or not.
- **How to Weed Electronic Resources:** The mechanics of weeding virtual items.

This chapter pairs well with its companion, Chapter 8, which discusses the assessment of serial subscription resources. The principles of data-driven decision making, as described in that chapter, are applicable here as well.

Collection Development of Electronic Resources

Even in a digital era, the fundamentals of collection development remain unchanged. When deciding whether to acquire content for the library, you consider a variety of factors:

- The quality of the content.
- The reputation of the publisher and author.
- Demand for the resource, as indicated by numbers of copies sold, box-office numbers, patron requests, and faculty recommendations.
- Currency, especially with nonfiction.
- Relevance to your community.
- Whether the item fills a collection gap.
- Awards, reviews, and buzz surrounding the item.

Once you've decided to collect a resource, you need to pick a medium. As recently as 15 years ago, the main formats for books were paperback, hardback, and large print; CDs were rapidly overtaking cassette tapes as the medium of choice for audiobooks; and with movies, DVDs had all but replaced VHS tapes. Now, in addition to those physical formats, you must consider e-books, downloadable audiobooks, and streaming films.

Or rather, you must consider them in *some* instances. A publisher might release a title as a print book but not as an e-book, or vice versa; or the publisher may have plans to release the book in both formats, but not at the same time. The audio version of a book, if it exists at all, is often released after the physical book, and movies are frequently unavailable for purchase or lease in streaming format.

With movies and audiobooks, streaming and downloadable options are becoming ever more attractive. Physical discs are comparatively inconvenient, and patrons are already largely familiar with streaming and downloadable media, thanks to popular consumer services such as Netflix and Audible. If cost permits (as discussed in the next section), libraries are often eager to choose electronic rather than physical movies and audiobooks. The electronic versions are accessible to homebound patrons and distance-education students, and in some cases, they are available to unlimited simultaneous users.

But although CDs and DVDs are waning in popularity, physical books are still holding strong. A 2016 Pew Research Center survey found that 65 percent of Americans had read a print book in the past year, 28 percent had read an e-book, and 14 percent had listened to an audiobook. As for college students, Millar and Schrier found that 57 percent of their survey respondents preferred print textbooks, 25 percent preferred e-textbooks, and 18 percent had no preference (Perrin 2015, 174). E-books and audiobooks constitute an important slice of the book market, but the death of the traditional print book has been greatly exaggerated.

PUBLIC LIBRARIES VS. ACADEMIC LIBRARIES: THE DIGITAL DIVIDE

Some academic libraries (Gonzalez 2016) and even some public libraries (Hays 2014) have transitioned to collections that are entirely, or almost entirely, digital. Although the patrons of academic libraries usually have the technological literacy necessary to use electronic resources, the patrons of public libraries might not. Digital collections pose a steep barrier to access for readers who are not comfortable with e-books. And in both public and academic libraries, some patrons do not have access to the high-speed internet connections that are required to use streaming media resources.

Knowing how many copies of a title to buy and in which formats is something that comes with experience—and even seasoned librarians encounter the occasional head-scratcher. In those cases, a good method is to buy conservatively at first and then gauge demand. Purchase one copy of a title as an e-book and another as a print book and then purchase additional copies if they develop long holds queues.

A similar strategy involves turnaways, a metric used mostly with e-books in academic libraries. If one person is using a resource and another person tries to access it at the same time, the second person is denied access or turned away. A high number of turnaways shows that many patrons were stymied while attempting to access a book and that you should consider increasing the user limits.

Format Selection

Although there is no secret formula for choosing a format and you must make a decision for each separate title, there are a few tips to make your choice easier:

Classics

Literary classics and seminal works within academic disciplines deserve a place in the library's collection, whether or not they circulate much. To save shelf space for higher-demand materials, consider replacing these titles with e-books.

Reading Experience

For books such as novels that are read cover to cover, many (though certainly not all) readers prefer the tactile experience of reading a physical book. For books readers refer to in smaller chunks, the digital version may be preferable, especially because e-books allow for keyword searching, an important consideration for students and scholars.

Durability

Electronic resources do not wear out. You cannot drop an e-book in the bathtub. Chubby little hands cannot crack a Disney streaming movie into pieces.

Cross-Format Duplication

In certain circumstances, you can choose not to spend money on a book because you already own it in a different format. This is particularly true in academic libraries, where the population served can be assumed to have the technological fluency to read a book in print or digital format. Some people might grouse about it, but they *can* do it.

Accessibility

On the one hand, electronic resources are inaccessible for patrons who are not comfortable with or do not have access to technology. On the other hand, electronic resources open up new avenues of accessibility. The text on e-books can be enlarged for the vision impaired, and some devices can even narrate the text, though not with the production values of a professional audiobook. Some streaming media platforms offer closed captioning as well as movie transcripts. And the automatic translation of texts into foreign languages, though still in its infancy, may someday become a standard feature of e-books.

Cost

In addition to the other factors we've already examined, there's one biggie that deserves its own section. The price of e-books, downloadable audiobooks, and streaming films could charitably be called "highway robbery"—or at least, that's what it seems like at first glance. In the library market, e-books are noticeably more expensive than their physical counterparts (Bailey, Scott, & Best 2015; Miller 2015), and the percentage of library budgets spent on e-books is growing (Sanchez 2015, 13).

The higher price of streaming films is easy to understand; unlike DVDs, they are typically accessible to unlimited numbers of people. With e-books and downloadable audiobooks, however, the price disparity seems especially egregious. They incur no material costs, and there's no need to ship them or store them. Shouldn't they cost *less*?

In truth, e-books and print books have similar production costs. Regardless of format, professionally produced books require editing and proofreading, page layout, cover design, and marketing. Printing and distribution comprise only a small part of the cost of producing a print book. And Michael Hyatt, former CEO of Thomas Nelson Publishers, explains that e-books come with hidden costs, including digital preparation to ensure compatibility with all major devices, quality assurance to ensure consistent formatting across those devices, and digital distribution to retailers (2010).

With e-books, the higher price sometimes comes with valuable benefits. Some publishers and distributors allow their e-books to be downloaded, printed, emailed, and shared among classmates and colleagues, though these perks are typically associated with scholarly titles rather than popular works. Another perk allows for unlimited simultaneous users. This, too, is uncommon for books from popular presses, though there are signs of change. For instance, there are no user limits in Hoopla, a platform that includes e-books, downloadable audiobooks, streaming videos, and other types of media.

Even without additional frills, the higher cost of e-books may be worthwhile. In examining popular reading at a mid-sized public library, Gray and Copeland found that the cost per circulation for e-books was $1.15, only four cents higher than the $1.11 cost per circulation for print books (2012, 338). And Jie Li's study of the University of South Alabama Biomedical Library collection is astonishing: in a five-year period, the contents of 60 e-books were used 370,695 times, whereas their corresponding print versions were used 93 times (2016, 44).

No library can afford to meet the demand for all titles in all formats, but even the most meager budget can make room for Project Gutenberg, a collection of free e-books (54,000 at the time of this writing). Most of them are from the public domain, and some are quite obscure, but libraries can take advantage of some or all of the collection, which includes perennial classics such as Jane Austen's *Pride and Prejudice* and Bram Stoker's *Dracula*. The website includes instructions on generating MARC records.

Hands-Off Collection Development

As with print books, e-books can be collected through approval plans. First you work with a book jobber to establish a profile with various parameters, such as "always send books published by Routledge" or "only send books in this Dewey range if they have a print run in excess of 2,000 copies." The book jobber notifies you when e-books match the profile, though you retain the option of declining titles that you do not want to add to the collection.

Similarly, you can establish parameters to receive MARC records through a use-driven acquisitions (UDA) profile. With UDA records, you do not pay for a book unless a patron triggers a purchase. The exact definition of a trigger varies among libraries and publishers; it might involve a minimum number of minutes the patron spends reading the book or the number of patrons who place holds on a record.

These automated acquisitions models relieve librarians of the need to do in-depth collection development—or, depending on your perspective, these models deprive librarians of the opportunity to do in-depth collection development. Chapter 4 discusses these approaches in more detail.

Access vs. Ownership

With some one-time purchases of electronic resources, the more accurate wording would be "one-time lease." Most vendors sell access to streaming films—and, less commonly, e-books and downloadable audiobooks—through leases rather than purchases. The lease may be for a set duration, such as one year, or for a set number of circulations. After the year passes or the item circulates so many times, the library must pay for the lease again or lose access to the item.

Though the end-user has no way to discern whether an item is owned or leased, there are both practical and theoretical implications for the library. In terms of budget, the library must pay again, and again, and again, in perpetuity, to maintain access to books and movies with enduring appeal. And from a philosophical standpoint, we who work in libraries must adjust to a new role: whereas once we sought to build and maintain collections, we must now focus on providing access.

Self-Pub

In the not-so-distant past, self-published books existed on the extreme periphery of the literary ecosystem. Authors would either pay a vanity press to publish their books or they would spend some quality time with a photocopier and a heavy-duty stapler. The resulting product typically looked unprofessional, and there was no way for librarians to know whether the book had merit, short of reading it themselves. Unsurprisingly, it was the rare self-pub book that got added to a library collection.

When e-books started to comprise a significant part of the market in the mid-2000s, self-publishing exploded. Authors now had newer, more affordable opportunities to publish their manuscripts, and internet sites such as Amazon and Goodreads made it easier for readers to discover, read, and review self-published titles. This new trend meant that libraries have had to decide whether to collect self-pub books and, if so, under what circumstances.

Especially at academic libraries, the answer has been "no" or "not yet." Academic libraries do not intensively collect fiction, and the qualities they look for in nonfiction books—credentialed authors, professional editing, and reviews from reputable sources—are often absent for self-published books. The one common exception is for textbooks that have been published by faculty members, especially because they tend to be less expensive than traditionally published textbooks (Holley 2015, 109).

Public libraries run the gamut from embracing self-pub to flatly rejecting it. Mark Coker, the founder of the self-publishing press Smashwords, understands why some libraries resist: "self-published books typically haven't survived the agent/publisher gauntlet of traditional gatekeeping" (2017, 45). And even when libraries want to add self-published books, it's not always practical: 48.9 percent of libraries responding to a *Library Journal* survey said they only collected e-books that were available from specific vendors (DiGirolomo 2016, 30). This puts self-published books at a disadvantage, because most of them are not available from book jobbers.

SELF-e, a platform created by a partnership between *Library Journal* and BiblioBoard, solves some of these problems. Authors submit their works to SELF-e for consideration, and *Library Journal* selects the best ones for inclusion on the platform. Libraries may then access those curated books by subscribing to SELF-e. And those books that are not chosen for distribution on the main platform can still be included on a statewide module, along with other books by local authors ("SELF-e: Frequently Asked Questions").

The Case for Weeding Electronic Resources

Weeding often takes a low priority in the bustle of daily library activities. In an ideal world, you would carefully consider resources for withdrawal on a frequent, regular basis, being sure to address all the formats, sections, and call number ranges in your stacks. In reality, weeding tends to get pushed aside until the shelves reach critical mass, at which point it becomes a proper emergency.

With e-books, of course, there are no space constraints forcing you to weed, and you never have to withdraw an item because of poor condition. Is it really necessary to weed out e-books, downloadable audiobooks, and streaming movies? That's a lot of effort for something you can't even put in your book sale.

Though it is true that some libraries have yet to weed so much as a single e-book, they can't put it off forever. You can't damage the third disc of a downloadable audiobook, but even so, electronic resources still need to be periodically assessed, the same as physical resources do, and for many of the same reasons:

- **Currency.** With nonfiction, topics such as medicine, law, test preparation, and personal finance do not age well. Older books and movies in these areas are irrelevant at best and potentially harmful to readers.

- **Relevance.** Books that used to be of interest to your community may go out of fashion. Usage statistics will indicate if interest in a title or topic has waned.

- **Superseded editions.** Do you have guidelines for withdrawing superseded editions in your print collection? If you automatically weed an older travel guide to Japan when a newer edition comes in, you should apply the same principle to your e-books.

And it may be that you have e-books you never wanted in the first place. This is quite likely in academic libraries, where roughly half of e-books are acquired as part of package deals (Walters 2013, 208). It's entirely possible that some of those packaged books were titles you would never have deliberately selected. If you acquire books through UDA, some duds will sneak in, even with the most carefully crafted profiles. The first user to read one of these undesirable books will unwittingly add it to the collection.

The considerations we've discussed so far apply mostly to nonfiction, but fiction titles should be assessed, too. Electronic resources will never clutter your shelves, but give them an inch, and they will overwhelm your catalog. In a few years, Suzanne Ward predicts, "users will face the same difficulty when trying to find a few recent and relevant e-books among dozens of less useful titles in their search results as they do today when browsing unweeded shelves" (2015, 132). The CREW manual for weeding puts it more succinctly: "We are wasting the patron's time if we make them sift through entries for e-books that will not serve their needs" (2012, 51). If you're not already routinely assessing your electronic resources for deselection, now is the time to get started.

Identifying What to Weed

With physical resources, there are two main ways to identify materials that need to be withdrawn. You can make your decision by looking at the physical objects, either by going to the shelves or by reviewing items when they're returned to the circulation desk, or you can run a report. That report might come from sophisticated software tools like collectionHQ or from your library's ILS.

Neither of those options works well for electronic resources. There are no physical shelves to visit. If you have MARC records for your electronic resources, you can generate a list of holdings in your ILS, but it will not contain circulation statistics. As we discuss in this section, the methods for assessing electronic resources are a little bit different.

When you purchase a physical item, your ILS tracks how many times it circulates. When you purchase electronic resources, the responsibility for tracking circulation lies with the vendor. Gathering this information is pretty easy if you only have a few vendors. This is often the case in public libraries, which might have only one or two vendors for their e-books, downloadable audiobooks, and streaming media. Academic libraries, however, may have dozens of vendors supplying them with electronic resources.

Once you have gathered your usage statistics, whether from 1 vendor or 20, you must interpret them. Levine-Clark (2006, 286) observes that e-book statistics do not distinguish between a quick click on a title and an immersive reading experience. This is not particularly important in public libraries, where end-users must go through several steps to check out an e-book and several more steps to download it, but it's noteworthy in academic libraries, where a routine catalog search can easily result in recorded e-book uses just from casual link-clicking.

Another factor to bear in mind is that circulation periods can throw off the numbers. If your library lends print books for four weeks but e-books for two weeks, you'll need to recalibrate your thinking. With a hefty book like George R. R. Martin's *Game of Thrones*, the patron reading the e-book may need to check it out twice, whereas the patron reading the print book only needs to check it out once. If you look at the numbers without context, you might think that the e-book version is twice as popular as the print version.

This effect is particularly pernicious with downloadable audiobooks, because it takes longer to listen to a book than to read it—and some libraries set their circulation period to one measly week for audiobooks. Worse, certain platforms automatically check out titles to patrons when their name comes up in the holds queue. If you already had an audiobook checked out and a hold comes in, you now have *two* titles you can't possibly complete within a week. You may have to borrow both books several times to finish listening to them.

Obviously, you would not want to weed books that are clearly in such demand. The takeaway here is that you should not assume that the electronic version of a title is more popular than the print version, even if it has more circulations.

USAGE STATS AND E-READERS

If you circulate e-readers to your patrons, usage statistics are nearly meaningless. They can only tell you how often the device circulated, not how often the titles on the device were accessed. This is not to say that it's a bad idea to circulate e-readers, but you won't be able to use circulation stats to inform your decisions about weeding titles or purchasing new titles.

As for streaming movies, you don't need usage statistics to make weeding decisions. Because these resources are almost always leased rather than purchased, you don't have to worry about cluttered catalogs or outdated information; you only have to decide whether you want to spend the money to lease the same title again. Usage statistics can be a good indicator, but again, context is important. If a film generated a lot of circulations last semester because it was required viewing for a class, you might not want to lease it for the coming year if that class isn't being offered again.

The Self-Weeding Collection

Sometimes electronic resources will weed themselves, whether you like it or not, whether you even *know* it or not; licenses for bundled e-book subscriptions usually allow vendors to add or remove titles without informing the library (Walters 2013, 203), though fortunately that does not hold true for e-books that the library purchases or leases.

Those electronic resources that are leased rather than purchased have a finite, predictable life span in the collection. When the lease is up, you must pay to extend the lease or lose access to the resource. This has become *de rigueur* for streaming media, but in 2011, when HarperCollins debuted the circulation cap model for e-books, public librarians reacted with outrage. The cap functioned as a lease, with the lifetime of the book defined as 26 circulations.

HarperCollins saw the model as a way to recoup lost sales, because libraries would never need to purchase replacement copies for worn-out e-books. Librarians saw the cap as an additional budgetary burden at a time when relations between publishers were already strained; Simon & Schuster and Macmillan, in fact, flatly refused to sell e-books to libraries (Jackson 2011). The introduction of the circulation-based lease led many librarians to call for a boycott of HarperCollins.

Tensions have relaxed in the intervening years. All of the major publishers now sell e-books to libraries, and although leases still exist, they show signs of receding; in 2016, for instance, Penguin Random House replaced its leasing models with purchase models (Sockel 2016).

In academic libraries, the emergence of evidence-based acquisitions (EBA) has added another type of self-weeding e-book. With EBA, a library pays for unlimited access to a collection of e-books for a set period. When the time is up, the library reviews the usage of the various titles, purchases the e-books it wants to keep, and forfeits access to everything else. This can be a disappointment to end-users who did not realize that these books were on probation. A professor who used an e-book a couple of times may be dismayed to discover later that the library no longer "owns" it.

How to Weed Electronic Resources

Because you can't chuck an e-book into the recycling bin, you must instead remove all paths of access to it. For most e-books, downloadable audiobooks, and streaming media, there are two paths of access. You can get to the items by going through your public catalog, or you can go directly to the vendor platform.

Eliminating access through the catalog is straightforward: delete or suppress the relevant MARC records, and you're done. If you acquire any of your e-books through UDA, remember to look at all of your UDA records, not just the records for the titles you've purchased.

Eliminating access through the vendor platform, unfortunately, is not nearly so easy. You will need to communicate your weeding wishes to the vendor, who may or may not get around to your request quickly. And, as the CREW manual warns, some vendors might not be able to honor your request at all (49).

Conclusion

Given the importance of e-books, downloadable audiobooks, and streaming media in contemporary libraries, it is astonishing that the library profession doesn't talk more about assessing them. It's as though we used up all our collection development energies with print books and e-journal packages.

Don't neglect your one-time purchases and leased resources. Give them the same level of consideration as you do when collecting physical materials. And if you take away only one thing from this chapter, let it be the knowledge that electronic resources need to be weeded. Old e-books never die: they just clutter your catalog.

Additional Readings

Carrico, Steven, Michelle Leonard, and Erin Gallagher. 2016. *Implementing and Assessing Use-Driven Acquisitions: A Practical Guide for Librarians*. Lanham, MD: Rowman & Littlefield.

Kaplan, Richard, ed. 2012. *Building and Managing E-Book Collections: A How-To-Do-It Manual for Librarians*. Chicago: Neal-Schuman.

Lukes, Ria, Susanne Markgren, and Angie Thorpe. 2016. "E-Book Collection Development: Formalizing a Policy for Smaller Libraries." *Serials Librarian* 70, no. 1–4: 106–115.

McGraw, Michelle and Gail Mueller Schultz. 2016. *Crash Course in eBooks*. Santa Barbara, CA: Libraries Unlimited.

Polanka, Sue. 2011. *No Shelf Required: E-books in Libraries.* Chicago: American Library Association.

Polanka, Sue. 2012. *No Shelf Required 2: Use and Management of Electronic Books.* Chicago: American Library Association.

Spratt, Stephanie, et al. 2017. "Exploring the Evidence in Evidence-Based Acquisition." *Serials Librarian* 72, no. 1–4: 183–189.

Texas State Library and Archives Commission. 2012. *CREW: A Weeding Manual for Modern Libraries.* www.tsl.texas.gov/sites/default/files/public/tslac/ld/ld/pubs/crew/crewmethod12.pdf.

References

Bailey, Timothy P., Amanda L. Scott, and Rickey D. Best. 2015. "Cost Differentials Between E-Books and Print in Academic Libraries." *College & Research Libraries* 76, no. 1: 6–18.

Coker, Mark. 2017. "How to Market Self-Published E-books to Libraries." *Publishers Weekly* 264, no. 13: 45–46.

DiGirolomo, Kate. 2016. "LJ's Self-Publishing Survey." *Library Journal* 141, no. 10: 30.

Gonzalez, Kelly. 2016. "Transforming an Academic Medical Center Library into a Digital Library and Learning Center." *Journal of Hospital Librarianship* 16, no. 3: 250–254.

Gray, David J., and Andrea J. Copeland. 2012. "E-Book versus Print." *Reference & User Services Quarterly* 51, no. 4: 334–339.

Hays, Alicia. 2014. "The Nation's First Fully Digital Public Library." *Public Libraries* 53, no. 2: 46–50.

Holley, Robert P. 2015. "Self-Publishing and Academic Libraries." In *ACRL 2015 Proceedings*, 706–712. www.ala.org/acrl/sites/ala.org.acrl/files/content/conferences/confsandpreconfs/2015/Holley.pdf.

Hyatt, Michael. 2010. "Why Do E-books Cost So Much? (A Publisher's Perspective)." www.michaelhyatt.com/why-do-ebooks-cost-so-much.html.

Jackson, Nicholas. 2011. "Boycott HarperCollins: Publisher Limits Library E-book Lending." *The Atlantic.* www.theatlantic.com/technology/archive/2011/03/boycott-harpercollins-publisher-limits-library-e-book-lending/71821/.

Levine-Clark, Michael. 2006. "Electronic Book Usage: A Survey at the University of Denver." *Portal: Libraries and the Academy* 6, no. 3: 285–299.

Li, Jie. 2016. "Is It Cost-effective to Purchase Print Books When the Equivalent E-book Is Available?." *Journal of Hospital Librarianship* 16, no. 1: 40–48.

Millar, Michelle, and Thomas Schrier. 2015. "Digital or Printed Textbooks: Which Do Students Prefer and Why?" *Journal of Teaching in Travel & Tourism* 15, no. 2: 166–185.

Miller, Laura Newton. 2015. "Print Books Are Cheaper than E-Books for Academic Libraries." *Evidence Based Library & Information Practice* 10, no. 3: 91–92.

Perrin, Andrew. 2016. "Book Reading 2016." www.pewinternet.org/2016/09/01
/book-reading-2016.

Project Gutenberg. 2017. "Free Ebooks—Project Gutenberg." www.gutenberg.org
/wiki/Main_Page.

Sanchez, Joseph. 2015. "Forecasting Public Library E-Content Costs." *Library Technology Reports* 51, no. 8: 8–15.

"SELF-e: Frequently Asked Questions." http://reviews.libraryjournal.com/self-e
/self-e-faq.

Sockel, Adam. 2016. "Penguin Random House Now Offers Simplified Lending
Models." OverDrive Blogs. http://blogs.overdrive.com/front-page-library
-news/2016/01/05/penguin-random-house-now-offers-simplified
-lending-models.

Texas State Library and Archives Commission. 2012. *CREW: A Weeding Manual
for Modern Libraries.* www.tsl.texas.gov/sites/default/files/public/tslac/ld/ld
/pubs/crew/crewmethod12.pdf.

Walters, William H. 2013. "E-books in Academic Libraries: Challenges for Acquisition and Collection Management." *Portal: Libraries and the Academy* 13,
no. 2: 187–211.

Ward, Suzanne. 2015. *Rightsizing the Academic Library Collection.* Chicago: ALA
Editions.

CHAPTER TEN

I Think the Internet Broke

Troubleshooting is probably the most time-consuming and frustrating aspect of managing electronic resources. You can't plan for it, and it interrupts your workday when you are trying to accomplish other necessary work. You probably never had any formal training in it, even if you attended library school (Lawson & Janyk 2014, 157). You need technological skills, obviously, but roughly 20 percent will be pure people skills (Resnick 2009, 114). And, according to the person reporting the problem, the fate of the world hangs in the balance.

Here's the first lesson of troubleshooting: the sky is not falling. New Electronic Resources Librarians tend to view every reported problem as a crisis, but with experience, you will learn to remain calm and take these reports in stride. Re-establishing service as quickly as possible is the goal, of course; you should be responsive in addressing the problem and getting a resolution. But keep your perspective. Lives are not at stake.

This chapter will discuss several aspects of troubleshooting:

- **Reporting and Tracking Problems:** So that people can efficiently report their problems.
- **What Went Wrong and How to Fix It:** The steps to take when troubleshooting.
- **Troubleshooting Scenarios:** Some common problems and ways to solve them.
- **The End of the Troubleshooting Rainbow:** Where troubleshooting ends and reference begins.

Bear in mind that different libraries have different organizational structures. The processes described in this chapter may be in the purview of an Electronic Resources Librarian, or they may be shared among other parties, including frontline staff, Systems Librarians, and IT support; or, if you work at a small library, your job duties might include all of those roles. As you create new troubleshooting workflows or review existing workflows, be sure that you and your colleagues are clear on the division of troubleshooting labor.

Reporting and Tracking Problems

The crucial first step for smooth troubleshooting is to establish the mechanisms for reporting problems. How will end-users and frontline staff let you know when an electronic resource isn't working? Methods can be casual or formal:

- Filling out an online form; this allows for easy tracking, but it may be onerous for end-users, and it does not work if the internet or local networks are down.
- Emailing or calling a specific individual; this method needs a backup plan in case that individual is in a meeting, at lunch, out sick, etc.
- Emailing a shared email account or a listserv monitored by several people capable of responding; this generally works quite well. Just be sure that the person who responds lets the rest of the list know so that multiple people don't answer the same problem.
- Stopping by the office of the Electronic Resources Librarian.

Also consider whether end-users and staff will use the same or different reporting mechanisms.

Whatever mechanism you pick should be prominently displayed where users are likely to see it wherever they may encounter e-resource problems. Give the mechanism a clear name that avoids lingo. "Report a problem" is good; "Report an electronic resource problem" is bad. If your reporting mechanism is form based, be sure to solicit good information. Consider gathering information about some or all of these factors:

- Location (in the library or on campus, or remote).
- Library card number (for public library patrons).
- Type of resource (e-book, database, audiobook).
- Name of the resource.
- Device (computer, tablet, phone, e-reader).
- Browser (Safari, Firefox, Chrome, Internet Explorer).
- URL of the page where they ran across the problem.

- How they got to the page where they encountered the problem: Did they search in the All tab? Did they go to the Database list?
- The text or screenshot of the error message they are seeing.
- Their name and contact information (phone number, email).
- If being sent by a library staff member: Initial troubleshooting steps they have taken.

At the same time, you do not want the person reporting the problem to get bogged down in bureaucracy. It's bad enough that the resource they wanted isn't working. Don't compound their frustrations by making them fill out forms in triplicate.

Regardless of the means of delivery, the person reporting deserves a response, whether it comes in the form of an automatic email, a webpage, or a spoken conversation. Let them know what to expect from you and what the turnaround time is, even if that turnaround time is "I have no idea." The downtime for an electronic resource can vary greatly depending on why access was lost, but users and staff are usually patient as long as they know someone is working on the problem.

You'll also want to decide whether or not to collect statistics regarding troubleshooting. For some organizations this may be an unnecessary extra step; for others, the data can be useful. Statistics can include the number of problems reported, the nature of those problems, turnaround times, and whether or not the end-user was satisfied with the solution.

The kinds of information you want to collect may influence your reporting mechanism, and will certainly influence what information you collect and retain from each reported problem. If you ask for the information through a form, you may be able to track the data in a simple Excel spreadsheet or have the form populate to a Google sheet. If your institution has an IT department that uses ticketing software, you may be able to be added as a queue in their existing system and get reports from the software. Even if you use something as low-tech as email, you can keep track of the information provided by transcribing it yourself into an Excel spreadsheet.

What Went Wrong and How to Fix It

Library users generally don't understand how access to library resources works, but they definitely know when something they want doesn't work. They will understandably be frustrated and unhappy that they can't get access—and in a way, this speaks well of the library. The library's electronic resources are generally so reliable that disruptions are noticeable and sharply felt. Things normally work well, thanks to invisible work behind the scenes.

> End-users may trip over library lingo. Someone reporting a problem with the "library website" may actually be referring to the catalog, a database, or a third-party platform like OverDrive.

Loss of access to electronic resources can happen for a variety of reasons, including:

- Internet outages
- Flaky wireless connections
- Problems on the vendor's side
- Payment and invoicing problems
- New URLs for content
- New vendors for content (especially common with academic journals)
- Changes to your IP addresses
- Changes to your proxy server
- User error

Sometimes there will be more than one possible way to fix a problem. Sometimes you will chase a wild goose when your time would have been better spent on a different solution. (Don't worry. This happens to everyone.) Although there are different steps and different possibilities for troubleshooting, the following steps are a good basic template for fixing problems with electronic resources.

Step 1: Replicate the Problem

First, see if you can replicate the problem using conditions that mimic the end-user's experience: insofar as possible, use the same browser and type of device. And if the person is accessing the resource remotely (outside of the public library or off campus of the academic library), you will need a way to simulate the remote experience.

Can you replicate the reported problem? If not, it may have been a temporary glitch or an error on the user's part. If you cannot replicate the problem but it persists for the user, consider these possible causes:

Remote testing can be accomplished using a smartphone if you first disable the wireless connection. Alternatively, your institution may opt to purchase a tool such as a Verizon mobile hotspot or other mobile Wi-Fi device. In that case, disconnect from your local area network (LAN) and local Wi-Fi and then log in to the remote connection. Check with your IT department about establishing a way to test remote access.

One other option, especially for problems that are not critically time sensitive, is to take your laptop to a coffee shop. This is by far the tastiest path to remote access.

- Username or password information that was entered incorrectly.
- Username or password information that was forgotten.
- User information that was invalidated. This includes expired library cards, library cards with excessive fines, or (especially with university students) blocks related to nonlibrary functions such as probationary status.
- Computer operating systems.
- Web browsers.
- Firewalls (common in computers in schools, businesses, and government).
- Disabled cookies and popup blockers.
- Internet access (due to local routers or problems from the internet service provider).

Frontline staff can and should be trained in this first stage of troubleshooting. There's no need to call in a specialist if the error was caused by a simple typo.

Step 2: Determine the Route of Access

If the troublesome electronic resource is a database or a journal, find out if the end-user attempted to access it through the library website. If so, move on to the next step—but if they attempted to access the resource circuitously, you may have your culprit.

Sometimes an internet search leads people to links that *seem* right. Searching in Google or Google Scholar may lead to content that looks to be affiliated with the local public or university library. In fact, that content may well be affiliated with the local library, but it does no one any good if the link is not proxied. (See Chapter 5 for a detailed discussion of remote access and proxy links.) To access a library's paid subscription content, the searcher must go through the library's website, not through a search on the open web.

When troubleshooting with users or when communicating your problems to a vendor, one tool that can be very valuable is the screen capture, or screenshot. A screen capture is an image of the end-user's computer screen. It gives you access to valuable troubleshooting information, such as the URL that is resolving in their browser, the search terms they used, and the exact syntax of an error message. Not all library users will have the technological savvy to send you a screen capture, but ask for one from those who know how to take a screen capture or who are comfortable following your directions.

A useful tool for screen captures that you may wish to use is Lightbox, a free download that creates high-quality captures. It has excellent markup tools for highlighting parts of the screen, which can be extremely helpful when you're trying to communicate the things you're seeing to a vendor.

Special screen-capture software is nice but not necessary, however, for you or your end-users. You can use a keyboard shortcut to capture the screen: On a PC it is PrntScrn, and on a Mac it is Command-Shift3. There is also a built-in, free capture tool on most PCs called Snipping Tool. After taking the screen capture, you can paste it directly into an email, or paste it into a program such as PowerPoint or Photoshop to edit it.

Step 3: Seek Out Reports of the Problem

If you conclude that the problem extends beyond one user, you'll want to check the gang of usual suspects. Go ahead and subscribe now to the ERIL (Electronic Resources in Libraries) listserv, and if you use EZproxy, subscribe to the EZproxy listserv. Even if you don't read them faithfully, you'll already be subscribed when you need answers in the future. You can check these resources to see if others have reported problems, or you can report problems of your own.

You should also go to the vendor website to look for known problems; if it's a Gale resource, for instance, check the Gale support page. An invaluable resource is "Down for Everyone or Just me" at www.downforeveryoneorjustme .com. This webpage can help you determine if an outage is affecting just you or if it is affecting people outside your library.

You'll want to report your outage to the vendor, but these tools are a good first step. They can help if you want to troubleshoot a bit while you are waiting on the vendor to get back to you. If you're the only institution reporting problems, you can begin working on possible local fixes, such as updating proxy stanzas or changing resource URLs.

Step 4: Report the Problem

After you've checked the likely causes of the problem and concluded that the cause is external, there are three parties you should report to:

- The vendor. If you're not sure who to contact, investigate the website or look to see if you have login credentials for a librarian administration portal.
- Your library colleagues, including frontline staff and IT staff.
- Library users. Put notices on the library website. For problems with the wireless connection or the internet, print out notices and put them on the doors.

Make sure your colleagues and your library users know which resources are affected and how long the problems are expected to last.

Troubleshooting Scenarios

Read through these scenarios carefully. They are not hypothetical. Any practicing librarian in public or academic libraries *will* encounter these problems.

Scenario 1: ProQuest Database Outage

Let's say all of your ProQuest databases have gone down. In most libraries, this counts as a major headache, and you'll need to drop everything to prioritize regaining access. Your formerly peaceful day will go haywire when library staff and patrons, both local and remote, begin reporting a ProQuest error screen. Routes of access that normally work have suddenly, inexplicably, stopped working.

You confirm the bad news by logging in—or rather, *attempting* to log in—to a ProQuest database, with both local and remote access. What should you do next?

1. Use whatever mechanism(s) you have to communicate the outage to your public. Include any information you have regarding when you think service might be restored. Place a notice on the library website, library staff email list, library Facebook post, etc. You wouldn't want to spam people through all these marketing avenues for smaller outages, but these are appropriate steps for big outages that will affect a lot of users.
2. Call ProQuest. Is this outage only you? Are they experiencing a larger problem? If this were a smaller ProQuest issue, you'd use the ProQuest support email form, but for something this serious, pick up the phone.

3. Based on what you find out from ProQuest, provide them with whatever information is needed:

- If ProQuest says you're the only institution experiencing this problem, try to think of any changes you've made that may have affected your setup. Have your IP ranges changed? Do you have a new proxy server? Do they have your correct proxy stanzas?

- If all of your ProQuest databases (but *only* your ProQuest databases) are affected and nothing has changed on your end, then the problem is likely on ProQuest's end, and you'll have to wait for ProQuest to sort it out. Other institutions will be reporting the problem soon, if they haven't already. Communicate the situation to staff and users and keep in contact with ProQuest. Be persistent. Don't assume they will contact you when there is a fix.

4. Notify your users and staff when ProQuest is back up and there is a resolution.

Scenario 2: Downloadable Audiobook Access Error

Upon arriving at work in the morning, you find a message from the person who closed last evening: please call patron Chris Kenneth, who was having trouble with his downloadable audiobook. You roll your eyes at the paucity of information in this message, which tells you almost nothing.

Even so, you know a few things already. With downloadable and streaming media (e-books, audiobooks, movies, and music), widespread outages are extremely rare. A quick glance through your listservs reveals no red flags about OverDrive or RBdigital, the two platforms for downloadable audiobooks. And because no other patrons of your library have recently reported difficulties with downloadable audiobooks, the problem is probably unique to the patron.

You pull up Mr. Kenneth's account to see if he has excessive fines or overdue materials. You also check to see if his card has expired. Patrons who borrow digital resources exclusively are always surprised to find their cards have been on probation for inactivity after one year. It's an unfortunate quirk of your ILS.

But Mr. Kenneth's account is active, and he owes only modest fines. You see that he has several books checked out from the library's print collection, but you don't know which electronic resources he has checked out, because the third-party media vendors do not share that information with your ILS. At this point you call Mr. Kenneth to find out more, and he offers to bring in his iPod so you can diagnose the problem.

When he comes to the library, you discover that he successfully checked out an audiobook from RBdigital, and he successfully downloaded it to his device. The problem is that the device will only play Chapter 1.

You breathe a sigh of relief. This one's easy. You hand the iPod back to Mr. Kenneth and walk him through the steps of turning off the "Repeat" setting.

Finally, you schedule a meeting to talk with the branch manager about staff training. Although you don't mind being the point person for troubleshooting, this was a simple fix that could have been resolved yesterday.

PUBLIC VS. ACADEMIC LIBRARIES: DOWNLOADABLE MEDIA

Patrons of academic libraries are, by definition, educated, but the patrons of public libraries come from every conceivable background. The person who needs help with an electronic resource may be literate, illiterate, or semi-literate—or literate in a language other than English.

Or the patron of the public library may be technologically illiterate. People often approach the reference desk to report a problem with accessing an e-book or a streaming movie. Very often, the technology is working flawlessly, and the only problem is a question of patron education. Should the Electronic Resources Librarian come to the rescue?

Maybe, depending on how your library is staffed. If you're an Electronic Resources Librarian who works with the public, you may be the default, go-to person when it comes to questions about downloading media and using apps and devices. But whether you work on the frontlines or not, your colleagues should be cross-trained. Everyone should know how to answer basic questions about how to operate devices; download content; and read, watch, or listen to library books, movies, and songs.

Scenario 3: Journal Access Error

A faculty member calls the library reference desk to report an error when trying to access the journal *Cancer Epidemiology, Biomarkers & Prevention* from home. The reference librarian tries to access the journal and has no problem getting in. She takes down the patron's number and forwards the user's error message to you:

Because the Reference Librarian was able to access the resource on campus, you immediately suspect the problem has to do with proxies and

> To allow http://cebp.aacrjournals.org/cgi/content/abstract/8/6/489 to be used in a starting-point URL, your EZproxy administrator must first authorize the hostname of this URL in the config.txt file.
>
> Within this database's section of config.txt, either the following line must be added:
>
> Host cebp.aacrjournals.org
>
> or, alternatively, a RedirectSafe for this host or domain may be appropriate.

remote access, and reading this error message confirms your suspicion. The message tells you that this journal publisher's EZproxy stanza was not added to your institutional instance of EZproxy, and so your EZproxy server is not allowing access to this journal.

This is a common error. New journal titles drop in and out of packages all the time, and they frequently change publishers and URLs. It can be difficult to keep up with all the changes. What should you do next?

Step 1

Consult the OCLC Stanzas List to see if there is a suggested stanza. Because this is a journal and not a database, there may not be any suggestions listed; in that case, you'll need to create a stanza yourself. Journal stanzas are usually fairly simple and follow the basic stanza protocol, as described in the textbox.

SAMPLE: BASIC EZPROXY JOURNAL STANZA

Title: AAUP Journal of Academic Freedom
U http://www.academicfreedomjournal.org
H www.academicfreedomjournal.org
DJ academicfreedomjournal.org

Step 2

But then you start second-guessing yourself. What if the problem is larger than just one journal? Is it possible you're missing an entire journal *package*? You dig deeper and go back to the OCLC EZproxy stanza list, where you find that the journal *Cancer Epidemiology, Biomarkers & Prevention* is actually in the *American Association for Cancer Research* package. Your institution is indeed missing the stanza for the *American Association for Cancer Research* package. You feel slightly embarrassed that you overlooked it, but this kind of thing happens even to meticulous record keepers, and it's an easy fix. You add the OCLC-provided stanza to allow access to the entire package:

TITLE AMERICAN ASSOCIATION FOR CANCER RESEARCH

URL http://www.aacrjournals.org/
HJ aacrjournals.org
HJ cancerdiscovery.aacrjournals.org
HJ cancerimmunolres.aacrjournals.org
HJ cancerpreventionresearch.aacrjournals.org
HJ cancerres.aacrjournals.org
HJ canimmessentials.aacrjournals.org
HJ canreviews.aacrjournals.org
HJ cdnews.aacrjournals.org
HJ cebp.aacrjournals.org
HJ cgd.aacrjournals.org
HJ clincancerres.aacrjournals.org
HJ cme.aacrjournals.org
HJ educationbook.aacrjournals.org
HJ intl-preventionportal.aacrjournals.org
HJ mcr.aacrjournals.org
HJ mct.aacrjournals.org
HJ preventionportal.aacrjournals.org
HJ www.aacrjournals.org
HJ www.canimmessentials.aacrjournals.org
DJ aacrjournals.org

Step Three

Now you reboot the proxy server to confirm that adding the stanza has solved the problem. You check access both on and off campus to several of the package's journals. When you are satisfied that the situation has been resolved, be sure someone contacts the faculty member who originally reported the problem. Depending on the process in place at your library, this job will fall to you or to the Reference Librarian who first took the call.

Scenario 4: Database Access Error

A remote library user emails the reference desk to report a problem with ScienceDirect. Although your library subscribes to ScienceDirect, when the researcher clicks on links to articles, she gets a prompt to add the articles to a shopping cart. She includes a screenshot to illustrate what she's talking about. The Reference Librarian who receives the email is able to click straight through to ScienceDirect articles without being asked to pay money, so she forwards the question to you.

You immediately home in on the URL from the end-user's screenshot:

www.sciencedirect.com/science?_ob=ShoppingCartURL&_method =add&_eid=1-s2.0-S0753332216321485&_ts=1497030097&md5=7037b cb9e20c7a00b8a59d70bb5753b7

Notice that the link does not contain proxy information. This is a problem, because the end-user is trying to access the resource from home. Proxy information would automatically appear in the URL if the user were logged in via the library's subscription. You suspect the library user arrived at ScienceDirect by way of a search on the open web.

You email the library user and confirm your hunch: this requires no technical fix, but only a quick bit of user education. You write back to explain that she'll need to access ScienceDirect by going first to the library's website. You include a link to your A-Z database page and invite her to follow up with you if she has any other problems.

Once the user accesses ScienceDirect via the library's subscription, she should have no trouble clicking through to articles. When she successfully gets to an article, the URL will show proxy information:

www.sciencedirect.com.proxy195.nclive.org/science/article/pii/S075333 2216321485

Scenario 5: Abundant Discovery Service Access Errors

Last summer, your statewide consortium wrangled a deal for a discovery tool, and you recently added this functionality to your website. Since then, the reports of access errors have gone through the roof.

Carter and Traill observe that the addition of a discovery service brings fresh challenges to the already complicated process of troubleshooting. They recommend that Electronic Resources Librarians spend time studying various aspects of discovery searching, including how the ILS interacts with the link resolver and the discovery layer and how local, remote, and full-text results are displayed (2017, 10).

There are a few things that are important to especially pay attention to when working with discovery layers that can help you pinpoint problems specifically. These tend to center around problems with content being accurately represented in the discovery service's knowledge base and issues with link resolvers. Depending on the service you use, these issues can either be fixed by you or need to be sent off to your discovery service provider.

Problems with the knowledge base manifest as search results that claim the library has access to something it does not, or search results never displaying content the library does indeed have access to (often only discovered when looking at usage statistics). The first problem is often caused by the knowledge base listing incorrect coverage dates or having titles turned on to be indexed that are not actually owned by the library. When you discover this sort of error, if possible, you can go into the knowledge base and manually change coverage dates or deselect incorrect titles. With many discovery services, though, the librarian is restricted from making those types of changes and must instead submit a ticket to the discovery service company explaining what needs to be changed and why.

Realizing something is not appearing in your discovery service results when it should be can be a bit more challenging. Sometimes it's because you forgot to turn on a collection or individual title, in which case fixing the problem is relatively simple. Sometimes, however, the problem is on the publisher's side:

- The publisher has chosen not to not make its material discoverable.
- The publisher's records do not conform to the format needed by the discovery service.
- In some cases, the publisher's material is not discoverable without a special widget.

In these cases, your best course of action is to reach out to the discovery service and see what you can do to put pressure on them to include these resources or to work around their default noninclusion.

Outside of knowledge base work, the other major problem you may encounter is that the link resolver built into the discovery service is not accurately routing patrons to full text. Unfortunately, most of the time this link resolver is not able to be fixed on the library end. The only recourse is to contact the discovery service directly. These errors often come from idiosyncrasies with how the publisher has formatted the page or from metadata the discovery service has created for the record, which can cause errors in the OpenURL request. It is frustrating that librarians cannot do more, but you have to know when to move on from some problems.

However, the best way to respond to the inevitable increase in errors is to get more training. Although it is true that many of the problems will be familiar (broken OpenURLs, authentication errors, vendor-side problems), the fact is that these errors will be more prevalent in a discovery environment. Integrated searching introduces new combinations of systems and new ways for things to go wrong.

Ideally, you will receive additional training, and so will your colleagues. Frontline staff will naturally develop some troubleshooting skills, just by the nature of their jobs, but it will help you—and more to the point, it will help the library patrons—if they can become more sophisticated in their troubleshooting capabilities.

The End of the Troubleshooting Rainbow

The end of your shift rolls around, and you get to go home and forget about your troubleshooting troubles for a while. Congratulations! You're done!

Only, not really. There's another component to consider. In your role as troubleshooter, you are in a unique position to notice if certain resources are prone to problems. You can make note of enhancement needs, functionality, and stability issues and report them to the vendor (Davis, Malinowski, Davis, MacIver, & Currado 2012, 31). You can also use this functionality, or lack thereof, as one of your considerations when it comes time to renew resources. It won't matter if you have *Best Database Ever* if the vendor's server is always crashing and you aren't getting your money's worth.

A final note: Not every problem with electronic resources demands the attention of the Electronic Resources Librarian. Sometimes problems should be routed to frontline staff, IT support, the Systems Librarian, or even the vendor's customer service support. This last one is sometimes the best route for the library patron, especially with third-party platforms. Your library will be unable to answer questions about a patron's forgotten OverDrive password, for instance.

No two Electronic Resources Librarians have the same job description and duties, but typically they are not responsible for *how* things work. For instance, a database with a quirky sorting algorithm is a problem for a Reference Librarian to untangle. This is not to say that you couldn't help with that sort of question, but rather that you don't *need* to help. Your primary role is to ensure that library users have access to electronic resources.

Conclusion

Perhaps more than any other aspect of managing electronic resources, troubleshooting is a skill you learn with experience. Even as you get more comfortable with solving problems, you'll still encounter odd resource errors that throw you for a loop. Fortunately, diagnosing and solving problems does get easier with time, and remember: This is a stressful part of the job, but no one's going to die. Relax. Breathe. You got this.

Additional Readings

"Demystifying Shibboleth—A Guide for Publishers." 2017. LibLynx. www.liblynx.com/demystifying-shibboleth-for-publishers.
Edgar, Lynne E. 2015. "EZproxy: Migrating from a Local Server to a Hosted Environment." *Journal of Electronic Resources Librarianship* 27, no. 3: 194–199.
Mann, Sanjeet, and Sarah Sutton. 2015. "Why Can't Students Get the Sources They Need? Results from a Real Electronic Resources Availability Study." *Serials Librarian* 68, no. 1–4: 180–190.
Mikesell, Brian L. 2004. "Anything, Anytime, Anywhere: Proxy Servers, Shibboleth, and the Dream of the Digital Library." *Journal of Library Administration* 41, no. 1–2: 315–326.

References

Carter, Sunshine, and Stacie Traill. 2017. "Essential Skills and Knowledge for Troubleshooting E-Resources Access Issues in a Web-Scale Discovery Environment." *Journal of Electronic Resources Librarianship* 29, no. 1: 1–15
Davis, Susan, Teresa Malinowski, Eve Davis, Dustin MacIver, and Tina Currado. 2012. "Who Ya Gonna Call? Troubleshooting Strategies for E-Resources Access Problems." *Serials Librarian* 62, no. 1–4: 24–32.
Lawson, Emma, and Roën Janyk. 2014. "Getting to the Core of the Matter: Competencies for New E-Resources Librarians." *Serials Librarian* 66, no. 1–4: 153–160.
Resnick, Taryn. 2009. "Core Competencies for Electronic Resource Access Services." *Journal of Electronic Resources in Medical Libraries* 6, no. 2: 101–122.

CHAPTER ELEVEN

Users Are People, Too

When reading a book about electronic resources, you might expect to learn about licensing, acquisitions, link resolvers, and all of the technical, behind-the-scenes components of providing patron access. These elements are all essential—after all, they make up almost all of this book—but they are not the end goal.

The ultimate point of all this work is to help your users accomplish the information-finding tasks they need to succeed in their lives. The focus on the workflows, processes, and systems risks losing sight of this purpose. With that in mind, this chapter will introduce user experience, usability, and user research techniques that can help bring the user back into our systems and products. It focuses on several key topics:

- **Overview:** Understanding the user experience in libraries.
- **Getting Started:** Laying the groundwork.
- **Setting Goals:** Figuring out what you want to learn.
- **User Research:** Learning about the people you serve.
- **Participatory Design:** Getting users to help design your products.
- **Usability Testing:** Studying the user experience.
- **Heuristic Testing:** Keeping up with the library Joneses.
- **Presenting Your Findings:** Letting other people know what you've discovered.

Many excellent and comprehensive books have been written about the user experience from within and outside the library, but it is still an emerging area of study and practice, and the particulars are not yet universally familiar. It is an area rich with potential for Electronic Resources Librarians who want to incorporate the principles of user experience into their everyday work.

Overview

Due to its broad nature and relative newness, there are many different definitions of user experience. For this book, we've chosen to use the International Organization for Standardization (ISO)'s definition: "The extent to which a product can be used by specified users to achieve specified goals with effectiveness, efficiency, and satisfaction in a specified context of use." Examining each of those terms separately, this means, according to Rubin and Chisnell (2011, 4–6), that something that is usable or has good user experience design is:

- **Efficient:** People can accomplish what they need to accomplish in a reasonable amount of time.
- **Effective:** People can complete desired tasks with few errors.
- **Satisfying:** People feel emotionally satisfied when they use the product.

What this means for libraries in general can be a bit foggy. Schmidt (2010) in his first "User Experience" column for *Library Journal* says that user experience for libraries means finding and removing pain points wherever they are in a patron's library visit. Narrowing this down slightly, the ARL "Library User Experience" SPEC report (Fox & Ameet 2011, 11) says that user experience in the library includes performing any of the following types of activities:

- Assessing or measuring the experience users encounter with the library's services, resources, facilities, and technology.
- Seeking user input to help design or guide improvements in these same areas.
- Collaborating with other library staff or campus/community partners to enhance library services, facilities, and resources in innovative ways.

As you can see, user experience is a way of looking at library processes, services, and resources in general, a lens that can be applied to most electronic resources work. As such, there are some guiding principles to consider:

- **Empathy.** Listening deeply and then empathizing with the user by understanding what they care about, need, and want is a core part of all user research.

- **You are not the user.** Understand that your thoughts, needs, and experiences aren't necessarily the same as the user's. We often get trapped in our own expertise, but the systems we are creating are not for librarians. We must understand that and think beyond ourselves.

- **Users should be included in all project stages.** Bring the user in early and regularly into any type of design process, from the earliest stages of paper prototyping through final bug testing. Testing is also done after a product is finished in order to make sure it is staying up to date with user needs. There are times when neither you nor the users can participate in each of the designing stages, such as when you are working with a product from a third party—but even in these cases, you can bring in the user to work with the finished product.

- **Products need to be useful, not just usable.** A product needs to fill a need for a user so that they have a reason to engage with it. It does not matter if something is beautifully designed and easy to use if it does not accomplish tasks that matter to your user.

- **User experience needs to be holistic.** It needs to be about how products fit together and communicate, and not just about a few parts at a time. Even if you are just testing one part of a larger site, the context of that part also needs to be considered. Never consider something in isolation, as that is how you end up with silos and workflow problems.

Because user experience incorporates so much of what the library does, it touches what we create as Electronic Resources Librarians. Moreover, Electronic Resources Librarians have a major role to play in any user experience program in a library. There are many aspects of our job duties that make us ideally suited to consider the user's needs. As Electronic Resources Librarians, we have a system-wide view of all of the methods patrons can use to get to resources and how they fit together to shape the user's research experience. Not only do we know the technical aspects of how these various systems speak to each other, but we also know firsthand which systems are isolated, how they could affect the user, and how the library might be able to overcome these stress points. Finally, we know how much things cost and what the stakes are if they don't get used. We can bring this understanding to user testing in order to determine the criticality of certain user tasks.

We might not realize it, but we have a lot of control over how patrons interact with and find resources. Electronic Resources Librarians tend to be the ones who manage Database A-Z lists, discovery services, catalog settings, and guides concerning the various types of electronic resources. Because we have so much knowledge about the back end of these systems and control over the content and design of their front ends, we have the context to play a role in improving the user experience of our patrons.

According to the ARL "Library User Experience" report, 50 percent of ARL libraries conducted some sort of user experience activity to better understand electronic collection use. We need to be leading this effort.

Libraries do not have full control over the user experience with electronic resources. We can design the website and the initial few layers of a search, but once a user has gone into the discovery layer or the vendor platform for content, we lose much control. And that is another reason for Electronic Resources Librarians to play a large role in user experience: we have close relationships with vendors. We are the ones who serve on advisory boards and who meet with vendors to talk about user experience with their products. Because of this close relationship, we can work with our providers and vendors to jointly run user tests.

An example of this sort of collaboration, between Simmons University and EBSCO's usability coordinator, is described by Clark et al. (2016). They worked together to run patrons through tests related to using EDS (EBSCO's discovery service) to find electronic resources. This allowed Simmons to better understand how their own configuration options and the placement of EDS on their website affected searching. It also helped EBSCO see first-hand how students in an actual college environment used the product. By coordinating on user testing in this way, the vendor and library work together to create a better experience.

Getting Started

Now that you know what user experience is and are convinced that Electronic Resources Librarians can play a leading role in introducing or strengthening its presence in the library, your next step is getting others on board. Some libraries may already have a User Experience department or a set user experience team. If this is the case, you will want to meet with the team or department and discuss how you would like to bring user research into your role. They can often help you set up and run your research.

Official User Experience departments are fairly uncommon, however, especially in public libraries. User experience may not be part of anyone's formal job duties, at least not explicitly. If user experience is written into someone's job description, it is often assigned to the Web Librarian, for whom it is only one part of the job.

Ask around your library, especially to staff who manage the website, to see if they have interest or already have done user experience work. If they do have interest or experience, ask if you could work with them to expand into areas concerning electronic resources. If not, talking to them about your plans and even demonstrating a small test can help convince them of the importance of user experience methods.

Getting the staff member who oversees the website and systems on your side can make the process smoother because, unless you are in charge of the website yourself, you will need their help to make any changes to the overall website structure, home page, or navigation. If you have a web team, volunteer for it. This will give you say on general website decisions and will also let you propose usability and user experience projects more easily.

If your website is controlled by your municipality, consult with them before you embark on any projects. If they are unwilling or unable to make significant changes, you'll first need to persuade the key players of the worthiness of improving the user experience.

If you already have staff who are interested in user experience, you are in luck, because you must do less work to convince others of its importance. Although you can run your usability tests as a lone wolf, it is best to have your important stakeholders on board. Higher-ups like supervisors or library heads need to understand that this work has value, and one of the best ways to convince them is to team up with one other person (like the webmaster, as discussed previously) to start doing small tests, focusing on one page, or even one icon, that you want to investigate.

These tests should often be short, no more than 5 to 10 minutes. Invite librarians to sit in on the test and watch users. Often seeing real users experience real problems is enough to convince people of its value. If you find it challenging to even begin testing, Wrubel (2007, 233) recommends performing a usability test at a staff meeting, just to demonstrate that it can be fast, low cost, and relatively easy for your library to implement.

If you do manage to get a test off the ground, be sure to share a report about the results of the test with the rest of the library. Reading about how many problems these tests find and how many news ideas come out of this process can help convince other librarians to not only let you continue this work, but perhaps bring some of its methodology into their jobs.

Setting Goals

When you are trying to bring user experience into the library, you need to be thinking about your main goals for your initial user research project. You should never just do user experience testing because it is cool and hip. Like all research, this format needs a purpose that drives it.

You might already have something that jumps out at you, but if not, there are a few ways that you can begin to form goals and research questions. A great place to start is by spending half an hour thinking about where you have noticed patrons struggling with accessing electronic resources. Write down a few of these problems.

Public Libraries vs. Academic Libraries: Focusing on the User Experience

In conferences and in the professional literature, the discussion on user experience is dominated by academic libraries. In part, this is because the university setting naturally lends itself to the research and testing components of user experience. Dedicated research is less feasible at public libraries, which do not always have the staffing and the culture to perform studies. Sometimes, just getting through the day without calling the cops is a win.

But user experience is part of public libraries, even if it's not immediately apparent. The work of observing and improving the experience of users may fall to the frontline staff, Digital Services Librarians, Web Librarians, or administrators.

You can also talk with stakeholders in your department and with library staff who work with users every day. Have some casual conversations about the main problems they observe in relation to users attempting to access electronic resources. If you want to be more formal, you could also set up a meeting with a group of frontline staff and conduct a problem-sharing discussion.

After you talk to your librarians, try to have some brief conversations with users. Ask people who are using computers at your library about problems they have experienced with accessing electronic resources. Document their responses.

Once you have a big list of possible issues, you need to prioritize them both by how frequently you believe these problems occur and by how severely they impair a user's search for electronic resources. A good suggestion from Schmidt (2015) is to look at all the issues that have been reported and categorize them along a line of low impact to high impact and low effort to high effort. Based on ranking, choose one or two issues that you want to focus on for your first user experience goals. Once you have done that, you can create your research questions based on these issues.

Although it is not necessary to have a detailed plan for every research question, writing a plan before you begin can be a great way to keep yourself focused and organized. This is especially true for bigger tests, including those that will take an hour of a user's time, examine a lot of different research questions, or require a bigger budget. Goodman, Kunviasky, and Moed (2012, 65–72) lay out a good outline for what you should include in any user research plan. Later in this chapter we'll discuss how to develop a usability test plan, as it requires a few more parts, but in general, all plans should include five components:

- **Expectations:** What research is being done, how is it is being done, and what form will the results take?
- **Schedules and Responsibilities:** Who is going to do what and when?
- **Research Goals:** What questions do you want to answer? How will this help the library?
- **Research Deliverables:** What will be the result of your research? A report? A set of recommendations? A new navigation system?
- **Budget:** Write down how much this all might cost, including what incentives you might want to offer for participants, cost of user experience software and equipment, and the amount of time it will cost in terms of staff hours.

User Research

User research either can take place before you begin deciding on goals or it can be used to help answer some of your research questions. Regardless, you'll want to conduct user research, or at least examine user research that others in your library have done, before launching into the techniques discussed later in this chapter. This is so you can identify the types of users you have and recruit effectively for your tests.

User research does not need to be incredibly extensive. It can be as simple as examining results from any surveys you may have done previously and using that information to determine who makes up your user group, what they consider important, and what they need to accomplish in terms of finding information.

The main techniques used for broad user research are surveys and focus groups. These techniques are covered extensively in Chapter 6. Note, however, that conducting user research for user experience, as opposed to marketing research, changes the focus. With marketing, you investigate how to get users to pay attention to a product; with user experience, you investigate how users find information using online tools. You are trying to more broadly explore their relationship to online information, framed by the research questions you have already developed. This information in turn will help you build personas, create realistic scenarios for usability testing, and conduct user testing.

Persona Creation

One of the classic ways to employ user research is to create user personas that you can then use to inform future design questions. Personas are mini biographies that describe unique fictional people who represent main user categories. They have a background, a photograph, three key needs or beliefs, and a quote to summarize their main focus. They should reflect the ages and genders of your users, and you can refer to them when you are wondering if your idea fits with user needs. In short, they help keep your users at the center of all design questions.

The user categories discovered during surveys and focus groups create the main groups you will base your personas around. Aim to create four to five personas. To do this, identify your user categories and then interview a few users who fall into those categories. These interviews should not be about the library, but instead about how that user finds information, their study and research habits, their reading habits, and whatever else is important to your library. It's best if you can get permission from the user to record the interview: this lets you not get too caught up in taking notes and helps with accurately capturing phrasing during later transcription.

After you have conducted your interviews, look through the notes you have taken and group behaviors together. This will take a long time, but these grouped behaviors are what you want to capture and illustrate when writing up your personas. When you turn to writing the full persona, you should first focus on user goals, which you base on what your surveys and user interviews have told you about their own research and information-seeking needs and aspirations. After you have written goals, you can then do the fun stuff like coming up with hobbies, occupation, websites regularly used, and things that make the personas more like real, unique people.

Once the personas are written, they can be used throughout the development of a product. They can even be used for the creation of anything related to the library's online presence, depending on how specific you were in their creation. Use personas regularly to ask things like "What does Padma need from this site in order to be successful in life (needs and goals)?" or "What does Mr. Schultz need from the site to be successful in using the library in this way?"

During this brainstorming process, do not think about technological limitations or politics. Go wild and let the user guide you. Once finished, look at the ideas you generated and rank them by how many personas have the same answers or concerns. Only after you have generated a list should you start focusing on what you can build or revise, based on your own program's constraints.

Recruiting Users

Now that you know who your users are and what you want to test, you can begin to recruit users for your research. Although corporate usability books talk about large numbers of recruits and screening, it's a bit more relaxed for libraries. We can draw from the people in our library buildings or from people on campus or in the community.

Finding people willing to spend time to participate in your research can be challenging, though. If you do not recruit using the right means and in the right places, you might find that no one responds, or that only people who fit a very narrow demographic respond. Because you want to recruit people across the user groups that you identified, you should ask questions of those you recruit to make sure they represent the spectrum of users you need. In library tests, achieving full representation can mean trying to get both library and nonlibrary users, technical novices and experts, and research novices and experts.

Within the library, you can use flyers or signup sheets near the door to recruit people as they enter the building. Beyond the physical library, you can advertise usability on your website, with a link to a sign-up form. You can also directly email groups you want to target, such as your teen advisory board or your teaching faculty.

Although direct emailing can reach beyond the library's main population, most of these methods will only reach your current library users. If you want to go after nonlibrary users, going into public spaces to recruit can be a good option. At a university, you can recruit for usability and user testing by setting up a table at a main student thoroughfare, such as outside the coffee shop or dining hall, and handing out information and getting people to sign up on the spot. In a public library setting, you could put flyers up around town, submit information to the community newspaper, or reach out to library users and ask them to recruit friends who are not library users.

Whatever methods you use, be sure to note which method gives you the best results. The next time you need to recruit, you can then focus your efforts on these high-performing methods.

Finally, when you do recruit, it is important to offer some form of incentive or payment for those who sign up. You want to pay or otherwise reward people for their time. In libraries, common incentives are food, gift cards for 20 dollars, or—for very quick usability tests—even just a candy bar. Hanrath and Kottman (2015, 5) offered gift cards with money for dining services on campus, which proved very popular. Duke University gives out a free drink of any type at their local coffee shop. Public libraries can offer gift certificates and early admissions to their book sales.

You'll want to recruit between five and eight participants. Research has found that using five users will expose 80 percent of usability problems. Extending up to between 8 and 10 should cover around 95 percent of all problems (Rubin & Chisnell 2011, 72). Again, make sure you have representation from all the demographics you are interested in, if possible.

Screening Users

Because you want a relatively representative sample of your user population, you will want to ask potential participants some questions before you begin testing. This does not need to be a long process. It can be as simple as asking people a few questions as they sign up. The other common method is to call up possible testers. Whatever method you choose, you do not want the screening process to take more than five minutes.

As you design your screening questions, there are a few rules you should follow. First, you want to order the questions so that the earlier a question is in the screening questionnaire, the more people it will eliminate from the pool. This allows you to see who will not fit into your target population quickly and not waste their time. You also want to end with asking an open-ended question to see how they respond. This lets you judge the potential recruit's willingness and ability to express their opinion easily

Although it will depend on the nature of your test, your community, and the target groups you have identified, there are a few key groups librarians tend to want to screen out of their tests. Because of their specialty knowledge, we don't want librarians, library school students, usability experts, or information scientists to take our user tests (unless, of course, they are the audience for which you are designing). We also generally do not want people who fall outside the community the library serves, such as out-of-town visitors at a public library or parents of students at a university library.

Finally, although novice researchers and even some novice technical users are of interest, those with no computer knowledge probably should not be in your sample. Including them will cause you to test their ability to use a computer, rather than the product itself.

After you have finished screening, you are ready to begin the test or schedule the test at that point. For tests longer than 10 minutes, schedule a time with the user at least one week out.

Having conducted preliminary user research, developed target audiences, and recruited users, you can now begin to determine what type of more in-depth user research you may want to conduct. Different types of user tests are best for different points in a design process and different research questions. The rest of this chapter will be devoted to describing how to use three different types of user and usability testing: participatory design (including card sorting and prototyping), usability testing, and heuristic testing.

Participatory Design

Participatory design is "a loosely defined series of techniques that encourages user participation in the design of interfaces and, in the process, sheds light on users' preferences and behaviors" (Pennington 2015, 197). Most of these techniques take place early in the design or redesign process, though card sorting can take place during any part of product development. These techniques, which allow the user to draw, design, and create interfaces and navigation systems, help incorporate user feedback into the process before anything has been coded. This means that using these techniques allows for early error discovery, before you waste time going down the wrong path.

Card Sorting

Card sorting is a technique that is useful if you have research questions based around the usability of any type of navigation system. In a card sort, users look through various terms, which are written on a set of cards, and sort them into groups based on what they feel is the clearest method of organization.

There are two types of card sorts: open and closed. Open sorts are where you do not have predetermined categories, but instead just a group of terms. These terms are sorted into groups by the user, who then creates an overall category name for each of their groupings. In a closed sort, the categories the terms need to fit in are predetermined. Users sort the items into each category.

Card sorts can be done either individually or with people working in groups. Once again, you generally only need between 5 and 10 people doing a card sort. The actual sort should run for about 15 minutes, but the whole process, which includes pretests and discussion after the sort, can take up to an hour.

Before you begin a card sort, you want to look again at your research question. Based on this, narrow your test down to a specific level of navigation. Whatever category you are most interested in examining, you want your cards to list terms from the navigation level just below that. So, for example, if you were trying to figure out what broad-discipline categories should exist for departments in a databases-by-subject list, you would have your cards list departments. In a closed sort, there would be a separate category for cards naming disciplines, whereas in an open sort you would just have blank category cards

In general, it is best to have around 50 cards to sort, though this is flexible based on the size of the project. Before you begin, you will need to write up a quick pretest to give to participants to gather simple demographic information about the user. If you have not prescreened users, make sure to ask them a few screening questions before inviting them to participate. Screening questions might ask if they have a library science or information science background, if they have done a card sort recently, or if they have ever used the library website. The first two questions can help you eliminate those with too much knowledge. The last question can help you understand the context of your results.

You should also use a script for card sorting, with a written introduction that provides detailed instructions about the process to the user; discusses why you are doing the study; and explains the length of time it should take, any incentives that will be provided, and the role of the moderator. During the sort, as a moderator, try to stay quiet and let participants concentrate. You can answer questions about logistics, but never on whether they are doing something "right." Do, however, pay close attention to their actions, and take notes and write down follow-up questions to ask after the sort is complete.

After the sort is done, take a picture of all the categories to document exactly where different items got sorted. Then spend the rest of the time, usually around 20 minutes, asking follow-up questions:

- Explain your thought process for each grouping.
- What were the easiest groups to make?
- What was the hardest group to make?

Ask about specific things you may have noticed during the sorting process, such as people making an "other" category or people switching cards mid-sort.

The last step is to analyze the data. Look at your notes and photographs, and compare cards across the numerous sorts. See if there are cards that always seem to be together or cards that always are hard to sort. For closed sorts, examine the top-level categories and determine the percentage of times that each term falls within each category; for open sorts, it is often best to look at what cards tend to go together.

The final report based on this analysis for card sorting can be short. Summarize your findings, point out main trends, and suggest a potential navigational scheme based on them.

So, how does this all work in practice, especially for electronic resources? One example comes from the State University of New York at Oswego, where the Penfield Library did a card sort for their entire library home page in conjunction with both the reference librarians and the Electronic Resources Librarian. Through this sort, they realized all the various parts of the library website needed to be connected. They developed links between types of content that had previously been in their own silos. Doing this sort helped provide solid evidence for connecting certain types of resources and created new connections that they would have never thought of on their own (Mitchell, West, & Johns-Masten 2015).

Prototyping

Prototype analysis is another type of participatory design that usually occurs before anything is coded; it consists of users examining sites, either low fidelity (generally paper sketches) or high fidelity (on a computer, with some basic functionality). The goal for these types of tests is to get feedback about the user interface design, navigation, and possible areas of confusion, preferably *before* committing development time to a faulty design.

A common early user research activity is to have groups start with a rough sketch, usually created by the interface designer, and work together to modify or even develop a new prototype based on the existing sketch. You can have different components of a page cut out, for example, and then have groups arrange them to reflect how they would like the final product to look. Even if you are not having users redesign a new interface, prototypes can be useful in early focus groups to give the users something to work with.

Fry and Rich (2011) describe an example of using a prototype for a quick usability test. Their library grabbed students who walked by and, using printouts of both their Database A-Z and home page, asked them to mark three types of things: links they used frequently, content they thought was not useful, and content they did not understand. Based on this, they discovered that their most used resources were EBSCO databases and their catalog, and that people did not understand what ILL meant. This caused them to change the wording of ILL to "get a book from another library." They also did not want tutorial information on Database A-Z pages, which led to them removing this element during redesign.

Usability Testing

When you think of user experience and usability, you probably envision a user sitting in front of a developed site, testing whether links work and whether concepts make sense. This is not a bad way to think about it. Although it is true that user experience research is a wide arena that includes numerous techniques and practices, the traditional usability test—in which a moderator collects "empirical data while observing representative end-users using a product to perform realistic tasks" (Rubin & Chisnell 2011, 21)—is still an incredibly important aspect of user experience research.

Types of Usability Tests

According to Wrubel (2007, 230–232), there are four main aspects of a classic usability test:

- The participants are representative of real users.
- The participants perform real tasks.
- The evaluators observe and record what participants do and say.
- The evaluators analyze the data, diagnose the problem, and recommend changes to fix the problems.

If a test you conduct meets these requirements, then—no matter how many formalities you use or how short your eventual report on your findings—it can be considered a classic usability test. There are three main types of usability tests: the formative test, the assessment or summative test, and the comparison or A/B test.

The Formative Test

Formative tests are done early in development, before much actual coding is completed. They are like prototype tests, except they are more focused on having one user complete tasks with the prototypes instead of actively helping with their design. To use these prototypes, the user indicates where they would click or what they would interact with to complete a task. The tester then manually moves onto the next paper prototype representing the next screen.

During these types of tests, there is a lot of back and forth between the participant and the moderator centered around broad research questions: How easily can users navigate the product? How useful is the product to the user? How well can the user make inferences about how to use the product just based on the paper design? As users go through tasks, they should be encouraged to talk aloud about their thought processes.

Formative tests can be readily applied to electronic resources product development. For example, when this chapter's author was at North Carolina State University, she helped create a knowledge base (the Global Open Knowledgebase) from scratch. Initial tests were conducted using numerous paper prototypes of possible interfaces, with the moderator asking the participants in this case to complete simple scenarios, such as how they would add a resource to the knowledge base and where they would go to look up whether they owned a particular journal package.

As the participants worked together to answer the questions, the moderator took a lot of notes, and this feedback was taken into account for the final design. Doing a test at this stage helped greatly because it revealed the designers' false assumptions, especially about which tasks were most important.

The Assessment or Summative Test

Another type of test is the assessment test, also known as the summative test. It takes place after coding has been done, generally midway through designs. This means that there is still time to make major changes, but the designs are advanced enough to run people through real scenarios. The main focus of this type of test is asking people to mimic actions they would perform in a nontest environment. Assessment or summative tests also can be used to examine an existing site in preparation for a redesign.

An example of this type of test was done by Mitchell, West, and Johns-Masten (2015) when they were redesigning their home page at State University of New York at Oswego's Penfield Library. Using a redesign that was already mostly coded, they directed students through numerous scenarios concerned with searching for electronic resources to try to learn how students used the home page and the discovery layer. They also wanted to investigate how to better integrate the discovery service with the rest of the website.

They set up hour-long tests with students individually and asked them to think out loud while they performed the various searching scenarios. During the tests, they recorded both the actions on screen and what the users said. As a result of the testing, they worked with the vendor to add widgets onto the discovery layer, which allowed students to better search by a citation or by a database name (Mitchell, West, & Johns-Mastern 2015).

The Comparison or A/B Test

The comparison or A/B test is a subcategory of the two previous types of tests. It asks users to look at two different products, one after another or side by side if possible. Users perform the same few scenarios on both products and then, at the end, state which they preferred and why. They also can rank the various aspects of each product.

The comparison test can be used early on to test two different prototypes; it can be used to allow users to choose between two configurations for a vendor-provided service; or it can be used to allow users to choose between two content providers to see which platform they prefer. Whatever you use it for, it does work best if the two products being compared are relatively different from one another. This challenges user assumptions and makes them think about the fundamental nature of the designs.

THE FIVE-MINUTE USABILITY TEST

If you are beginning a user experience program, it can be useful to conduct a fast and simple usability test. Duke University has established an entire program of quick usability tests, in which they recruit people by setting up a table near the coffee shop on campus and catch people as they pass by. They have usually just one research question that they test with one scenario. It can be anything from testing a new look for the database page to seeing if students know how to find DVDs on their site. They generally use screen-capturing software to get images of the test.

Because you are testing something so small in such a non–time-intensive way, it is also easier to write up a quick report on the findings, present it to administration, and convince them about making a small change. If you feel overwhelmed, remember that testing doesn't need to be formal or time intensive to get useful results.

Creating a Test Plan

Usability testing, like all other forms of user research, should have a test plan to keep you focused on your goals and research questions and to make sure your process is organized. Because usability tests are more complicated than the other types of user tests covered in this chapter, we'll go into some depth about the actual process of planning, moderating, and running these tests.

Develop Research Questions

Based on the goals you have for your product and user research, you want to develop research questions for the test to answer. These questions should be measurable, actionable, and relatively precise. A good example comes from a study Imler and Eichenberger (2012) conducted, in which they looked at the specific research question of what led patrons at their institution to print out abstracts instead of full-text articles. You can test numerous research questions per usability test, but in general you want to focus on at most five. More than that can become very unwieldy and cause the test to lose focus.

Divide Tasks

After you have stated your research question, you want to decide how tasks will be divided among participants. A popular method called "within-subject design" calls for all participants to complete all the scenarios. This does mean there is a possibility that people will learn some of the system as they complete tasks, which could make later tasks easier. You can work against this by having each participant complete the tasks in a random order, if they do not need to be completed sequentially. But you may prefer to assign tasks in sequential order, because this helps the test feel more realistic and lets you catch whether early errors hurt the completion of later tasks. In this case, accept that you might have a bit of a bias for ease on later tests and mention that in the report.

Create Scenarios

In your test plan, list the tasks you want to test and then create scenarios that group them together in a realistic way. To begin developing scenarios, first list all tasks you are interested in seeing users accomplish. Brainstorm this with any developers working on the project. If you are the only person working on a project, it is often good to get another person to bounce ideas off, perhaps a frontline staff member who is familiar with the target audience's behavior.

Based on this list, decide how to measure success for each task: How many errors could be allowed? How long should it take? Does the person just need to reach the final point in the task to have it be successful? Write out what steps should be taken to complete the task so you can see where the user might differ. Any divergence from the regular path can be considered an error.

Your list will probably have more tasks than you can realistically test, so you'll want to prioritize them. Review them and think about which tasks are either fundamental to using the site (for example, using the search box to find articles) or critical to the functioning of the site (for example, if a user cannot find a way to get an item via any method). Test those first.

Once you have prioritized and chosen your tasks, you need to join them together to form realistic scenarios. Scenarios are activities that you ask your participants to attempt to complete. When coming up with scenarios, you want to consider how people might perform these tasks in the library so they don't feel artificial. You also want to observe how people go from task to task in the completion of a major goal.

For example, Zhang (2014, 56) tested the search interface of Medline with this scenario: "One of your friends told you that she been exposed to hepatitis B because her husband is positive with hepatitis B. She was immunized some time ago with a hepatitis B vaccine. But now she is wondering how long a hepatitis B vaccine is usually good for. Please attempt to help your friend!"

This scenario takes the user through a regular search, allowing the testers to see whether users can navigate the interface and correctly identify the right place to find this information. It tests numerous tasks—browsing for basic information, placing a search in the right area, scanning through results, and clicking on results to read the full text—but it does so in a way that is realistic.

Scenarios form the backbone of your testing, so taking care to write good ones should be a priority. When writing out scenarios, there are a few things to keep in mind:

- Don't use jargon and don't name the buttons, menus, or items you want people to use in the scenario. Using the actual names of things on the interface can bias people.

- Provide a substantial amount of work for all scenarios. You want processes to be complicated enough that they demonstrate the weak points in the chain of actions. A scenario should take at least two minutes and incorporate numerous steps.

- Be specific. Give people names, identify specific journals, and refer to real college classes or after-school clubs that people need to find information for. These details make the scenario seem more realistic.

Determine the Setting

The next step in your test plan is to discuss the setting and logistics of your test. Here, you want to describe where you are performing your test, what exactly you will need, and how you will have it set up when participants arrive. Although you can use a usability lab, most tests can simply be done in an office where there is a computer and enough room for two chairs. For equipment, most usability tests require a computer and either audio recorders to capture the dialogue or video recorders if you decide you need to capture the entire session. If you want others to observe the test, doing a video capture is generally the best method.

Choose the Type of Data to Collect

Having described what you will use to collect data, you now should list what type of data you are looking to collect. In usability testing, there are two main types of data: performance data and preference data. Performance data is the quantitative data that you can gather through this type of testing. Common forms of performance data include how many errors occur during each task, how many tasks actually were completed, how often the facilitator had to give hints to the participant, how many steps the participant skipped, the time the participant spent recovering from errors, and time spent reading versus completing a task. This data explores how well someone performs on a task and has the advantage in that it is easily comparable across participants. It is almost always gathered while the person is doing the test (Rubin & Chisnell 2008, 166–168).

Preference data, on the other hand, is "subjective data that measures a participant's feelings or opinions of the product" (Rubin & Chisnell 2008, 166). This type of data is generally gathered via questionnaires or debriefing sessions after the participant is finished with the main scenario part of the test.

Although all this data is potentially useful, when deciding what type of data to collect, you need to go back to your specific research question. Look at it and think: What information from this test would help answer this question? For example, if you wanted to know if people could find the streaming media list of resources from the home page, you might want to look at failed completion and number of errors per task or how many steps it took to finish that task. You probably would not care if they omitted a step that you thought of but they did not see as necessary.

Choose How to Collect the Data

After deciding what data you want to collect, you need to decide how you will go about collecting it. There are a variety of options, running from the efficient and expensive to the free and time consuming. On one end of the spectrum are software programs that automatically record all interactions with a product, requiring no manual interaction or note taking. They record keystrokes, items clicked, and audio. They even record the person's face while interacting with the product via a web camera. These programs are very comprehensive but very expensive.

A less technologically intense method is where the moderator has an online form into which they enter task metrics—like time to completion, number of errors, and number of times the patron needed hints or prompting—often while the test takes place. This helps you keep everything organized, though it does take more preparation time and requires the moderator to have access to a computer during the test.

Probably the most common form of data collection, especially when you're just starting out, is manual note taking during the session. It is the simplest to set up and the cheapest, though it does require the most effort to decipher, code, and analyze.

Write Pretest and Posttest Scripts

The last steps are to write a pretest and posttest script, if you feel that you need them. They can be extremely helpful for almost all tests, even for tests consisting of a few questions that take the participants no more than five minutes each to complete.

Pretest Scripts. A pretest is a written survey or form that participants fill out before they begin completing scenarios. It serves a few purposes. It can act as another form of screening, asking people about their demographics, experience with similar products, etc. It can also get at more specific information that might influence the user's behavior, such as experience using similar systems or if they have ever attended a library instruction session. You can then take this experience into account when analyzing the results.

Pretests can also be used to get open-ended first impressions of a site— like what users think certain icons, links, and terminology mean—before they begin interacting with it. This will alert you to misunderstandings or possible areas of challenge before the test begins.

Zhang (2014, 57) did a pretest before conducting a usability test of Medline's searching and browsing interface. Users were asked about their experience searching for medical information online, their computer use history, and their current profession or major. This helped Zhang better understand user performance during the test.

Posttest Scripts. Posttests tend to be more extensive than pretests and provide a bit more flexibility. The purpose of the posttest is to ask follow-up questions, get a person's overall subjective impression of the tool, inquire why they went a way they did during the test, and get rankings of different aspects of the product (efficiency, learnability, aesthetics, usefulness). This is also the point in a comparison test where you ask participants to rate both products and explain their rankings.

You might try using a two-part posttest. Directly after each scenario, when users' actions are still fresh in your mind, ask follow-up questions that occurred to you during observation. Then ask questions concerning users' overall feelings about the product, their ranking of elements, and if they would use this product in their work.

Clark et al. (2016, 196) used this type of posttest as part of their user tests conducted on EBSCO's discovery layer. They created a script of five questions that were asked of participants aloud:

- Prior to this test, had you used Library Search before?
- What did you like most about Library Search?
- What did you like least about Library Search?
- Based on the websites that you currently use for research, was it easier or more difficult to find full text using Library Search?
- On a scale, 1 to 5 (1 easy/5 difficult) how would you rate this test?

The Nuts and Bolts of Moderation

Having finished up your posttest, you are now done with your test plan. You should be ready to start pulling out components to create a moderator script and begin testing participants.

The Moderator's Script

Once you have written your test plan, you should gather your materials and prepare to run the test. The main part of this preparation is to write a script for the moderator. Scripts should include standard language for introducing the entire test, the pretest, each scenario, and the posttest. The introduction to the entire test should include why the participant is here, what the expectations will be, how long the test will take, and how they will be monitored and recorded. It should also emphasize that the purpose of this is to test the product, not the participant.

In addition to instructions, the script should include the text of the scenarios, accompanied by the path users should follow to complete the scenarios. Be sure to leave space for moderators to write down whether the scenario was completed successfully, the number of errors per scenario, and the time of completion. Writing a script for what the moderator will say helps ensure that all users receive the same instructions and background information. This assists in removing variation in testing due to moderator inconsistency.

Along with the script, you may wish to create a moderator packet. This contains a checklist of everything that needs to be present in a room before user testing begins, a copy of the pretest for users to fill out, scenarios for users to read as they complete the test, and any informed-consent paperwork needed for recording.

Tips for Moderating

Before you jump into testing, you need to understand what it means to be a good test moderator. The test moderator has the most control over how well the test goes and how valid the results are, so understanding how you can be a good moderator is essential. Follow these tips as you moderate:

Watch out for bias. Don't attempt to help people, and watch your body language and tone of voice. It is hard, but you want to remain as neutral as possible for every participant to make sure you don't let them know if they are doing something wrong or encourage them if they are going down the right path. This also means you want to ask neutral questions when you notice something interesting. Don't ask something like "why did you go to that page?" Instead ask "What were you thinking when you used that feature?"

Be patient. You might want to jump in to help or give them hints, but let them struggle. Often that awkward struggle time is when you get lots of good insight. If you are concerned, don't ask directly if they are frustrated but instead ask something more neutral, like "How is it going?" Only stop the test when they encounter a bug that is program-ending or if you have given them an amount of time to continue trying and you have reached the end of that time limit.

Don't force it. Don't automatically end a scenario when they find the "right" end. You want to see if they recognize that they are finished. Count to 20. If they have not said anything but have not done anything new, move to the next scenario.

Be encouraging. Ask people what they are thinking if they fall quiet during a test. If they are very frustrated, let them know how much longer you want them to try until you move to the next test. Always let them know that it is not them that is being tested but the product.

Be flexible. Things might go off script, and that is okay. You need to think on your feet.

Be warm, casual, and inviting. You want people to feel comfortable around you so they don't get flustered and have more trouble than they would otherwise.

Have a good memory. You need to remember what people do, you need to remember when they look particularly flustered, and you need to remember to go back and ask about questions that occurred during the testing. You can't write it all down. In fact, you don't want to; if you are constantly taking notes you will miss visual cues. And if you just rely on recordings, you will spend a long time listening to hours of testing.

Executing the Test

Finally, you are now ready to run your test. When scheduling your time, you should provide an hour to run a full formal usability test. Make sure to get to the room before the participant arrives to ensure that you are organized and that all technology works. Follow the script in general, but be willing to answer any logistical questions the participant may have. The main thing you should do as the moderator during the test is to lead the users through the script, administering all parts while observing and taking notes.

A good method for testing is called "think aloud," though it does require a bit more guidance and active participation from the moderator than mere observing. Using the think aloud method means that participants are asked to talk about their thought processes while they go through the scenarios. With this method, you can capture preference data and performance data at the same time. It also gives you a greater window into *why* people do what they do, instead of just *what* they do.

Talking out loud about what they are thinking can feel weird for many users. This is where your role as a moderator comes in. You can do several things to help:

- Be sure to explain the technique and give a demonstration of it before you ask participants to do it themselves.

- As the test progresses, you can repeat back what participants say in a different form to show that you are listening and care about what they are doing.

- You can ask participants what they are feeling or thinking as they are doing X, prompting them to talk.

- You can ask things like "What are you expecting to happen here?" and "Was that what you were expecting to happen?"

Summarizing the Data

After you have run all your tests, written or recorded all your data, and thanked all your participants, it is time to make sense of your results. This can be a time-consuming process: even with just five participants, you will be left with lots of notes and observations to process.

As you begin to make sense of all the information you gathered, summarize the data first. The sooner after a test you write, the easier it will be, as it will still be fresh in your mind. Write down your thoughts and what you noticed so you don't forget. After this, look back through your data and begin to put information into a more standardized format and calculate key measures.

Summarizing Performative Data

When summarizing performative data, look at each task and write down the percentage of people who successfully completed it, regardless of whether they needed assistance or went over the set time benchmark, as well as the percentage of people who completed the task successfully without needing assistance or going over a time benchmark. Further calculations you might want to perform include calculating task error rate (total number of errors / total number of attempts × 100) and task completion rate (number of successful completion / total number of attempts × 100) for each task.

As you write down all the errors that occurred for each test and try to make sense of them, one method of organization you could use is to categorize each error as minor, major, or catastrophic. Minor errors are ones that the user notices right away and cause little problem. Major errors are ones the user corrects eventually, but only after significant effort or time. Catastrophic errors are ones that cause a participant to fail at the task. You can then look at each task and see what the ratio of the three types of errors are for each task. The ones with the most catastrophic errors are the ones you should focus on first.

Summarizing Preference Data

Preference-type questions are a bit harder to compare, but there are a few methods you can use to make it easier. When looking at limited-choice questions, such as ranking questions, you can sum how many people listed each possibility so you can see which answers were the most common. Freeform questions are the trickiest and least specific. The best way to deal with freeform questions is to write down all questions with their answers, read through them all, and then group answers into meaningful categories that you develop after reading them. This allows you to quickly scan for trends during your analysis stage.

Analyzing the Data

Before you write a report, the last stage is to analyze all the data that you have summarized.

Once you have your data all sorted, go through everything, task by task, and see what the data is telling you. The tasks you want to focus on are those that have less than a 70 percent successful rate of completion. These are your trouble areas. When you find these, go back, look at your recordings, and examine all the errors made. Looking at the errors, try to understand where the root of the misunderstanding was for each individual error made by each person.

This is time-consuming and subjective work, but it is very important to understand the product-related reason why a mistake was made. Even if not every user made a mistake on the task, you still want to go back and look at every user's run-through of that task. This is so you can try to understand what caused the difference between users, why one made an error and the other did not. All of this will help you get into the mind of your user and discover the true issues underlying their problems.

Once you have identified the errors for each task, you want to prioritize them so you can highlight the most important to fix in your final recommendations. When you look at errors, consider both the criticality of the error and how frequently you expect the error to arise. For criticality, you want to ask if it caused the entire product to stop working or if it prevented participants from completing the task without moderator intervention. Errors that resulted in tasks that could not be completed are critical to fix.

Frequency is not as easy to determine. Looking at the tasks you thought would occur the most frequently (from your task list rating), examine the errors that occurred during these tasks. These errors are a good place to begin. Rank the errors in order from highest to lowest priority. Once you have done that, you are ready to write up your final report and present it to your stakeholders.

Heuristic Testing

All the previously mentioned forms of user research involve talking to the user in some way, even if it is just short interviews for persona creation. Heuristic evaluation, however, does not involve the user directly at all. This technique consists of comparing your site to an established usability standard, called a heuristic. A person very familiar with usability, often an outside consultant, looks at each site of interest and analyzes it according to predetermined standards. They then usually rate each page using a Likert scale. Often these ratings are tracked in a spreadsheet. Once the expert looks through all the targeted sites, they review their ratings and highlight areas where the ratings are low, and thus where problems exist.

There are many standards you can use for evaluation, but one of the best-known user interface heuristics is the Nielsen Heuristic (Nielsen 1993). These measures, listed next as an example, are what a heuristic evaluator would use to rate an entire product of interest. You can use them to create your own evaluation of a product or service.

Visibility of System Status: Check if users are always aware of what is happening in the system. Do they know if something is loading or if they are being taken to a new page? Users need to get a lot of feedback from a product.

Match Between System and the Real World: This measures how well the system speaks the user's language. Does it avoid jargon or technical (or in this case library) terminology that is unfamiliar?

User Control and Freedom: The product needs to let the user make mistakes and undo those mistakes in a clear and not time-consuming way. It needs to provide a way out if the user finds themselves where they don't intend to be.

Consistency and Standards: Terms, headings, and other phrasing should follow from the first page of the site. There should be no changing of what something means from page to page. This will leave the user confused.

Error Prevention: Look to prevent errors in the first place through good design. The design should locate and then remove aspects of the design that would cause errors regularly or put in a step for the users to complete that asks if they want to go through with a potentially error-causing action before they commit.

Recognition Rather Than Recall: Objects, options, and actions users can perform should be very clear to the user. This can manifest in numerous ways, be it easily identifiable icons that are used consistently, descriptive hovertext that appears for each item, or short, easy-to-follow instructions provided to the user about what things mean.

Flexibility and Efficiency of Use: There should be shortcuts, personalization, and other tools that can be employed by expert users to complete tasks with greater speed and efficiency than the default. This allows a design to scale and be valuable to multiple user groups.

Aesthetic and Minimalist Design: There should be no piece of information that is unnecessary. Every bit of extraneous information competes with the important information and reduces its value.

Help Users Recognize, Diagnose, and Recover from Errors: Any error message should be written clearly and without jargon. They should describe why the error occurred and help the user solve that error.

Help and Documentation: Support documentation should be easy to find and easy to search.

After conducting a heuristic test, the expert (who might be you) should provide a report describing each problem discovered, what heuristic it violates, and how the library might fix it. If possible, the provided descriptions should be in-depth descriptions of what brought about the problem: what was clicked, what was typed, what steps the user had taken just beforehand, etc.

Heuristics are most often used for websites, but can be used for other product evaluations. An example of a heuristic evaluation that examines vendor-provided material comes from Purdue University (Stonebraker 2015). Purdue had subject liaison librarians use a heuristic evaluation based on the Nielsen rating in their yearly evaluation of database renewals. Each subject librarian was presented a sheet with the different categories and the instructions to rate every database on a 1 to 5 scale. Purdue's collection management team then averaged the ratings for each category across all reviewers. This allowed them to directly compare database usability across products, which did eventually lead to the cancellation of one database due to its low usability scores across the board.

Presenting Your Findings

This section will touch briefly on some overall processes and techniques to consider as you write any report, but especially the longer, more formal reports that are written for usability testing. You generally want to tell stakeholders what you have discovered after any kind of test. When writing a report, you need to think about what your administration and other stakeholders value. The goal is to create something that will be read and that will convince the powers that be that they need to make the changes or go in the direction you are suggesting.

If you do a bunch of usability testing but the designers and the library administration don't believe in or even read the findings, you will not make much of a difference. So, you want to know what your people respond to: Do they like graphs and numbers? Do they want to hear user stories? Will they only look at slide decks or do they want to read a report? Think about the politics and how your stakeholders like to consume information, and shape your report to fit those constraints.

Another important tip is to keep it short, no matter how much you want to say. Focus on the things that affect the entire site first, that are broad themes and universal issues. Then move into specifics. Always provide a concrete way to fix things, and don't forget to add the positive. If you find a site does something well, be sure to add that!

Divide suggestions into both short- and long-term goals for the site. Short-term goals are things that can be fixed quickly without delaying any kind of schedule for the project. Long-term fixes are important but much bigger in scope and will require substantial coding or redesign.

Finally, there are many ways to organize your report, but it's generally easiest to organize it by findings, which are one-sentence summaries about the root cause of an error you observed. Underneath the finding heading, the discussion is expanded by specific examples of where users made errors and illustrated with user quotes about the task.

At the end of each finding, you should present a potential solution. The hope here is that if you make your findings short, easy to read, and clear, with practical, implementable suggestions, they will be more likely to be adopted and all of that testing and research that you put into this final report will have not gone to waste.

Conclusion

Although you might have not considered user research, usability testing, and user experience techniques to be part of the toolkit or the mission of the Electronic Resources Librarian, our knowledge of the entire information environment, our say in resource access points across the library's online presence, and our connection with vendors all make us natural fits for this type of work. This chapter provided you with the terminology, best practices, and techniques to begin implementing user experience techniques in your job and perhaps into your library for the first time. Bringing user experience into our regular work can make users feel that they are valued, make sure our resources can be found and used, and all around improve the value of what we invest in as a library.

Additional Readings

Bettencourt-McCarthy, Aja, and Dawn Lowe-Wincentsen. 2016. "How Do Undergraduates Research? A User Experience Experience." *OLA Quarterly* 22, no. 3: 20–25.

Blakiston, Rebecca. 2015. *Usability Testing: A Practical Guide for Librarians*. Practical Guides for Librarians 11. Lanham, MD: Rowman & Littlefield.

Fuller, Kate, et al. 2009. "Making Unmediated Access to E-Resources a Reality: Creating a Usable ERM Interface." *Reference & User Services Quarterly* 48, no. 3: 287–301.

George, Carole A. 2008. *User-Centred Library Websites: Usability Evaluation Methods*. Oxford, UK: Chandos Publisher.

Kupersmith, John. 2012. "Library Terms That Users Understand." *EScholarship*. http://escholarship.org/uc/item/3qq499w7.

Lehman, Tom, and Terry Nikkel. 2008. *Making Library Web Sites Usable: A LITA Guide*. New York: Neal-Schuman Publishers.

Nelson, David, and Linda Turney. 2015. "What's in a Word? Rethinking Facet Headings in a Discovery Service." *Information Technology & Libraries* 34, no. 2: 76–91.

Robertson, Richard. 2015. "From Paper to Pixels: Evaluating the Usability of Digitised Books Online." *New Zealand Library & Information Management Journal* 55, no. 2: 14–22.

Schryer Norris, Sonya. 2016. "Encore Duet: How the Michigan ELibrary Tweaked Configuration Options to Improve the User Experience." *Computers in Libraries* 36, no. 8: 11–13.

Tidal, Junior. 2015. *Usability and the Mobile Web: A LITA Guide*. LITA Guides. Chicago: ALA TechSource.

References

Clark, Andrew R. et al. 2016. "Taking Action on Usability Testing Findings: Simmons College Library Case Study." *Serials Librarian* 71, no. 3–4: 186–196.

Fox, Robert, and Doshi Ameet. 2011. *Library User Experience*. SPEC Kit 322. Washington, D.C.: Association of Research Libraries.

Fry, Amy, and Linda Rich. 2011. "Usability Testing for E-Resource Discovery: How Students Find and Choose e-Resources Using Library Web Sites." *The Journal of Academic Librarianship* 37, no. 5: 386–401.

Goodman, Elizabeth, Mike Kuniavsky, and Andrea Moed. 2012. *Interactive Technologies: Observing the User Experience: A Practitioner's Guide to User Research.* St. Louis, MO: Morgan Kaufmann.

Hanrath, Scott, and Miloche Kottman. 2015. "Use and Usability of a Discovery Tool in an Academic Library." *Journal of Web Librarianship* 9, no. 1: 1–21.

Imler, Bonnie and Michelle Eichenberger. 2011. "Do They 'Get It'? Student Usage of SFX Citation Linking Software." *College and Research Libraries* 72, no. 5: 454–463.

Mitchell, Emily, Brandon West, and Kathryn Johns-Masten. 2015. "Revitalizing Library Services with Usability Data: Testing 1, 2, 3 . . ." *Computers in Libraries* 35, no. 4: 11–14.

Nielsen, Jakob. 1993. *Usability Engineering.* Cambridge, MA: AP Professional.

Pennington, Buddy. 2015. "ERM UX: Electronic Resources Management and the User Experience." *Serials Review* 41, no. 3: 194–198.

Rubin, Jeffrey, and Dana Chisnell. 2011. *Handbook of Usability Testing: How to Plan, Design, and Conduct Effective Tests.* Hoboken, NJ: John Wiley & Sons, Inc.

Schmidt, Aaron. 2010. "The User Experience." *Library Journal* 135, no. 1: 28–29.

Schmidt, Aaron. 2015. "Setting UX Priorities." *Library Journal* 140, no. 18: 23.

Stonebraker, Ilana R. 2015. "Measuring Usability in the Database Review Process: Results From a Pilot." *Journal of Library Innovation* 6, no. 2: 15–34.

Wrubel, Laura S. 2007. "Improving Access to Electronic Resources (ER) Through Usability Testing." *Collection Management* 32, no. 1–2: 225–234.

Zhang, Yan. 2014. "Searching for Specific Health-Related Information in Medline Plus: Behavioral Patterns and User Experience." *Journal of the Association for Information Science & Technology* 65, no. 1: 53–68.

CHAPTER TWELVE

No Librarian Is an Island

Libraries have always had a culture of sharing. We're famous for loaning books to patrons, obviously, but we also have a rich tradition of sharing with one another. We share our professional expertise with one another, and we share our resources through cooperative efforts such as interlibrary loan.

We do not share because we are altruistic beacons of moral virtue. We share because we don't have any other choice. We couldn't possibly serve our patrons' needs without sharing resources among ourselves. Even the largest research institutions, with the most expansive collections and the biggest budgets, borrow from other libraries.

As discussed in Chapter 8 and at various other times throughout this book, the cost of electronic resources is growing at an unsustainable rate. The introduction of the Big Deal, which bundled electronic journals into an affordable package, temporarily assuaged the serials crisis that loomed in the late part of the 20th century, but that détente is beginning to crumble. And although public libraries are less affected by the spiraling costs of subscription resources, their budgets must somehow stretch to accommodate e-books, downloadable audiobooks, and streaming media.

In response to these budget woes, libraries are finding new ways to share with one another. This chapter looks at consortial sharing and collaboration in the age of electronic resources. It also looks at sharing and collaboration for the individual librarian. These concepts are discussed in two separate sections:

- **Consortia:** Collective groups that can save your library time and money.
- **Professional Development:** Listservs, organizations, conferences, webinars, journals, and mentors.

Collaboration is not a panacea for flat budgets and rising prices. It is, however, part of the solution. Use the ideas in this chapter as inspiration for growing your collections and expanding your professional horizons.

Consortia

Partnerships among libraries are not a new phenomenon. Melvil Dewey wrote on the topic of "Library Co-operation" for *Library Journal* in 1886, and by the 1970s, the word "consortium" had become part of the library vocabulary (Kopp 1998, 7–8). A visible example of library cooperation is interlibrary loan (ILL), an excellent solution for physical items that a library can't or won't purchase. By borrowing the item from another institution, the library opts to provide access without committing the funds and shelf space that would be needed for ownership.

With electronic resources, however, ILL is rarely the solution. Although some (but not all) publishers permit e-journals to be loaned between institutions, almost none of them permit the interlibrary loan of e-books or downloadable audiobooks. Nor do they permit interlibrary access to databases. This poses a problem, because electronic resources can be exorbitantly expensive. A single e-book won't break the bank, but the price of some databases and journals can be out of reach for libraries, with certain disciplines being notorious offenders. A year's subscription to a particular science journal might exceed the annual salary of the library director, and vendors of business databases, accustomed to making deals with Fortune 500 companies, may have little interest in adjusting their subscription rates for library budgets.

Because temporary access is usually not a viable solution for electronic resources, libraries must opt for long-term access (in the form of subscriptions) or ownership (outright purchases). To make these options more affordable, libraries have banded together to share costs and to bargain for better prices. Indeed, library consortia now commonly serve a variety of roles, including bargaining for discounts and deals on resources; sharing ILS software, discovery services, or digital repositories; developing shared collections; and transporting physical materials among libraries as a small-scale ILL cooperative (Machovec 2013, 200–201).

Writing in 2001, Uma Hiremath observed that libraries liked the idea of consortia, but didn't necessarily know how to make them work: "It seems clear that the need for consortia is felt by libraries, but that the processes for filling that need remain uncharted and idiosyncratic" (80). In very many ways, this remains true today. We will discuss some of the basics of consortia, but we recommend that readers do their homework before jumping headfirst into cooperative agreements. An excellent starting point is with the International Coalition of Library Consortia (ICOLC), which provides support and resources for library consortia.

Advantages

Consortial purchasing of electronic resources can save libraries substantial amounts of money. Whether through shared or discounted subscription costs, direct purchases, or collective acquisitions models such as demand-driven acquisitions (DDA) or evidence-based acquisitions (EBA), consortia often (though not always) generate a handsome return on investment. Harloe, Hults, and Traub describe how 17 of 18 academic libraries in New York realized positive financial returns from a consortial DDA e-book program. They were also able to negotiate superior terms, including waived participation fees, waived platform fees, and waived setup fees (normally in the range of $5,000 per library). As the authors note, "vendors pay a lot more attention to $244K than they do to $2K" (2015, 254).

In addition to increasing market leverage, consortial purchasing allows for other benefits such as shared staffing (Machovec 2017, 583). Individual libraries do not need to each employ a skilled negotiator, for instance, as long as there's an expert somewhere within the consortium, and libraries that work together can strengthen their relationships (Carter & Ostendorf 2017, 60–61; Machovec 2013, 205). And consortial purchasing of e-books not only increases libraries' purchasing power but also expands the pool of available titles and results in broader subject coverage (Harloe et al. 2015, 254–255).

Participating in a consortium is a simple way for your library to earn political capital. Consortial work demonstrates to stakeholders that you're working collaboratively to maximize efficiencies and to stretch your dollars. Joining a consortium makes you look good, and leaving a consortium makes you look standoffish and difficult. These political considerations, combined with the potential for monetary savings, increased purchasing power, and shared staffing, make consortia look very attractive indeed.

Disadvantages

As budgets tighten and prices increase, library administrators understandably want to explore consortial purchases of electronic resources to stretch available funds. The decision should not be made lightly, however. Even in the best circumstances, consortial acquisitions of electronic resources are difficult because of complicated licenses and "multiplex or opaque pricing models" (Carter & Ostendorf 2017, 58). Some vendors do not offer their resources to consortia or cannot provide usage statistics at the institutional level (Machovec 2013, 206). And although one library might be interested in a niche product, it may be the only institution within the region that wants to acquire it (Machovec 2015, 73).

Moreover, consortial purchasing is sometimes simply not worth the money. "Cost savings have been touted as a benefit of cooperative collection development," writes Christine N. Turner, "but in fact, cost sharing and containment more accurately describes the reality" (2014, 37). Her study of five academic library consortia found mixed results. Some of the participating libraries found their participation to be financially beneficial, but others saw no substantial savings, either in terms of money or staff time (44–45).

In Colorado, the Marmot consortium saw similarly mixed results when it implemented consortial e-book purchasing (Thomas & Noble 2016). Consisting of 16 public library systems, 6 academic libraries, and 5 school districts, the consortium quickly discovered challenges with staff workload, ILS incompatibility, e-book readability, available content, and acquisitions nightmares. "Marmot is not much interested in more ebook experiments in 2016," the authors conclude (33).

Let this be a warning to libraries that are considering consortial purchases. Consortia can and do reap rewards for their members, but success is not guaranteed. Consortial purchasing is not a magical cure for a tight budget. For consortial arrangements to be effective, libraries must plan ahead, as we'll discuss in the next section.

How to Make Consortia Work

A consortial deal can be as simple as getting a few other libraries to join you in bargaining for a vendor discount on a subscription—even a subscription you already have. You can form or join consortia locally, at the state level, or nationally. Whether your aims are modest or ambitious, Carter and Ostendorf recommend that you begin with a charge consisting of "background information, purpose, scope, sponsors (usually administrators or directors), members, goals, expected outcomes, deliverables, and timeframe" (2017, 64). They also point out that licensing is easier when consortia acquire resources that are new to each member library rather than resources that some members already have access to (66).

Consortia need to consider budgeting questions from the very start:

- **Membership fees:** Some consortia charge fees. Some do not.
- **Financial contributions:** Will libraries contribute money to shared collections in proportion to their budgets? In proportion to actual use? In proportion to population served?

- **Staff contributions:** Who will bear the burden of staff costs? These can be incurred at every stage of the electronic resources life cycle, including licensing, acquisitions, collection development, cataloging, access setup and maintenance, and assessment.

The library literature is rife with examples of consortia that didn't work or consortia that sort of worked, but not as planned. "We learned a lot, but we didn't actually save any money" is a common refrain. And this is not necessarily a bad outcome, because consortial arrangements often result in nonmonetary benefits. What is important is that you assess your outcomes and decide whether you've met your goals.

In some cases, formal assessment is not necessary. If by joining a consortium you get 10 percent off of a subscription resource that you were going to acquire anyway, you should still assess the performance of that resource (as described in Chapter 8), but you do not need to spend a lot of brain power to conclude that you benefitted from a pricing discount. For collective purchases, however, you should pay closer attention. After the first year and periodically thereafter, assess the costs and benefits of your consortial purchases:

- **Quality of Selections.** Did the consortium select electronic resources that you would have chosen on your own? If not, are the resources welcome or unwelcome additions to your collection?
- **Return on Investment.** Are your financial contributions commensurate with the quality and quantity of electronic resources you received? Did you get more value for your collection dollars? Less?
- **Staff Costs.** What about your staff contributions? Did your consortial membership cause your library to spend more time or less time working with electronic resources?
- **Hidden Benefits.** Did you develop stronger relationships with other libraries or with vendors? Did you become better at your job or learn new things? Did you generate political goodwill by working with other institutions in your region? Did you satisfy a grant requirement that you work collaboratively?
- **Alternative History.** If you had not committed funds to the consortium, how would you have spent them instead?

Effective consortial arrangements take work. Without proper planning and assessment, they probably won't deliver the results you want. But consortia can and do work very well for electronic resources, as we'll see in the next section.

Consortia in Action

Consortial arrangements that serve public libraries often focus on popular e-books and downloadable audiobooks. The Listen Up! Vermont project (LUV), for instance, makes downloadable audiobooks accessible to patrons of Vermont public libraries. Participating libraries have access to a shared collection in OverDrive, with pricing based on a formula that factors in the number of registered borrowers and the number of circulations from the previous year. It is a boon to Vermont libraries, which each receive funding from their individual towns and not from the regional systems as are commonly found elsewhere. The LUV arrangement allows libraries to provide resources they simply would not be able to afford otherwise.

Consortial arrangements that serve academic libraries have somewhat different aims. For example, although the Washington Research Library Consortium (WRLC) does offer some shared collections of e-books, it serves several additional purposes, including the digitization of resources unique to its nine institutional members. And CARLI, the Consortium of Academic and Research Libraries in Illinois, provides access to a core collection of databases while brokering discounts for others.

In contrast, the Colorado Library Consortium (CLiC) serves all types of libraries in Colorado, not just public libraries. Members enjoy access to shared e-book collections, discounted subscriptions to databases and OCLC, and the option to join AspenCat, an open-source ILS. Likewise, NC LIVE serves all types of libraries in North Carolina, though it differs in approach from CLiC. Rather than offering discounted services, the consortium bargains directly with vendors and uses state funds to pay for access to electronic resources. Thus all libraries in the state, regardless of budget, have access to a collection that includes databases, e-books, downloadable audiobooks, streaming videos, e-journals, and more.

Professional Development

In the first part of this chapter, we looked at collaborations among libraries. Now we look at resources in the library community that focus on you as an individual. If you've got a healthy professional development budget at your library, fantastic—but if your budget is maybe not so healthy, don't despair. This section covers free and low-cost means of professional development as well as traditional, pricier options.

Whether or not you've benefited from formal education about electronic resources in libraries, whether you've got years of experience or you're starting from scratch, you're going to want and need more information, more training, more support. At no point will you achieve mastery of electronic resources. There's always more to learn.

Listservs

Joining a listserv is a low-tech way to tap into the collective wisdom of hundreds or thousands of your colleagues from around the world. Listservs sponsored by organizations are sometimes restricted to dues-paying members, but the six listed here are free to join. If you find yourself distracted by an onslaught of listserv traffic, set up subfolders within your inbox to siphon the flow. Alternatively, some listservs allow you to sign up for a digest version that consolidates conversations into a daily or weekly email.

colldv

Topic: Collection development and collection management

Sponsor: ALCTS Collection Management Section

Sign up: lists.ala.org/sympa/info/colldv

Posting address: colldv@lists.ala.org

ERIL-L

Topic: Electronic resources

Sponsor: Electronic Resources & Libraries

Sign up: www.eril-l.org

Posting address: eril-l@lists.eril-l.org

EZproxy

Topic: EZproxy

Sponsor: The State University of New York (not OCLC, which sells EZproxy)

Sign up: www.oclc.org/support/services/ezproxy/documentation/list.en.html

Posting address: ezproxy@ls.suny.edu

Liblicense

Topic: Licensing

Sponsor: The Center for Research Libraries

Sign up: liblicense.crl.edu/discussion-forum/subscribe

Posting address: liblicense-l@listserv.crl.edu

Libstats

Topic: Usage statistics

Sponsor: JISC

Sign up: www.jiscmail.ac.uk/cgi-bin/webadmin?SUBED1=LIB-STATS&A=1

Posting address: lib-stats@jiscmail.ac.uk

SERIALIST

Topic: Serials, including databases and journals

Sponsor: NASIG

Sign up: http://www.nasig.org/site_page.cfm?pk_association_webpage_menu
=308&pk_association_webpage=4955

Posting address: SERIALST@listserv.nasig.org

Organizations

Membership in professional organizations is hit-or-miss. Done right, membership in a professional organization offers you the chance to stay abreast of trends; network with colleagues; sharpen your skills; and develop a professional reputation locally, nationally, or internationally. Done wrong, membership in a professional organization is $200 you'll never see again.

Some of the experience is beyond your control. The organization's elected leaders might be ineffective, or the literature they publish might not apply to you, or your library's travel budget might preclude you from joining a committee or running for office. But in some respects, what you get out of your membership depends on what you put into it. If you automatically chuck the organization's publication into the recycling bin, ignore its emails and listserv messages, and never attend its conferences or webinars, the only benefit you'll get is a line on your résumé.

Your state or region may have organizations, interest groups, committees, and consortia for people who work with electronic resources. At the national level, professional groups such as the American Library Association (ALA), the Public Library Association (PLA), and the Association of College & Research Libraries (ACRL) are broad in scope. Because they offer resources and support for many areas of librarianship, they may be the better choice if your job duties include work outside of electronic resources. But if you would like to join a national organization with more direct applicability to electronic resources, you have several options:

- **ALCTS:** A division of ALA, the Association for Library Collections & Technical Services is "for information providers who work in collections and technical services, such as acquisitions, cataloging, metadata, collection management, preservation, electronic, and continuing resources" (ALCTS website).

- **NASIG:** Formerly known as the North American Serials Interest Group, NASIG "promotes communication, information, and continuing education about serials, electronic resources, and the broader issues of scholarly communication" (NASIG website).

- **ER&L:** Electronic Resources & Libraries "facilitates the communication and collaboration for information professionals around issues related to managing electronic resources in the digital world" (ER&L website).

- **LITA:** A division of ALA, the Library & Information Technology Association is for "new professionals, systems librarians, library administrators, library schools, vendors and anyone else interested in leading edge technology and applications for librarians and information providers" (LITA website).

Conferences

If you're unsure of which conferences are worth attending, you might start with your state and regional groups. Local travel is less expensive, and you'll find opportunities for "continual learning, leadership, and mentoring but also for networking with professionals who deal with similar issues and concerns in terms of local funding and availability of technology" (Goldman 2014, ii). As for national and international organizations, there are several of interest to Electronic Resources Librarians.

ACRL

A division of the American Library Association, the Association of College & Research Libraries meets every April. Programming covers a variety of topics for academic librarians, including robust offerings on topics related to electronic resources.

- **Audience:** Academic librarians
- **Location:** Varies

ALA

The American Library Association holds two conferences every year. The main ALA Annual Conference is held in June and typically attracts 25,000 people. The ALA Midwinter Meeting is held in January and attracts 11,000 to 12,000 people (ALA website). It's easy to be overwhelmed by the sheer size of the conferences, so you may wish to focus on a subset of the offerings. The LITA and ALCTS divisions offer programming of interest to Electronic Resources Librarians.

- **Audience:** Public, academic, and school librarians (and everyone else in the library world)
- **Location:** Varies

Charleston Conference

The Charleston Conference, held every November, is designed for everyone who works in library technical services. In addition to ample programming for electronic resources, there are programs for acquisitions, collection development, cataloging, and all the other functions that go on behind the scenes in the library. The conference attracts roughly 2,000 attendees each year (Charleston Conference website).

- **Audience:** Mostly academic librarians
- **Location:** Charleston, South Carolina

Computers in Libraries

Held every spring, Computers in Libraries covers all aspects of library technology. It has a cutting-edge vibe, with programs that showcase new trends and innovative ideas. If you've been in a rut, this is the conference to revitalize your spirit.

- **Audience:** Public, academic, and school librarians
- **Location:** Arlington, Virginia, or Washington, D.C.

ER&L

The annual Electronic Resources & Libraries conference, held in March or April, offers programming devoted to every aspect of electronic resources. Topics covered include licensing and management, collection development and management, user experience, and scholarly communication (ER&L conference website). There is noticeably little programming for public librarians, but this is the preeminent conference for Electronic Resources Librarians in academic libraries.

- **Audience:** Mostly academic librarians
- **Location:** Austin, Texas

LITA Forum

The Library and Information Technology Association, a division of ALA, hosts an annual forum for people from all types of libraries. Roughly 300 people attend the forum each year, so the smaller size is less overwhelming than some of the other national and international conferences.

- **Audience:** Information professionals from all types of libraries
- **Location:** Varies

NASIG

Held in June, the NASIG conference offers programming related to library technical services. Most of the program sessions are related to electronic resources in some way. Like the Charleston Conference, the NASIG conference is geared toward academic librarians.

- **Audience:** Mostly academic librarians
- **Location:** Varies

PLA

Unfortunately, there are no conferences on electronic resources designed exclusively for public librarians. The general Public Library Association conference, however, includes plenty of programming about electronic resources. It is held in March in alternating years.

- **Audience:** Public librarians
- **Location:** Varies

Webinars

The advent of the internet did not kill the traditional conference. We now have the technology to attend teleconferences in real time with people around the world, but we haven't stopped attending in-person meetings. Watching a presentation over Skype does not have the same impact as seeing a presentation in person. It's the difference between listening to an album in your home and attending a concert.

That said, webinars have a lot to recommend them. There's no travel hassle, no time away from work, no need to hire a cat-sitter while you're out of town. In many cases, webinars are free. And although it's not the same as attending a conference in person, recordings of conference presentations are often live-streamed or made available after the fact.

Some organizations, like OCLC and ACRL, routinely hold webinars. So do many vendors. EBSCO, Gale, and ProQuest all host frequent webinars, some related to products and training, others of a more general nature. Vendors will commonly offer to host an on-demand webinar at your convenience to showcase a new electronic resource. Announcements for webinars may be posted on listservs or sent to you via email from a company or organization. You can also visit the websites of vendors and organizations to see if they have any archived webinars available for viewing.

Journals

Journals of interest to Electronic Resources Librarians abound. Titles to consider reading include, but are certainly not limited to, *Against the Grain, Collection Management, Journal of Electronic Resources Librarianship, Library Technology Reports, The Serials Librarian, Serials Review,* and *Technical Services Quarterly.*

Libraries do not always have the budget to pay for subscriptions to professional journals, however. Academic libraries may have access to these titles through journal bundles or database aggregators. Public libraries are less likely to have access to them, though it is not unheard of.

It should be noted that the content of most of these journals is written by and for academic librarians. Public libraries would do well to subscribe to a general title such as *Library Journal*, which always includes content of interest to Electronic Resources Librarians in both public and academic libraries.

Mentors

The tools of professional development we've already discussed—listservs, journals, and organizations and conference—are focused on helping you, as an Electronic Resources Librarian, with the technical aspects of your job. In contrast, a mentor may have nothing to offer you whatsoever regarding electronic resources. It's wonderful if you can find a mentor who understands the minutia of your job, but that's unlikely to happen. Few libraries employ more than one person who has expert knowledge of electronic resources. Even if you've just started in your position, that one person is probably you.

And that's okay. In a survey of librarians in Illinois, respondents ranked availability and personality fit as the most important characteristics of a mentor (James, Rayner, & Bruno 2015, 535). This makes sense, when looking at the list of mentoring benefits for the mentee in Julie Todaro's *Mentoring A-Z*. Entries on this list include exposure to new ideas and interests, feedback and critical analysis, heightened awareness of challenges at different levels within the organization, and development of one's own self-awareness (2015, 50–51).

Furthermore, as mentor/mentee team Kenefick and DeVito observe, "learning how to manage politics and social attitudes effectively is challenging for everyone, but especially for new librarians with expectations that may be in conflict with the organization" (2015, 91). A good mentor is someone who will help you navigate those organizational politics and attitudes, not necessarily someone who understands the particulars of electronic resources.

A great deal of literature has been written about implementing and evaluating formal mentoring programs, both inside and outside of libraries. If such a program does not already exist at your library, your administrators may wish to establish one. However, you may actually have better success with informal mentorship. Less has been written about informal mentoring, but it's quite possible that you as a mentee would derive more benefits from an informal mentoring relationship (James et al. 2015, 535).

If you're looking for a mentor, there may be someone suitable within your workplace. You can also look further afield. There may be mentoring programs on your campus or in your community that can match you with someone who does not work in libraries, or you can seek mentoring opportunities through the organizations discussed earlier. And remember, you do not need to be a novice to benefit from mentoring. Formal mentoring programs tend to focus on people who are new to libraries, or even on students who are considering librarianship as a career, but seasoned veterans can benefit from the guidance and advice of a trusted colleague.

Conclusion

Collaboration cannot solve everything. You can participate in shared collections and join in on consortial discounts and still come up short in your budget. You can have a brilliant mentor and attend great conferences and read the latest trade publications and still go through phases where you're frustrated with your job and wish you'd never heard of electronic resources.

But collaboration can help. Collaboration between libraries can open up new possibilities with collections, and collaboration between people can lead to enriching professional development opportunities. You don't have to do it all alone.

Additional Readings

Farrell, Bridget, et al. 2017. "Addressing Psychosocial Factors with Library Mentoring." *Portal: Libraries and the Academy* 17, no. 1: 51–69.

Hale, Dawn, ed. 2016. *Shared Collections: Collaborative Stewardship.* Chicago: ALA Editions.

Machovec, George. 2015. "Consortial E-Resource Licensing: Current Trends and Issues." *Journal of Library Administration* 55, no. 1: 69–78.

Todaro, Julie. 2015. *Mentoring A-Z.* Chicago: ALA Editions.

References

ALA. "ALA Conferences: Q&A." www.ala.org/aboutala/offices/conference/conf services/ccc/faq.

ALCTS. "About Us." www.ala.org/alcts/about.

Carter, Sunshine and Danielle Ostendorf. 2017. "Processes and Strategies for Collaboratively Purchasing Electronic Resources," *Collaborative Librarianship* 9, no 1: 58–71.

Charleston Conference. "About." www.charlestonlibraryconference.com/about.

Computers in Libraries. "Computers in Libraries 2018." http://computersinlibraries .infotoday.com/2018.

ER&L. "About Us." www.electroniclibrarian.org/about/.

ER&L. "ER&L in a Snapshot." www.electroniclibrarian.org/about/erl-in-a-snapshot/.

Goldman, Crystal. 2014. "The Benefits of Local Involvement: Professional Development Through State and Regional Library Associations." *Practical Academic Librarianship: The International Journal of The SLA* 4, no. 2: i–xi.

Harloe, Bart, Pat Hults, and Adam Traub. 2015. "What's the Use of Use?: Return on Investment Strategies for Consortial DDA Programs." *Journal of Library Administration* 55: 249–259.

Hiremath, Uma. 2001. "Electronic Consortia: Resource Sharing in the Digital Age." *Collection Building* 22, no. 2: 80–87.

ICOLC. "About ICOLC." http://icolc.net/about-icolc.

James, Julie M., Ashley Rayner, and Jeannette Bruno. 2015. "Are You My Mentor? New Perspectives and Research on Informal Mentorship." *Journal of Academic Librarianship* 41, no. 5: 532–539.

Kenefick, Colleen, and Jennifer A. DeVito. 2015. "From Treading Water to Smooth Sailing: Mentoring for New Academic Librarians." *College & Undergraduate Libraries* 22, no. 1: 90–96.

Kopp, James J. 1998. "Library Consortia and Information Technology: The Past, the Present, the Promise." *Information Technology and Libraries* 17, no. 1: 7–12.

LITA. "About LITA." http://www.ala.org/lita/about.

Machovec, George. 2013. "Library Consortia: The Big Picture." *Journal of Library Administration* 53, no. 1: 199–208.

Machovec, George. 2015. "Consortial E-Resource Licensing: Current Trends and Issues." *Journal of Library Administration* 55, no. 1: 69–78.

Machovec, George. 2017. "Trends in Higher Education and Library Consortia." *Journal of Library Administration* 57, no. 5: 577–584.

NASIG. "Annual Conference." www.nasig.org/site_page.cfm?pk_association _webpage_menu=700&pk_association_webpage=1228.

NASIG. "Vision and Mission." www.nasig.org/site_page.cfm?pk_association _webpage_menu=308&pk_association_webpage=186.

PLA. "Conferences and Continuing Education." www.ala.org/pla/education.

Thomas, Jimmy, and Mark Noble. 2016. "The Douglas County Model in Western Colorado." *Journal of Library Administration* 56, no. 3: 326–334.

Todaro, Julie. 2015. *Mentoring A-Z*. Chicago: ALA Editions.

Turner, Christine N. 2014. "E-Resource Acquisitions in Academic Library Consortia." *Library Resources & Technical Services* 58, no. 1: 33–48.

Appendix

University Library Survey to Distance and Online Faculty

Adapted from a survey administered by Jackson Library at the University of North Carolina at Greensboro

Dear Faculty and Instructors,

We are seeking your honest feedback about the university library's online resources and services. Please help us improve our services by completing this brief survey. It should take 10 minutes or less. At the end of the survey you will have the opportunity to enter a drawing for one of four $25 Barnes & Noble gift cards. Please respond by October 1st. All responses will be kept strictly confidential. Thank you!

All responses are confidential. However, absolute confidentiality of data provided through the internet cannot be guaranteed due to the limited protections of internet access. Please be sure to close your browser when you finish so no one will be able to see what you have been doing. You may choose not to answer any question that makes you feel uncomfortable, or you may stop at any time. There are no risks or benefits for participants. You may print or email this letter for your records. Thank you so much for your time! If you have any concerns about your rights or how you are being treated, you may contact the Office of Research Compliance. Questions about this survey or your benefits or risks may be directed to surveys@university.edu.

Q1. Please tell us about yourself:

- Tenured Professor
- Tenure-Track Professor
- Lecturer
- Adjunct
- Other _____

Q2. How much of your course load is online?

- All classes
- Most classes every semester
- Half online every semester
- One class every semester
- Not regularly, a few classes over numerous semesters

Q3. What is your subject area?

- Business, Management, Marketing
- Humanities
- Social Sciences
- Visual or Performing Arts
- Health Sciences
- Sciences
- Education
- Other _____

Q4. What resources would you recommend to your students if they wanted to:

- Find a topic for a class assignment or research paper _____
- Begin a literature search for a class assignment _____
- Get help citing references _____
- Find primary sources (archival material, data, original research) _____
- Learn more about class content _____
- Find material for a multimedia assignment or poster (pictures, video, audio, etc.) _____

Q5. Where do you go to find information to:

- Bring into class as an assignment _____
- Conduct your own research _____
- Keep up to date on the literature in your field _____
- Properly cite references _____
- Consume for fun _____

Q6. Please rate the following in order of how often you use the resource to find new information for your classes and research from 1 to 6, where 1 is the most used and 6 is the least used:

- _____ Fellow researchers
- _____ University libraries
- _____ Professional organizations
- _____ Social media
- _____ Other campus resources
- _____ Recent literature in your field

Q7. Please rate the following in order of the method you use to learn about new resources and content you could use in your class from 1 to 8, where 1 is the most used and 8 is the least used:

- _____ Conversation (face to face, text, or chat based)
- _____ Email
- _____ Social media
- _____ Flyers/posters
- _____ Library website/catalog
- _____ Web browsing (Google, Bing, etc.)
- _____ Canvas
- _____ RSS feeds/BrowZine/listservs

Q8. What reasons prevent you from using the library's electronic resources more frequently? Select all that apply.

- My classes or research do not require use of library materials
- I get all of the information I need on the internet
- I use a library outside of campus: _____
- I get all or most of the information I need from other students/ colleagues
- The university library does not have the information I need
- The library's electronic search systems are too difficult to use
- I do not have the proper equipment to access the library's electronic resources
- I can't get help when I need it from library staff
- I have problems with electronic access to library resources because of proxy server, firewalls, etc.

- I prefer print resources over electronic resources
- Other (please specify) _____

Q9. Please enter your email to be entered into a drawing to win one of four $25 Barnes & Noble gift cards.

- Email:

University Library Survey to Distance and Online Students

Adapted from a survey administered by Jackson Library at the University of North Carolina at Greensboro

Dear Students,

We are seeking your honest feedback about the university library's online resources and services. Please help us improve our services by completing this brief survey. It should take 10 minutes or less. At the end of the survey you will have the opportunity to enter a drawing for one of four $25 Barnes & Noble gift cards. Please respond by October 1st. All responses will be kept strictly confidential. Thank you!

All responses are confidential. However, absolute confidentiality of data provided through the internet cannot be guaranteed due to the limited protections of internet access. Please be sure to close your browser when you finish so no one will be able to see what you have been doing. You may choose not to answer any question that makes you feel uncomfortable, or you may stop at any time. There are no risks or benefits for participants. You may print or email this letter for your records. Thank you so much for your time! If you have any concerns about your rights or how you are being treated, you may contact the Office of Research Compliance. Questions about this survey or your benefits or risks may be directed to surveys@university.edu.

Q1. What is your student status?

- First-Year Student
- Sophomore
- Junior
- Senior
- Master's Student
- PhD Student
- Other (please specify) _____

Q2. What is your subject area?

- Business, Management, Marketing
- Humanities
- Social Sciences
- Visual or Performing Arts
- Health Sciences
- Sciences
- Education
- Other (please specify) _____

Q3. Are most of your classes:

- Online?
- Face to face?
- Mixed?

Q4. Where do you go to find information to:

- Understand information covered in class _____
- Start researching for an assigned project_____
- Gain basic understanding of a field to choose a research topic

  _____

- Properly cite references _____
- Consume for fun _____
- Conduct your own independent research _____

Q5. How often do you search for new information to:

	Daily	A few times a week	A few times a month	A few times a year	Never
Understand topics covered in class					
Start researching for an assignment					
Gain basic understanding of a topic					
Cite references					
Consume for fun					
Conduct research for personal interests					

Q6. Please rate the following in order of how often you use the resource to find new information for school from 1 to 5, where 1 is the most used and 5 is the least used:

- _____ Friends
- _____ Faculty/instructor
- _____ The library

- • _____ Professional organizations
- • _____ Social media

Q7. Please rate the following in order of the method you use to learn about new information for school from 1 to 7, where 1 is the most used and 7 is the least used:

- • _____ Conversation (face to face, text, or chat based)
- • _____ E-mail
- • _____ Social media
- • _____ Flyers/posters
- • _____ Library website/catalog
- • _____ Web browsing (Google, Bing, etc.)
- • _____ Canvas

Q8. What times do you normally work on your course assignments?

- • Early morning weekdays
- • Afternoon weekdays
- • Lunchtime weekdays
- • Between 5 and 8 p.m. weekdays
- • 8 to midnight weekdays
- • Saturday mornings
- • Friday or Saturday evenings
- • Sunday mornings
- • Sunday evening
- • Other _____

Q9. What reasons prevent you from using the library's electronic resources more frequently? Select all that apply:

- • My coursework does not require the use of library materials
- • I get all of the information I need on the internet
- • I use a library off campus: _____
- • I get all or most of the information I need from other students/ colleagues
- • The university library does not have the information I need
- • The library's electronic search systems are too difficult to use
- • I do not have the proper equipment to access the library's electronic resources

- I can't get help when I need it from library staff
- I have problems with electronic access to library resources because of proxy server, firewalls, etc.
- I prefer print resources over electronic resources
- Other (please specify) _____

Q10. Please enter your email to be entered into a drawing to win one of four $25 Barnes & Noble gift cards.

- Email:

Public Library Survey of Research Habits

Thank you for taking this quick survey about research at Main Street Public Library. When you are done, return your survey to the Reference Desk for a $5 voucher good for use at the MSPL Friends of the Library Book Sale. Limit one voucher per person.

Q1. Do you have a library card with Main Street Public Library?
- Yes
- No
- Don't know/Not sure

Q2. What resources do you use to conduct research? Circle all that apply.
- The internet
- MSPL databases
- The MSPL online catalog
- Printed books
- E-books
- Printed newspapers, magazines, and journals
- Electronic newspapers, magazines, and journals
- Microforms or microfiche
- Other: _____
- I do not conduct research/I am not sure if I conduct research

Q3. Have you ever attended one of MSPL's free database classes?
- Yes
- No, but I've heard of them
- No. I haven't heard of them
- I don't know/I'm not sure

Q4. What subjects are you interested in? Check all that apply.
- _____ Books and reading
- _____ News and current events
- _____ Genealogy
- _____ Health, medicine, and wellness
- _____ Local history

- _____ Homework help
- _____ Computers and technology
- _____ Cooking and gardening
- _____ Travel

Please return this survey to the Reference Desk.

Glossary

Access-Only Journals
E-journals that the library doesn't specifically subscribe to, but that are available through e-journal packages and databases. Access to these journals can change at any time.

Aggregators
Databases that collect content from various publishers into one searchable platform.

APC
Article processing charges are fees charged to authors to publish their articles in open access journals.

APIs
Application programming interfaces are sophisticated tools for customizing or improving existing software so that data can be shared across software applications.

Assessment Test
A type of usability test that takes place after the service or product has already been designed. It focuses on leading users through realistic scenarios that mimic actions they would perform in a nontest environment.

Authorized Users
Patrons who have permission to access a given resource.

A-Z List
The public view of the library's holdings of a given type of electronic resource. It is commonly used for databases in public and academic libraries and for journals in academic libraries.

Backfiles
The archives of a serial publication (newspaper, magazine, or journal). Often sold in packages, backfiles are available for a one-time purchase rather than a subscription price, though they may come with a maintenance fee.

BATNA
The best alternative to negotiated agreement is the solution you would be willing to use if negotiations with a vendor fail.

Big Deals
Bundled collections of journals, usually marketed to academic libraries. As with cable television packages, some content will be more desirable than other content.

Brand
A recognizable visual style that expresses, in a general way, what your library considers its mission, goals, or ethos. Branding includes a color palette, specific fonts, and logos.

Business Terms
Parts of a license agreement that describe information like price, renewal cycle, authorization method, title lists, late fees, ownership, access methods, and definitions of the licensee and licensor.

Card Sorting
A type of user experience technique in which users examine possible navigation terms and categories and arrange them in way they feel makes the most sense.

Click-Through Access
An unpopular, cumbersome model of providing access in which terms appear when users try to access an electronic resource. Users must agree to the terms before they can proceed.

Comparison Test
A type of usability testing in which users perform tasks in two different products and then explain which they prefer.

Consortia
Nonprofit state- or library-run groups that work together to negotiate price and sometimes license terms for their members.

COUNTER Statistics
Project COUNTER (Counting Online Usage of Networked Electronic Resources) establishes standards for usage statistics so that librarians may compare like measures across different resources. Not every vendor has adopted COUNTER statistics.

Databases
Thematic collections of electronic resources. Some offer original content, whereas other databases are aggregators that pull together many disparate resources into one searchable interface.

DDA
In the demand-driven acquisitions model of collection development, the library sets parameters for books it would like and loads MARC records for e-books that

match that profile. The library does not pay the vendor unless a title is triggered by patron use, at which point the library either purchases the book or, in some cases, borrows it through short-term loan.

Discovery Service

A commercial product designed to replace the public catalog. Features can include improved search interfaces; relevancy-ranked search results; faceted searching; metadata and full text from local collections, open access repositories, and subscription resources; and bibliographic and holdings information from the library's catalog.

DOAJ

The Directory of Open Access Journals is a clearinghouse of open access journals.

DOI

The digital object identifier is a unique string of letters and numbers that identifies an article or book chapter.

Downloadable Audiobooks

Digitized audiobooks that may be downloaded to a computer or handheld device.

DRM

Digital Rights Management refers to copyright management for electronic resources. DRM is set by the publisher or distributor and can include restrictions on the number of users and the ability to save, print, and share.

EBA

In the evidence-based acquisitions model of collection development, the library pays to access a collection of e-books for a set length of time. At the end of the contract, the library can purchase books from the collection, using usage data from the preceding year to inform their title selections.

E-books

Short for "electronic books," e-books are digitized books that may be read on a computer or handheld device.

EBSCO

One of the three biggest database providers, along with Gale and ProQuest.

E-journals

Also called electronic journals, these are digitized journals that may be read on a computer or handheld device. They include popular magazines as well as scholarly journals.

Electronic Reserves

In academic settings, these are online course readings, usually chapters and articles, that have been put in a central place for student access. The reserves are often administered by the library.

Electronic Resources
Digitized versions of intellectual content, as compared to physical versions such as print, microfiche, and DVDs. Common examples are databases, e-books, e-journals, and downloadable audiobooks.

Entitlements
The journal holdings, including date coverage, that a library has access to, based on individual and package subscriptions.

Environmental Scan
A technique used to examine the current political, economic, social, and technological state of a library in order to identify strengths and weaknesses.

E-readers
Handheld devices that can be used to read e-books and other digital media. Some devices, such as the Kindle and the NOOK, are dedicated e-readers, whose primary or exclusive function is to serve as a platform for e-books and e-journals. Alternatively, multipurpose smartphones, tablets, laptops, and computers can be used as e-readers.

ERM tools
Electronic Resource Management tools allow tracking of electronic resources through their entire life cycle, from ordering and licensing to access setup and ongoing maintenance. Common features include custom alerts, linking licenses to resource records, and usage statistics retrieval, all in one integrated system.

EZproxy
Sold by OCLC, EZproxy is the dominant proxy server in the library market.

Fair Use
An aspect of United States copyright law that protects the use of copyrighted materials in specific cases. The fair use clause allows educational and nonprofit institutions to use copyrighted materials more freely than would be otherwise possible.

Flipster
A platform for e-magazines provided by EBSCO.

Focus Groups
A research technique in which a researcher leads a guided conversation among a group of people.

Formative Test
A type of usability test that uses prototypes of services or products. It happens very early in the design process.

Freegal
A service for downloading music, mostly from the catalog of artists in Sony Music Entertainment (www.freegalmusic.com/questions).

Gale
One of the three biggest database providers, along with EBSCO and ProQuest.

Global Update
A process for applying a common change to multiple catalog records.

Gold OA
An open access standard. Gold OA articles are freely available upon publication, without an embargo period, and without access restrictions.

Green OA
An open access standard. Green OA articles become openly available "at some point after formal publication . . . The publisher allows authors to self-archive a version of the published work for free public use in their institutional repository" (publishing.gmu.edu/communication/scholarly-communication-basics).

Heuristic Testing
A user experience method in which a usability expert compares a website or product to a pre-established usability standard.

Hoopla Digital
A provider of streaming and downloadable movies, music, e-books, audiobooks, comics, and television shows.

ICOLC
The International Coalition of Library Consortia provides support and resources for library consortia.

ILL
Interlibrary loan is a system in which libraries loan content to other libraries on behalf of their patrons.

ILL PoD
Interlibrary Loan Purchase-on-Demand is a means of filling user requests by purchasing content rather than borrowing it.

ILS
The Integrated Library System is the software that allows for library acquisitions, cataloging, circulation, and reporting. It comprises, at a minimum, the public catalog and the back-end catalog.

Indemnification
A legal term that means compensation, or what a party agrees to pay, in case a violation of the contract occurs.

Institutional Repository
An online open archive for collecting, preserving, and freely sharing the scholarship of an institution such as a university.

IP Address
An Internet Protocol address is "a unique string of numbers . . . that identifies each computer" in a given network (en.oxforddictionaries.com/definition/ip _address).

IP Authentication
The use of an IP address to verify that an end-user has the right to access an electronic resource. This is the most common type of authentication for electronic resources.

IP Range
A range of IP addresses for a network. In libraries, this includes the IP address of the proxy server, the IP address of branch libraries, and the local campus IP address.

Journal Packages
A collection of electronic journals served from one platform that are purchased, licensed, and maintained as a group. They often share a publisher or content area and may share a search interface. Most journal packages are sold as Big Deals.

Kanopy
A provider of streaming movies, mostly documentaries and classic films.

Knowledge Base
A collection of bibliographic information and metadata for a library's holdings in electronic journals (and sometimes e-books). The knowledge base delivers linking to full text via openURL standards. Sometimes abbreviated as KB.

LibGuide
A content management system for designing online course and subject guides. The person using it does not need to know coding.

License
A written contract, agreed to by both parties, that outlines the legal rights and restrictions of the use of an electronic resource.

Licensee
The party (usually the library) that agrees to a license in order to access something.

Licensor
The party (usually the vendor) that offers the product that needs to be licensed.

Limitation of Liability
A license term that designates the amount a library or company can be ordered to pay by the courts if the contract is violated.

LOCKSS
A peer network of libraries that works together to preserve digital content, especially e-journals and e-books, by having each library keep a copy of the content. Stands for Lots of Copies Keeps Stuff Safe.

MARC Records
Machine Readable Cataloging Records are the standard format for library catalog records.

Marketing
An organized method of communicating what libraries provide in a way that demonstrates to patrons the benefits of using library resources.

Marketing Campaign
A time-limited marketing effort targeted at a specific population.

Marketing Research
Techniques used to better understand the needs and consumption patterns of a target market.

Material Breach
A violation that occurs when a party knowingly goes against a contract.

NASIG
An organization that promotes the distribution, acquisition, and long-term accessibility of information resources.

NISO
The National Information Standards Organization develops, maintains, and publishes technical standards.

OCLC
A cooperative library that got its start with interlibrary loan. It remains best known for facilitating ILL, but it also provides many other services and products, including EZproxy.

ONIX-PL
A standard method of encoding licenses using XML in order to make them machine readable.

OPAC
More commonly referred to simply as "the catalog," the Online Public Access Catalog is the public interface of the library's ILS.

Open Access (OA)
Refers to intellectual content that is freely available to end-users, often with few or no restrictions for its use.

Open Educational Resources (OER)
A subset of Open Access Resources used in the classroom and other academic settings. They are particularly popular in distance-learning classes.

OpenURL Link Resolver
Parses the elements from a link to a bibliographic citation through an OpenURL knowledge base and provides a target that resolves to full text at the article level.

OverDrive
A provider of downloadable e-books and audiobooks.

Participatory Design
A group of techniques, including card sorting and prototyping, that encourages user participation in the design of services, systems, and interfaces.

PDA
Patron-Driven Acquisitions. See DDA.

Performance Data
Quantitative data gathered during usability testing.

Permalink
The permanent, static hyperlink to a specific webpage that should be used when creating proxy links to library resources.

Perpetual Access
An acquisitions model that allows for continued access to content that has already been purchased, even if a subscription to that content lapses in the future.

Persona
A common technique in user research and user experience, personas are miniature biographies that describe unique fictional people who represent main user categories.

Portico
An archive that preserves mostly journal literature, making it available to all member libraries when that journal's vendor is no longer able to maintain an electronic version themselves.

PPR
Public performance rights grant permission to play media in public.

PPV
Pay-per-view is a temporary acquisitions model in which the library purchases access to unsubscribed/unowned content on behalf of a patron.

Predatory Journals
Open access journals that are not legitimate scholarly journals. They flout scholarly norms such as peer review and the editing process and solicit article content from authors in exchange for payment.

Preference Data
Subjective data that measures a participant's feelings or opinions of a product gathered during usability testing.

Project Gutenberg
A collection of free e-books, mostly from the public domain.

ProQuest
One of the three biggest database providers, along with EBSCO and Gale.

Prototyping
A model that is used to test user interaction with a design early in the process. It can vary in roughness from a sketch to an almost complete, actually coded product.

Proxy Server
Authenticates end-users and connects them to electronic resources.

QR Codes
Barcodes designed to be read by a special app on smartphones that will then take the user to a specific URL.

Query String Link
A link that shows in the address bar during a database or e-journal session that may contain search terms and other information unique to that session.

RBdigital
A provider of downloadable audiobooks and e-books from Recorded Books. Formerly One-Click Digital.

Rule of Five
The de facto rule on quantitative limits on ILL lending. It states that, within a calendar year, a borrowing library should not borrow more than five articles from the same periodical published within five years of the request.

Scenarios
In usability testing, a scenario is a group of tasks that mimic an activity that a user might perform with the product being tested.

Script
In usability testing, a script contains directions for running the test and the exact words that the test runner should say to the participant.

SELF-e
A platform for self-published e-books.

Self-pub
Short for "self-published." Many self-pub books are available exclusively in electronic format.

Serials
In most contexts, synonymous with "journals." The term is a holdover from the time when all serials were journals and all journals were serials. Serials can also refer to databases, however, because most databases have dynamic content and require an annual renewal fee.

SERU
Shared Electronic Resource Understanding is a standard that, with the agreement of both parties, may be used as an alternative to licensing. It is not a legal document.

SHERPA/RoMEO
Database that tracks the copyright and self-archiving policies of open access journals.

Simultaneous User Limit
The number of users who can access a particular electronic resource, such as an e-book, at the same time.

Social Media
Any type of media that allows for users to create and share content with others and then allow others to comment on this content.

STL
The short-term loan is a variation on the DDA model of collection development. The first time an end-user triggers an e-book record, the library pays a fraction of the full cost of the book. Not until the second trigger (or third, or fourth; the library gets to decide) does the library purchase the book.

Streaming Media
Refers to resources that are "streamed"—continuously delivered over a live connection—as opposed to resources that are first downloaded and then watched by viewers. Films and television are the most common types of streaming media in libraries.

Style Guide
A collection of templates, images, and rules that help fellow librarians understand and use a brand.

Subject Alternative Name (SAN) Certificates
A security certificate that uses the Subject Alternative Name field to specify additional host names to be protected by a single certificate.

Subscription Agent
A company that acts as an intermediary between publishers and libraries. The agent takes library orders, transfers them to the publisher, and makes sure payment and access are set up correctly.

Subscription Resources
Resources for which libraries pay a yearly cost to maintain access to the content. Databases and journals are normally subscription resources.

SUSHI
The Standardized Usage Statistics Harvesting Initiative facilitates the automatic retrieval of COUNTER statistics. It is a protocol, not a piece of software.

Swank
A provider of streaming movies, including feature films.

SWOT Analysis
Stands for Strengths, Weaknesses, Opportunities, Threats. It is a marketing technique for identifying internal and external strengths and weaknesses.

Target Market
The group of patrons that a librarian has decided to focus on for a marketing effort.

Task
In usability testing, a task is a specific action that a user is asked to perform using the product.

TEACH Act
Legislation that was developed to help interpret what counts as fair use for teachers in distance and online classrooms.

TERMS
Techniques for Electronic Resource Management. Consists of six stages that describe the life cycle of electronic resources.

Think Aloud Method
A method of usability testing in which the test runner asks participants to talk about their thought processes while they go through the test scenarios.

Turnaways
A usage metric. Each turnaway represents one time a user was denied access to an electronic resource, usually because of simultaneous user limits.

UDA
Use-driven acquisitions is a form of purchasing that aims to maximize collection budgets by providing "just-in-time" collections instead of "just-in-case" collections by purchasing based on user need. Includes purchase models such as demand-driven acquisitions (DDA), patron-driven acquisitions (PDA), evidence-based acquisitions (EBA), ILL purchase on demand (ILL PoD), and pay-per-view (PPV).

URL
Uniform Resource Locator. Often called a web address, a link, or (less commonly) a hyperlink.

Usability Test
A method of user experience research for testing how users perform tasks using a real product or service.

User Categories
Part of user research. The different segments of your population that have similar needs and uses for the library

User Experience
A user-focused method for designing library services, processes, and resources.

User Research
The study of how patrons interact with, view, and possibly ignore the library and its processes, services, and resources.

Vendor
A company that sells content to a library.

Warranty
A company's guarantee that they have the permission of copyright holders to license the materials on offer.

WHAT Method
A four-step method of negotiation that advises the negotiator to understand why the other party is invested in its position, hypothesize possible solutions, provide answers to the other parties, and then listen carefully to their responses.

Wildcard Certificate
A digital certificate that is applied to a domain and all its subdomains, used most often for securing HTTPS-enabled websites.

Word of Mouth Marketing
A type of marketing in which the marketers identify people who are important to their target community and get them to adopt and spread the product or message on their own.

Zinio
A platform for e-magazines.

Index

About the Authors

Jessica Zellers worked in public libraries small, medium, and large before switching to academic libraries. Formerly an Electronic Resources Librarian, she is now the Collection Development Librarian at Western Carolina University. She is the author of *Women's Nonfiction: A Guide to Reading Interests*, and she frequently contributes to NoveList, the readers' advisory database. She is a sucker for fantasy novels.

Tina M. Adams, the Electronic Resources Librarian at Western Carolina University, has worked at mid-sized to massive academic libraries and is a former Reference, Instruction, and Distance Education Librarian. Her experience in both public services and online and distance education brings a patron-centric vision to technical services. She has published in areas such as online instruction, library support of distance education students, and the history and pedagogy of distance education. She has recently contributed encyclopedia articles related to electronic journals, e-books, and e-reader technologies.

Katherine Hill has worked in academic libraries of all types, from the small liberal arts Edgewood College in Wisconsin to the massive, research-focused North Carolina State University. Now the Electronic Resources Librarian at the University of North Carolina at Greensboro, she focuses on bringing the user into the equation of electronic resource management, whether it is through outreach, marketing, or user experience research. She has presented and written on this topic, on serial and knowledge base data management, and on the role of professional education in training future Electronic Resource Librarians at the Charleston Conference, NASIG, ER&L, Serials Review, and most recently in the book *Migrating Library Data: A Practical Manual*. When not being a librarian or hanging out at home with her husband and cats, she can be found either rolling dice pretending to be a character or running around pretending to be a character, often a wizard librarian. She is still trying to figure out how to bring this into library scholarship.